Sarah

Roselle Angwin

WRITING THE BRIGHT MOMENT

inspiration & guidance for writers

wishing you many bright moments...

Rosele

Devon, February 2007

Fire in the Head
Devon
UK

First published in Great Britain by *Fire in the Head*, 2005
www.fire-in-the-head.co.uk
P O Box 17
Yelverton
Devon
PL20 6YF

Cover image by Eloïse Sentito; cover design by Fred Hageneder, Dragon Design
Internal artwork by Amy Shelton
Copy editor Julie-Ann Rowell
Layout and typesetting by Susanne Worsfold
Printed on recycled paper by Bookchase, London

This book has been made possible with the support of the Arts Council of England

A catalogue record for this title is available from the British Library

Roselle Angwin is a poet, author and course director of the *Fire in the Head creative and reflective writing* programme. She read Anglo-Saxon, Norse and Celtic at Cambridge, and followed this with a training course in Transpersonal Psychology. In 1991 she brought together her own long-term writing practice and her lifelong studies of various wisdom traditions and the human potential movement to facilitate workshops in personal growth and creative and reflective writing. Formerly founder and artistic director of a literary festival on Dartmoor (*Writing on the Wild Side*), Roselle is a writing tutor for Arvon, the Open College of the Arts and her own Two Rivers poetry group. She leads groups and undertakes residencies, indoors and outdoors, throughout Britain and abroad, the most recent being a six-month residency at Sherborne School. Her own work is widely published, and she often collaborates with other writers, visual artists and musicians. As writer member of the occasional environmental arts group Genius Loci, she has been involved in projects at Hestercombe Gardens and the Cotswold Water Park. Her books include *Riding the Dragon, Creative Novel Writing, A Hawk Into Everywhere* (with Rupert Loydell), and *Looking for Icarus*. Roselle has a daughter, and lives in Devon.

For this book, which collects together some of her workshops and ideas from fourteen years of *Fire in the Head*, she has also invited contributions from a number of respected and inspiring writers and course facilitators; their biographies appear at the back of the book.

WRITING THE BRIGHT MOMENT

CONTENTS

PART 2 THE PRACTICE OF POETRY

PART 3 STORYMAKING

PART 4 WRITING FOR LIFE

FOOTNOTES & REFERENCES

NOTES ON CONTRIBUTORS

INTRODUCTION – LIVING THE WRITING LIFE

For a long time I thought – I hoped, perhaps, as it would make my job as a facilitator easier, and also my course descriptions – that you could differentiate writing from living; or creative writing from reflective writing; and of course, in one way, you can. A novel, a play, a poem speaks its own language, out there in the world, self-sufficient, finding its own way. And at the same time, the distinction is false. The more I work with people, and the more I explore my own creative processes, and my life, the more I recognise that fundamentally the separation is illusory.

For me, writing is a way of meeting the world; of becoming and staying more conscious, more open, more imaginative; and then expressing that experience in whatever form is appropriate to the context. That expression will then feed back into the way I meet the world; a kind of Möbius strip.

Clearly, writing is, or often is, an expression of creativity, a thing-in-itself. But I believe it's more than this. It is also a form of intimacy: becoming intimate with the world, with others or another, and with oneself. It is also, therefore, a way of connecting or reconnecting, which means that it is as much a path of practice, a psychospiritual journey, as it is an art form.

No matter what result you're looking for – and I hope that this book will help you to stronger more exciting results – to my mind the writing *process* matters as much as the 'product'. The act of putting words on paper is one of the most potent acts available to humans. We take language for granted, and we can forget that words can change lives. Writing at its best can be a way of making your world larger; and that of your reader, too.

This book takes a holistic approach to the writing process. We all write, in the course of our daily life; and we all improvise with words every time we open our mouths to speak. Creativity is part of life, an aspect of being human, not just the province of those few artistic geniuses who live permanently at full creative tilt. And creative self-expression has an important contribution to make to full health and wellbeing. In addition, how you live shapes how you write. And as a writer, how I write also shapes how I live.

Nonetheless, creative writing is a discipline with its own requirements, its own parameters and its own tools and skills, and this book, I hope, will encourage you to explore these things further. The exploration never stops: my own experience is that one is perpetually apprenticed to the practice of writing.

Much of our writing is a response to the world, to the experience of being alive. Humans live on many thresholds at once. It's the job of the writer to be conscious of this and to find ways of articulating it. What ends up on the page is partly a response to the world we perceive through our senses, the feelings, thinking, intuition, life experiences – our own and others' – and the memories we bring. It is leavened and made into something other by the imagination's ability to read even more into everything, by our ability to put ourselves into the shoes of another, to question and to respond, to ask 'what if?', to transmute the raw ingredients into something new. The work comes in the shaping of all those things so that the result is as near to what we want to say, in language that sings, as possible.

No matter how innovative our work, we are also writing from within, or extending, a tradition, even when we are challenging it. That tradition uses the power of imagery as its foundation, and leads back through the written canon to the oral culture to the pictograms, stories, myths and archetypes of our prehistoric ancestors, elders, bards and shamans amongst them. We are drawing not only from our own conscious and unconscious wells, we are also drawing from the limitless well of what Jung named the collective unconscious.

What this means is that the images we use and the language we employ are all freighted with decades, centuries and even millennia of meaning. As writers, we can excavate that meaning and bring it into daylight. We can also lay our own nuances over the top of it; a word, especially a noun or verb, is a kind of palimpsest. By changing the context of that word, assigning new tasks and neighbours to it, we can allow our reader to see new faces in everyday language. This is particularly true, perhaps, of poetry. 'An individual word', says writer and academic Peter Abbs, 'will carry ancient poetic sediment, and one of the poet's tasks – as language is the poet's medium – is to shake the hidden pollen and seeds that lie there, to allow for a new and quite unexpected fertilisation... Not to work the deep geology of language is to fail the medium.'[1]

This book is for anyone who is interested in any form of creative and reflective writing for any reason – to make something new with words, to communicate something important, as self-expression, self-exploration, as a personal record or journal – or simply because you have to, because nothing else fills that space, because that's what you do.

Nonetheless, I am addressing the poet in every writer, and an exploration of poetry forms much of the substance of this book. Poetry, in a way, is a process of distilling, heightening and refining experience, and therefore is a core practice.

Robert Frost described poetry as 'a way of remembering what it would impoverish us to forget'; and its place in history has been about just that: it is the oldest form of verbal art, once indistinguishable from storytelling, and universally crucial in the preservation of important cultural wisdom.

'I believe we need good poems,' says Andrea Hollander Budy, writing in *Resurgence* 207, 'because they are both entertaining and useful: *entertaining* in that they are rooted in the human traditions of telling stories and making music; *useful* in that they disturb our lives enough to reinforce our humanness. I don't believe there's another literature that does it quite like that.

'Poems speak the heart's language, an aesthetic language that is both spiritual and musical. It is a language that forms questions much better than it poses answers. It cradles the tongue and the heart but exists in the ear... poems provide one of life's few defences against inevitable grief and intolerable, unfathomable disaster. Yet poetry is equally the language of celebration, of unexpected joy, and of human love...'

In short, poetry addresses every aspect of being human; and there can be few people who haven't turned to it as reader or writer, however briefly, at moments of extreme feeling in their lives. For many reasons, and in many ways, poetry goes where other things can't. Its terrain is unique. It is also crucial, in my view, to the life of the soul, as a revivifying medium, a force for reconnection; perhaps especially in a secular dislocated culture. Peter Abbs says that in the present state of cultural dissipation 'an inner connection to a larger symbolic world is essential for the imaginative life'. We suffer collectively from a failure of imagination. Without the imaginative life we become, as individuals and as a people, desiccated; and, worse, incapable of empathy. Adrienne Rich says that poetry is a means of saving your life. Poet William Stafford said:

It is difficult
> to get the news from poems
>> yet men die miserably every day
>>> for lack
of what is found there.

My poet friend Brian puts it like this: 'Liverpool manager Bill Shankley said that football isn't just a matter of life and death; it's more important than that. Speaking as a footballer myself, I say that poetry's even more important than football...'

Whether or not poetry is your own medium, as a creative writer you will live with a poetic consciousness. This implies a simultaneous immersion in the life of the imagination and the life of the senses. There's something shamanic about poetry and about poets. A poet flies across the thresholds of many worlds, goes to where the veil is thin, but lives fully in this: he or she also looks deeply, listens deeply, feels, touches and tastes the world in all its moods. The poet conveys through a deep-rootedness in the sensory dimension, the concrete world and the physicality of experience, the existential, the spiritual, and the intangible. The profound is more effective if carried in the simple. If this is done skilfully enough, the poem will carry within it and convey to its audience its own true terrain of subtle non-physical meaning.

Writing undertaken in this spirit is both a tool to achieve this, and the process itself. How to enhance this practice and ability is the focus of this book.

So writing is both an end in itself and a means to an end, both journey and destination. As I said at the beginning, it may also be a spiritual practice. In some traditions – the bardic, that of Japanese or Chinese sages, the Sufi, the Christian contemplative, the troubadour – poetry has been a crucial aspect of a spiritual path – a container for processing, refining and shedding light on the experience of being human, and of communicating that – both back to oneself and to others. It has its own psychology, spirituality, philosophy, history, cosmography and ecology.

But this source book is 'hands-on'. I don't want it to be merely theorising, although there will be times when I use discourse to explore the nature of writing. Nonetheless the emphasis is to help facilitate in you, the reader, the shaping of your creative voice. It is intended to inspire, to guide, and to remind you that though writing is a solitary path you are not alone in your practice.

This means there are many suggestions and exercises to that end. This is a practical manual – a manual of practice.

What I aim to explore in this book are three interlinked things.

The first is those *moments of inspiration* that lead us to create words on a page (or in the ear), a largely subjective and usually solitary pursuit or phenomenon.

How can we find, enhance, and commit to that process?

The second is the *shaping* of those creations so that they do their job well. What does this require?

The third is a *holistic perspective*, and underpins, overlays and surrounds everything contained in this book – living the writing life: a wonderful, terrible, gruelling, rich and all-embracing journey.

All three perspectives are ones that I have spent the better part of my life exploring; and this source book is a way to collect, collate and reflect on the work I have done with groups of writers over fourteen years now, in the hopes that the final distilled result will create something inspiring.

Most of the material in here has been tried out and refined on the people with whom I have worked. That way, I know that it does its job.

It's also a record, in some ways, of my practice. And it will be a celebration of not only the writing process, but of the writing companions, friends, colleagues and students, who have travelled alongside me throughout my own solitary writer's journey; in many ways it is *our* work, not *my* work.

The book contains a series of short essays. Many are pieces I have commissioned from creative writing practitioners who take their work out into the world by inspiring and supporting others as they themselves explore their own creativity. The contributors who have generously given their time to this project are people whose work – personal creative work as well as professional facilitation – I respect and admire, and whose approach chimes with my own. (Their contributions are named in the Contents list and at the heads of their essays; the unattributed pieces are, of course, mine.)

My own pieces have been written over several years. Some of these are directly connected to various aspects of the writing process, what you might call the river; and many are 'tributaries' – less overtly related to writing but important 'feeders' into my approach to the whole adventure.

Most of the essays are followed by relevant suggestions and exercises. I recommend that you take one of the topics and work with it and around it and through it and within it over a period of days, allowing your own imagination and associative memory to suggest new directions in relation to this topic. Allow the work to take you deep, to settle inside you, to suggest its own directions. Allow it time before moving on.

You don't have to work through the book's contents sequentially. It may be more inspiring to take a serendipitous approach and open the book at random; then use that essay and any associated exercise(s) as a starting point for the week's musings.

Can writing be taught? Is it about learning? I don't know. That's a continuing debate. I believe that while talent may be innate, technique – and, even more importantly, insight – can be learnt or acquired, and talent can then be manifest. It will require continuing dedication and commitment, clearly. The art is in the practice. Learning how to *read*, how to *look*, how to *listen*, properly and wholeheartedly, and then to reflect on what you've noticed is all part of that practice. *The art of really paying attention.*

There's the story about the sculptor, asked how on earth he managed to carve a life-size elephant. 'I simply chip away everything that's not elephant,' he replied.

Maybe writing's like that too. Maybe it's about peeling away everything that's not what you want to say. As you work through this book, what I hope you will find is the courage to be the writer you could be as well as the writer you already are; and to allow your writing to feed your life, as your life feeds your writing.

PART 1

MAPPING THE TERRITORY

Only if words are felt, bodily presences, like echoes or waterfalls, can we understand the power of spoken language to influence, alter and transform the perceptual world.
David Abram

Picking grapes

My workshops are built around the idea of finding ways to encourage the imagination to yield up its fruit, to open and maintain a passageway from the unconscious to the conscious mind. Because I believe that, like anything else, this is a practice that needs constant repetition in order to keep the relevant 'muscles' flexed and in shape, I start most of my workshops with 'free flow' or 'stream-of-consciousness' writing.

This 'opening the doors' work is fundamental to the creative process. Many writing tutors employ similar tactics: Natalie Goldberg in her inspirational books, Julia Cameron's 'morning pages' in *The Artist's Way*, and before that Peter Elbow all recommend this kind of work.

Here's how it goes: you pick a time for you that works, where you will have minimal distractions. It's most effective at hypnagogic times when you are naturally closest to the world of the unconscious: close to drifting off to sleep, or drifting out of it. The best time is very first thing on waking on the morning (though some people find last thing at night is more fruitful for them). Then, without setting yourself any agenda other than to get words down on paper swiftly, you write and keep writing for a specified length of time. Don't be fooled by the apparent simplicity of the technique: it's both harder than it sounds, and often surprisingly profound in its results.

When you are immersed in creative activity at such times, you are most likely to be in what athletes call 'the zone' – a state of calm alertness where your attention is defocused but you are still sensitive to your environment as well as to the inner world, similar to that state produced in meditation. It's a kind of lucid entrancement, a relaxed liminal state where your awareness is heightened but you haven't yet switched into the day's activities and demands. (More of this in a later chapter.)

What's important is that you don't bring an agenda to this writing. This is a process; it isn't intended to produce brilliant writing (although as it happens it often does offer up the most surprising and original insights and phrases, and some of the best poetry that my regular groups produce come from this work). It's intended to get you into the groove of writing – to encourage you to allow yourself to just write on a regular, preferably daily, basis. If you can make a practice of it, your writing will, before too long, become broader and deeper and more exciting. Not all of it, of course – these flow sessions will produce rubbish and monotony too. Probably often. That's OK. It's the process that matters.

There are a couple of things that are important.

1 *Be good to yourself.* Set yourself a manageable amount of time: say ten minutes daily, five days a week. If you do exceed that, great! Increase the time if you like; but it's essential for motivation that you set a manageable target and feel good about achieving it rather than an optimistic one at which you fail – and beat yourself up.

2 *Don't stop writing.* Once you start, keep going. Just follow your pen. Allow it to dictate what you write about – leave your conscious mind and ordering intellect out of this – they can come in later. So once you've put down the first few words, just *go*. Follow the impulse, fly, duck, weave, burrow, jump, trapeze. It doesn't matter that it's rubbish or doesn't make sense or isn't grammatically or syntactically correct. What matters is following the flow. If you're bored, write *I am bored* over and over, until you get bored with it... If it's the same old stuff, notice: *Ah! Same old stuff! Must be something in there still for me;* and keep writing. Take a phrase from your writing above if you get stuck and just follow that.

3 *Don't read back, censor, correct or delete.* Just let it happen.

4 This one's the hardest of all. *Don't think.* Later, yes; later you can think or correct or edit. Or bin. But not here – this is primary process; this is 'first thought right thought'. You'll probably need to educate (unlearn) yourself into this one – it's tough for most people.

Just get it down.

Think of it – to borrow an idea from Ben Okri – as a way of sitting quietly on the banks of the pool of the imagination and gently casting your net for fish.

So to the 'how': first of all buy yourself a good notebook, and a pen that pleases you. I use substantial A5 spiral-bound notebooks with various coloured card covers – they're pleasing enough for me to enjoy writing in them but not so expensive that it's daunting to approach them. As you gain confidence you might want to find different notebooks – handmade paper, handbound, fabric covers – or make your own.

Pick up your notebook the moment you wake – before you get out of bed for your first cup of tea; if possible before going to the bathroom; especially before you speak to anyone. Pick up your pen and – just go.

Write the first thing that comes into your head, and then follow it for ten minutes (or three pages, or whatever you've set yourself). Record your dreams, your early morning feelings, your thoughts about the day that has passed or the day to come or your stiff legs or your hunger or what someone said to you yesterday or that memory that just popped into your head about buying an ice cream in the park and the chestnut leaves falling around you or the sound of the rain on the window or your anger or despair at the state of the world or your anxiety about that argument you had or the fact that you don't want to go to work and what you'd rather be doing is paragliding or reading and eating chocolates by the fire or drinking coffee with a friend or that dream of yours about trekking in Chile... just write. This is not an attempt to capture factual sequences of events. Let fantasies run away with you; let nonsense, surreal images and bizarre ideas hijack your pen.

If it feels too difficult to start right in like that, than there are a couple of other things you can try.

Make a list in the back of your notebook of all the things you might one day want to write about. Add to the list when you think of something new. Starters: childhood garden; first kiss; an evocative song/piece of music; first encounter with death; my mother's dress; first day at school; if I could go anywhere; meeting a lover; the most important place; challenging things I've done; things I've never done; things I've never told anyone; places I've lived/places I haven't lived; first car, and so on. You'll see that all these have the potential to grow into something else – memories, associations, feelings, desires, secrets all have a lot of potential energy.

Another starting point is to flip through a book at random and pick out an image or short phrase as a beginning.

Or you might choose to put on some music and allow your hand to follow it, and see where that takes you.

Once you've done one day's worth, there's another possible starting point: look back over that day's piece and pick an image or a phrase, and let that take you off again, somewhere different this time.

Don't feel you have to be neat and tidy in your notebook/journal, by the way, or keep it only for this kind of work. In fact, the looser you are with it, the better for your imagination. Stick things into it. Punctuate it with quotes and poems. Write sideways, upside down, diagonally, in hieroglyphs. (One of my group participants habitually writes in curves and spirals.) Make sketches, even if you think you can't draw (especially if you think you can't draw).

Filling the vat

The 'flow' stuff can be left at just that – stuff, in your notebooks. Some people suggest that you don't look back over what you've written for weeks or even months. Keep your notebooks, at least for a while. If you're interested in therapeutic writing, then (dated) notebooks like this kept over some time can be invaluable at enabling you to pick up long-distance themes and patterns in your psyche and your life.

Creatively, too, your notebooks will undoubtedly offer some plump fruit. When you do look back, you may want to pick out ideas or phrases that seem strong to develop at a later time. Some people transfer these into an electronic 'dump' file, or a 'rainy day' notebook (see 'The Sudden Glint' chapter).

Meantime, in addition to letting the notebook writing 'cook' for a few weeks or months, here's a secondary reflective process, to apply spontaneously and immediately, that can prove both creative and insightful.

Take a little while to apply these three questions to the passage you've just written:

> What do I notice?
> Anything that surprises me?
> What am I really writing about?[1]

These questions are some of the most useful tools for a writer. That last question in particular can be, at times, like a firecracker. You might think you're writing about a pair of shoes – to quote a recent exercise I set a group – and find you're actually writing about your marriage, or your anger (these two things are not necessarily connected!), or the calluses and bunions on your life. The words may not reflect this, but the subtext might.

So there's another possible direction to explore in a second piece of writing.

Then move on to the next section...

Distilling the vintage

Now comes the refining, the distillation.

When I was a student I worked one early autumn picking grapes in the vineyard of a chateau in the beautiful Cognac area of France – all misty morning lakes, silent ducks and harlequin falling leaves. (Great for the poetic imagination, of course.) That area, and that castle in particular, were known for their *pineau* – which is a delicious and heady blend of white wine and its distilled cousin, cognac (also not bad for the poetic imagination).

Cognac is a distillation of the grape must. In terms of this piece of writing, then, it's time to look for the essence. The distillation is an alchemical process – the stage of pure magic.

What are you *really* writing about? Yes, I know I've asked you that already. But what I want now is the essence of that recorded moment, that vignette, that piece of writing... in thirty words maximum. (You can write fewer, but not more.)

This isn't about 'précis' and 'summary'. This is a more intuitive and imaginative process than that, and the final result may have no apparent bearing on the first piece at all; or it may use some of the same phrases. Whichever way you go is OK; you can't get it wrong. But I'm asking you about the heart of the matter; the kernel, the burning shining core.

A good way in for some people is to start by underlining the words and phrases which hold the most creative or emotional 'charge' for them, or which they simply like best. These may then form part of the final short piece; or they may simply light the way.

I guarantee you will be pleased, and surprised, at the result.

Maturation

Now it's time to let the substance – the words – sit and age gracefully.

At some stage down the line, maybe weeks on, when you judge that everything's ripened nicely and your subconscious has worked away below ground on it, look at your final 30-word piece of writing again (and/or the original piece, too).

This time you're looking at the form the writing wants to take. Is it complete, or does it need reworking in any way (in a less restricted way, maybe?)? Is it a paragraph of prose, or does it have the smell of a poem? What does it need? Can anything be added or is there more to pare away? Can you refine the words and tighten the way you've used language any further? What are your verbs like? Are they as alive and active as you can make them? Is there a superfluity of 'little' words? Where does this piece want to go? Does it have colour, texture, smell? Now taste it, savour it, make it your own... Then rework it if you need to, forgetting my 30-word rule.

30-word workshop poems from free flow writing

> She is the breeze
> a hunter of spaces between lines
> she is scarlet
> licking her lips with the blood of lust
> and life drips from her tongue
> *Jo Bellchambers*

> Bridge of trees –
> something dangerous in the fractured light.
> This cusp
> between what has been lost
> and what is still to lose.
> You open your mouth:
> the future tumbles out.
> *Roselle Angwin*

> I prefer the wind blowing
> against me
> like a cushion
> sometimes it catches
> reflected sunlight
> and juggles
> the stream giggles
> everything is nothing
> when we are nothing
> we are everything.
> *Brian King*

See the shifts to daylight
shifts to dark…
the shift to death
(although it aches)
is only change
a hesitation
in the distance
Mary Gillett

Velvet throat
holds me:
dances Spanish
in cool colonnades.
My heart is drying up,
needs soul linctus,
needs someone to pour
the music.
Jennie Osborne

Beneath a crouching bridge
       the fish,
           shadow among shadows,
           noses the drift:
working to shape its space
           exactly there:
dreaming the source
         the spawning burst
         of death.
Elisabeth Rowe

Devenish Island[2] (40 words)

These stones have made
a compact with earth,
the rain, and the kiss
of fingers: some penitent hands
and hands like mine.
The island goes on
pushing up grass
for the next man's cattle.
We leave through the reeds.
Julie-Ann Rowell

Sometimes, when I lie in a state of half-waking half-sleeping, I am conscious of a stream of words which seem to pass through my mind, without their having a meaning, but they have a sound, a sound of passion, or a sound recalling poetry that I know. Again sometimes when I am writing, the music of the words I am trying to shape takes me far beyond the words, I am aware of a rhythm, a dance, a fury, which is as yet empty of words.

Stephen Spender

TELLING TALES

Reading

Periodically with my regular writing groups I return to two fundamental questions: why do you read? And its corollary: what do you want from a book? There are a number of reasons for asking these questions, but two are relevant to my purposes right now. What I hope to do with these questions is to ask people to return to the passion and pleasure, the breadth and depth, the *aliveness* that a good book will bring. The second question returns them, via the 'what', to the 'how'; and is also a way of encouraging objectivity in order to apply that to their own writing.

Of course, there are numerous possible answers to these questions; some pretty much universal, others mitigated by personality, life experience, situation, age and immediate circumstances. So some answers might be: to be amused; to be entertained; to learn; to increase my understanding; to lose myself; to find myself; to be moved; to feel less alone; for insight; to escape; to enter another world; to revisit something; to see how other people do it. (These are some of many actual answers.)

Writing and reading writing is a way of connecting or reconnecting with the world. It's a kind of engagement. In E M Forster's analysis, books are a way of gaining entry into other people's secret lives. In real life, he says, we can know each other only imperfectly. In books, we can know people completely[1].

This feels important to me. There's something here about gaining a foothold in this slippery world of ours; coming in at our own life through the tangent of others'. To this extent, fiction is as 'real' as non-fiction: the events and experiences of the characters in a novel in some way mirror our own, even if only the lives of our imaginations, the lives we haven't lived; how it might be. A good story will take us further into our own lives at the same time as taking us out of our life into another. It might – arguably should even – address or invite us to ponder some of the continuing questions of the 'human condition' – though this does not have to be overt, heavy or humourless.

While I acknowledge that escapism and entertainment are of course both valid reasons to read, the books that I remember are those which have in some, even minute, way imprinted themselves in me to the extent that they have shaped and revisioned the way I see or live my life. In these books I as reader collaborate in my imagination with the writer in questioning and exploring what it means to be alive, with all its falterings, failings, frailties and complexities of needs, desires and feelings. Richard Eyre in *The Guardian* of 17 January 2004 mentions two of the greatest writers of the last century, Joyce and Conrad, as exhibiting 'an insistent, stubborn desire to examine lived experience, to provide a moral frame for it rather than take refuge in a maze of whimsical fantasy'. Exploring the nature of being human, questioning the choices and decisions we make, the consequences of these actions and what we might – or don't – learn from them, and examining these things in the company of other questioning minds – all this forms a bundle of tacit expectations, and is part of the delight, with which I approach literature.

As both reader and writer I take nothing for granted. I want to be drawn into the adventure. I want to be taken into the corners of life as well as into the high and deep places. I want, as Rainer Maria Rilke puts it, to live the unsolved questions in the human heart and to share in this with at least one other person – the writer, or if I am lucky a reader.

Starting point

So why do *you* read? And by what qualities do you judge what you read?

I invite you to take a moment and think about this. Find your notebook and write down all the reasons for reading, and criteria for evaluating, books that you can think of.

Next time – and the time after that – you read something, see how many of your criteria it fits. Be aware that you might have one or two over-riding requirements: that it moves you, for instance; or that it absorbs you completely. Other qualities may then be subservient to this criterion; or might be determining features of your engagement or otherwise: perhaps it is in a certain literary style, or of a certain genre, or certain aesthetic, or there is a poetic quality to the prose; or maybe for you it must have a strong plot, or well-rounded characters, and so on. Maybe there are specific themes that attract you?

Look back at your list. What is it fundamentally and specifically that determines whether a book is strong or not for you? What do you tend to admire in writing?

Now take one of your own pieces of writing; preferably one you completed a while back. Being as objective as you can, have a look at that piece of writing as if encountering it for the first time.

One by one, go back through the points on the list(s) you've just made. As honestly as you can – and it might be better to exchange work with a writing friend whom you trust – see how many of them you could apply to this piece of writing.

Writing

The next question is, inevitably of course, why you write. Without thinking or looking back at the 'why you read' list, brainstorm this question. Don't stop until you feel that your list is as complete as it can be.

Somewhere on your list, I hope, will be a phrase like 'because I have to'. While this compulsion alone won't necessarily make you a good writer, it is perhaps the only thing that will make you write 'authentically'. What's more, it may well be the only thing that keeps you going through the harder times. Writing's tough. When people arrive on my workshops – as often happens after some well-publicised literary coup: J K Rowling's rise and rise is a good example – with stated aims like 'to be published' or 'to write a bestseller' or 'to be able to make enough money to retire on' as their primary motivations, I gently let them know that this is not reason enough. Unless there is more substance behind that stated aim, as well as the idea and the tools or at least a willingness to learn and develop them, these same people are also the ones who melt away very fast. Of course we all want to be published. Of course we all want to write the next bestseller and have film-makers fighting over the purchase of our rights. Of course we would all like a five- or even four-figure advance. But what is more likely to make good writing is a writer's total belief and immersion in and passion for what he or she is writing.

'Discover the motive that bids you write,' says Rilke; 'examine whether it sends its roots down to the deepest places of your heart, confess to yourself whether you would die if writing were denied you. This before all: ask yourself in the quietest hour of your night: *must* I write? Dig down into yourself for a deep answer... if you may meet this solemn question with a strong and simple "*I must*", then build your life according to this necessity; your life must... become a token and a witness of this impulse.'[2]

Writers have an irresistible urge to *correspond with everything*. Everything fills them with the need to record, answer back, relate, connect, respond. It's partly our way of staying alive. 'Each thing, just by looking at it, aroused in me an irresistible longing to write so I would not die,' said Gabriel Garcia Marquez.

A work of art is good if it has grown out of necessity.
Rainer Maria Rilke

Freedom. It isn't once, to walk out
under the Milky Way, feeling the rivers
of light, the fields of dark –
freedom is daily, prose-bound, routine
remembering. Putting together, inch by inch
the starry worlds. From all the lost collections.
Adrienne Rich

It's Friday; not-quite-dusk and I'm driving the few miles through the beautiful Devon lanes and along the banks of the Tamar to run another weekend at one of my favourite venues. As I bump down the track with my windows open and hear the curlews and see the silver light on the incoming tide, I know once again that it couldn't get much better than this – doing something I love and believe in, in a place that is as close to paradise as I ever need to be.

Nonetheless, the first evening of a course fills me with a certain amount of terror. My friend who hosts the course feels, I know, a similar sense of apprehension. Will this be the course from hell? Will we maybe this time get it wrong? Will the group 'gel'? Will the participants even find us?

And there are the usual snags: it's nearly seven o'clock, and we eat at seven-thirty and then I run the first session. Someone arrived earlier than we can easily cope with; someone else is lost across the border in Cornwall; others are delayed a hundred miles away in traffic; someone has to withdraw at the last moment through illness; someone else misses her connection to the little branch railway line and the next train's in three hours. We also discover we have one more vegetarian than we'd catered for; and will there be enough wine?

Finally we're all here.

I look around the group – great people, but all so undoubtedly different that I cannot imagine how we will possibly be able to find common ground. My nervousness increases. So this time, surely, our nearly-foolproof recipe will fail... *And then I'll be finished,* runs the script. *I won't be able to pay the bills, I'll be exposed as a fraud, and no one will ever come to my courses again.*

Of course, it doesn't happen. I've done enough of these courses to know that what I do is set in motion an 'opening' process that has its own life. What's more,

I should trust by now that I can wing it if I have to, and it comes out right anyway. The creative process is very forgiving: it only needs the tiniest drop of petrol on the tinder at the edge of the bonfire-material. And the house, and the welcome participants get from our hostess, and my counselling training and the courage of the people who arrive from all over, strangers to me and to each other more often than not, simply don't fail. Between us, we create a place of safety. What's more, our common humanity is stronger than our apparent differences. We all share the same needs; we all seek belonging, love, meaning, truth, fulfilment, joy; we all share fears of suffering and death, lovelessness, loneliness, abandonment, inadequacy and meaninglessness. It's only the outer trappings that change.

Writing is about being alive. After the course one of the participants sends me a book of poetry by W S Graham; in it I find the perfect quote for what we have been doing this weekend: 'What I am making is / A place for language in my life / Which I want to be a real place / Seeing I have to put up with it / Anyhow', he continues. 'What are Communication's // Mistakes in the magic medium doing / To us? It matters only in / So far as we want to be telling // Each other alive about each other / Alive...' Language, writing, he goes on to say, is a way of finding out 'what it is I want'.[1]

So often we don't know what we are thinking or feeling until we have said it, or written it. What I know, but the participants possibly don't, is that on this course, drawing on autobiography, it's not the stories that they think they want to write that will emerge; but the stories that need to be written. I know this, but don't let on. I also know that people tend to come on these courses during, or after, a period of significant and frequently challenging life events; and sooner or later these deeper stories, the ones that are scary but which really need telling, will emerge. And it says a lot about the courage of the people concerned that it's usually sooner. This process I trust absolutely. The psyche knows what it needs; and often, all that we need to do is to listen: to our own stories, to those of others.

And sure enough, despite people's declared intentions of being here to see if they can write, or amuse and entertain others, or find a publisher, the real business takes over. We laugh. We weep; one by one, or sometimes together. We write – of course. We share a rare and trusting intimacy as we listen to story after story of courage, of adventure, of danger, of loss and lost dreams, of love and joy, of death and illness, of heartsplitting choices and shocking events. It is hard to imagine where else in one's life such a depth of shared secrets and intimacies can take place in such a short span of time; and this begins just the next morning.

One of the course participants emails me later that week: '[There was] a very strong reinforcement that I came away with – the strength of the human spirit ... you asked about significant moments in life. I experienced one last weekend when [K...] touched my arm in a gesture of compassion during an emotional moment of mine! That one small gesture left an indelible mark upon me. I feel a bit daft saying this but I had not appreciated that writing from life is more about humanity than it is about recalling events!'

And this is how it is. The stories of our lives can stir in a reader or listener a profundity of compassion, of empathy and humility. The place we make for this language, the shared language of our lives, is, to quote Graham above, a real place. Somewhere, underneath the surface differences, beneath the clothes, real and metaphorical, that we choose, we share one skin.

Starting points

The stories of the present moment

1

Who are you? What are your virtues and your vices?

2

Who are you *really*? I don't want 'outer' facts; I want your passions and secrets and longings. What makes you sing? What do you love? What makes you angry? Where do you feel most alive? If you were an animal, what would you be? Why are you here, reading this book at this time? What are you hoping for?

3

Your life both ends, and starts, in this moment; and this, and this.

a) Tell me about this moment. Now. Before reading any further. Tell me in detail: Tell me about the coffee ring on the table and the sound of the pen on the paper of your notebook – or the flicker of the cursor on your screen. Where are you? What's the view from there? Note it all: the sweep of your room – smells, colours, textures, details, the things that are important to you in this room, that mean something; then tell me about the light outside the window, the sounds in and around the house, what you're wearing on your feet, the smell of soup from the kitchen. Tell me about the traffic splashing through puddles outside, the neighbour's dog barking, the things you left on one side in order to do this. Then tell me about your hopes and fears and dreams and yearnings that lie behind this moment.

b) Then slide back a little in time. What did you do before sitting down to read and write this? Tell me about the thread of your day unspooling from first thing this morning to this moment.

c) Stand back a bit: tell me about the different colours in the braid of your daily life – what do they stand for? Who else is plaited in there with you?

d) Now pan: allow your attention to alight on *six* disparate moments from the last 24 hours. Whatever they are, just note them in brief and vivid detail – one paragraph each, no more. This is writing practice – recording how it is, fluidly but succinctly.

The moments don't need to be significant: just close your eyes and allow the memories to surface. Perhaps one is the closing of the door on the busyness of your habitual world right now in order to sit with quietness, with relief. Perhaps one is the chaos at suppertime tonight with all the kids competing for noise levels and the point at which you lost it. Perhaps one is something funny or bizarre you witnessed in the traffic jam. Or maybe it's the baguette you had at lunchtime, the one that oozed mayonnaise and avocado all over your fingers; the one you swore you wouldn't have because today you were absolutely going to start that diet, really truly. Or perhaps that first moment of waking, drinking tea quietly in bed with your partner in the moments before the working day erupted.

Get it all down in the kind of detail you would want from your lover if you were the other side of the world and homesick. Life's built of these tiny ordinary details; and so, often enough, is good writing. The ability to observe and conjure a scene and the life in it for a reader in a few carefully chosen phrases is paramount.

At the end of the day we only have our experience of life to write from. There is nothing else. In order to write it is necessary to be alive... to the awakening of sensory and psychic perception. Stick at the business of being alive. Don't be defeated by the idea of writing. Get used to writing in a way which can take you anywhere. Don't try to control everything you write, but establish a process which takes you from an impulse to raw material, to a more refined form...
Graham Mort

WRITING FROM LIFE 2

The long view

We are, at least to some extent, the sum of our pasts. One of the ways of moving forward is to see where we've come from, and what we might want to change. 'If you do what you've always done,' someone said, 'you will get what you've always got.'

Words make magic; speaking or writing words is a powerful magical act. The Nazis burnt books; Rushdie had a *fatwah* placed upon him. Words change lives. I think of them as a kind of currency, and if you think of them in this way, it's less easy to squander them.

The reason I mention this here is because the act of writing something down changes it, and changes the writer. (If it's strong, of course, it may also change the reader.) If there is someone to whom you feel safe and comfortable reading your life stories, so much the better – witnessing someone's story is also a powerful act. However, you might feel yourself freer to express difficult feelings when writing about your past if you don't have to censor your writing.

Last time, we circled the present, pretty much. I think of this as mouse-eye view. Now it's the turn of the hawk – taking the distance to look at the bigger picture of your life, picking out significant details.

Starting points

1

Eight incidents

For the moment, make brief notes on each – or several – of these eight kinds of incident just to hold the thread in your mind. Maybe a paragraph each; two at most (you can elaborate later):

    a) An experience you'll never forget
    b) A loss or ordeal
    c) A serious misunderstanding
    d) A funny or embarrassing incident
    e) A mistake

f) A major turning point or life event

g) A significant dream

h) Meeting a significant person.

You might then choose to concentrate on one at a time, and write the incident out in detail, as it happened, but making it as vivid and interesting as you can. This means selective editing – choosing what to leave out, and what to intensify or highlight. Think also about where to start in the telling – make the opening as interesting as possible. Writing in the present tense makes it more immediate, and might help you recall more. Remember the impact of sensory detail in creating a picture for a reader.

In the 'Stranger Than Fiction' chapter there are suggestions for further developing this piece of writing, using the original incident as a basis for creating fiction.

2

Memories

Short sketches – a paragraph or two each – including details, the life of the senses, feelings and atmosphere.

Here are some starting points:

Write about:

An object from your childhood

An item of clothing of yours as a child

Your grandfather's toolshed/vegetable patch/allotment

Your grandmother's kitchen/larder/garden

A piece of jewellery belonging to your mother/an item of her clothing

A jacket/tool/pipe/car etc belonging to your father

A childhood holiday or trip out

A significant place of your childhood or adolescence (and: what happened here?)

Your first love

Your first loss

A significant crossroads as a teenager or young adult

3
Topics

The idea behind this exercise is to map a particular object or type of object, person, animal, topic or place throughout your life. Choose *one* of the following topics or items (or make up your own):

A particular object or kind of object (e.g. clocks or watches, torches, boats, cars, chairs, books etc)
A particular person
A particular smell
A particular place
Pets: dogs, cats, horses
Food
Footwear
Gardens

Make notes around your chosen topic, but starting with a very distant memory in connection with this topic and bringing it to the much more recent past, so that you end up with a string of short pieces focusing on the *same* topic at different times in your life. In effect, what you write about will end up as a symbol for aspects of your life.

Don't be too literal. The object may only be peripheral; a trigger or springboard. For instance, a book might simply be an indirect way of talking about the houses you've lived in – where it was on the bookshelf – or a way of talking about a shared intellectual companionship or a relationship, or it may represent something you and your siblings did together – *Swallows and Amazons* might suggest a den known only to you and your brothers as a child, which you then write about to mirror change – for example, a new car park built on a riverside meadow. (As always, follow your imagination rather than my 'rules' when writing.)

What shape might these pieces take if you redraft them either as prose or poetry?

The following poem was written in a workshop in response to a childhood object in 3 above:

Bone China

At nose level
on the ridged table
the light diffuses through
the frightening translucency
of exotic birds
bounces off the fairy tale gold
of scalloped rims

this is the ritual wash
rinse drain and polish
of the tea set
kept for best

but best never comes

re-stacked at the rear
of the white wooden cupboard
on wobbly floorboards
they rattle as I walk by
threaten to tumble crash
chip and crack

carted carefully
with every move
through our
then her life

they are stacked still
on glass shelves
in a bow fronted cabinet
the light diffusing through

too precious for hot tea
too fragile even to dust
now her hands
are losing their grip.

Susie Shelley

If you don't already, get into the habit of watching your mind at work, without judging. Learn how to step back and simply monitor what's going on, rumbling away beneath the surface of 'thinking'. Elsewhere I've talked about the steady stream of everyday consciousness, or 'monkey mind'; and of course much of what you tell yourself will be uninspiring – that tedious and gross (in the sense of unrefined) trivia: *Must just do... did I tell so-and-so what...damn, forgot to put that... wonder about supper tonight... where did that book go... what did John mean when he said... what is that in the corner... must phone so-and-so...* all punctuated by registered or unregistered flashes of inspiration and intuition, imaginings and fantasies, and coherent consequential thought to some greater, or lesser, degree too. It can be shocking and dispiriting to realise quite what passes for 'thought'; or, if you're an optimist, perhaps profoundly illuminating!

And, more helpfully for a writer, you will also see how you make up stories without even knowing you're doing it.

It's early morning, and wild, squally, invigorating spring weather – showers one minute, sun the next, storms of cherry blossom everywhere. Everything's green, blue, green, pink, green, yellow, white. I'm walking with the dogs down a steep narrow path through dark woodland. At the bottom it opens out; there's a stream in the valley. I lean on the bridge and lose myself in the May lushness: bluebells, fresh beech leaves, campions, broom, gorse. Early sun on my face; the fragrance of damp soil, wet new foliage, wild garlic and bluebells that's particular to spring.

A moment of stillness and unthought.

Suddenly my eyes are caught by a movement maybe a hundred yards away: the haunches of a big animal slinking swiftly away up the bank into the trees, one long dark slender leg then the other. In my May-mesmerised state my mind registers and simultaneously almost with the seeing I assume it's the bigger of my two dogs, the deerhound; then a nanosecond later realise it can't be as she's right by my feet (as is the other one – unusually). My mind says 'it must be a deer' even as my memory/imagination throws up the image of a long smooth big-cat tail. Again almost simultaneously with these two 'thoughts' my head says that deer don't slink leg by leg up steep banks into undergrowth but bound, forelegs together and hind legs together.

Approximately two seconds later I have written, in my mind, without any conscious intention, the news item, headlined: WOMAN EATEN ALIVE BY BLACK BEAST OF DARTMOOR, and am well on the way to syndicating the rights. And planning my funeral. (What's left of me, that is.)

The whole process from sight to complete story has taken about five seconds.

I am aware that I am oversensitive (melodramatic) and I tend to overreact. Some might call me paranoid; I prefer to think of myself as possessing a very vivid imagination. For me, that piece of sacking in the road is always part of a torso, and that unexplained sound is probably the local volcano erupting for the first time since prehistory.

I am a writer. A sense of melodrama goes with the territory – in fact it's a positive bonus to be a neurotic. Why hear hoof beats and assume 'horse' when it would be so much more exciting to see a wild zebra, here in Britain?

You are a writer. Milk it. Notice all those hundreds of potential stories quietly incubating away under all those so much more 'sensible' thoughts... and don't let anyone talk you out of your paranoia.

Starting points

Unlocking the cages
These are simply ways of using free association to loosen and exercise your imagination. It's helpful to use them frequently as warm-up exercises. They might also suggest further pieces of writing, but it's most useful not to approach them with this expectation. What is important is that you allow wild thinking... Don't try and make sense.

1
You might want to use coloured pens – recent research at London University shows that more of your brain cells 'light up' when you're using colour.

a) Take an image or object (ordinary domestic objects are often the most fruitful). Write or draw it at the centre of a large sheet of paper.

b) Without thinking, write all your associations and memories in relation to that word in a large rough circle around it, however bizarre or surreal they appear. Don't censor any of your writing. As you allow yourself to be drawn into it, you will find that it becomes quicker; and also that you become 'looser' in the way that you relate to it. This in turn allows more lateral connections to be made.

c) Take the most interesting of those responses and do the same again; and again.

d) At some stage, stop and look. Which of these words have an emotional charge for you? How might you develop something further from any of this?

2
Without thinking, write a sentence. Allow it to include interesting words, and to be bizarre.
Now write a second separate sentence, without following on in any way at all from the previous one. Do this until you have ten or twelve sentences.

3
Now do the same thing as above, but this time allow the sentences to follow on.

4
And again; this time incorporating a word from the previous sentence in the following one, but not necessarily looking to make the sentences follow each other; e.g.:

> They lay curdled and separate in the belly of their marriage
> Moonlight curdled the words they hadn't yet spoken
> The words fell into the cur's waiting eyes
> The eyes became saucers into which she poured the sentence of herself
> Herself is one alone again, a loose petal floating
> The Milky Way looses pollen on the night
> Dunked in pollen the bee is a gospel choir of one
> To bee or to wasp is not the right question
> A wasp squad is an off-key singing of spears
> The rain is singing of nowhere we know

5

Finally, take a sentence from a book. (Try using something that is not obviously creative, like a DIY or car manual, or a cookery or bird book. *National Geographic's* always good... Or try a book of fairy tales.)

Run with that sentence as far as you can in five minutes...

STANDING IN THE RIVER

When I was a child, my father taught me the 'scouts' pace': a rhythm that I could maintain over quite large distances, consisting of alternating 100 hundred paces at a walk with 100 paces at a jog.

As I reflect on my own practice, both as writer and facilitator, I realise that much of my work cycles between these poles of comparative tautness and slackness. I like this metaphor: the drift between states of being. Creating, resting. Editing, resting. Creating, editing. Facilitating a group workshop; dreaming into being and preparing a new workshop in solitude. Poetry, prose. Writing, not writing. Being indoors, working. Being outdoors, incubating. Being with friends; being alone. Fallow, fruitful. Fruitful, fallow.

So I'm thinking of rhythmic patterns: inbreaths and outbreaths, action of systole and diastole, ebb and flow of moon and tides, of course, and their echo in the body.

I'm thinking about the contraction and relaxation of muscles.

I'm thinking of moving between the tight weave of a poem and the loose knit (well, looser knit) of prose. I'm thinking that poetry is a taut muscle and prose is that same muscle slackened off a little.

I'm thinking about moving between inner and outer. And back again.

I'm thinking about standing in the stream, its endless and immeasurable flow of water running to the sea, and dipping a jar in to catch a few millilitres (fluid ounces) of water (which I know will be thrumming with organisms and micro-organisms, seen and unseen. If I were a fisherman I would be thinking in terms of minutes or hours standing motionless, and then one quick flick and lift, and part of the river's treasure on the end of my line.)

I'm thinking of a video running on a loop and the option of freezing a frame.

I'm thinking about shifting perspective between far-sight and near-sight: I speak of this in the chapter on perspective – shifting between the broad picture and the close-up (or buzzard and mouse).

I'm thinking about how a writer needs to be able to shift between a number of pairs of totally different perspectives and their demands: creating and editing; passionate immersion and objective evaluation; the pace of an action scene, and that of a narrative passage.

Especially important is the shift between detail, and overall picture or context.

I think writers need to strengthen or develop a particular way of looking that embraces the whole world and also allows them to focus in on what's important for their purposes. We train our eyes to really look, and then we combine what we have observed with what we already know, and then project this combination onto an inner imagined landscape with its own stories. So much of writing is about this conjunction between what can be observed, what we can't observe but know to be there, and what is imagined.

The river's a good metaphor. When you're in it, standing in it, you are only aware of its flow around you; or maybe not even that – maybe you perceive yourself as part of it. When you examine it in close-up, you notice its patterns and variations, its plant life, insect life, fish life, mineral life, colour, texture, music. When you look at it from a distance, you get some sense of its scale, size and speed, its proportions in relation to the surrounding landscape. Step back further again, and it takes on a different form: it seems frozen, immobile. I've recently come back from the Isle of Mull, where there are often bodies of water cascading furiously down slopes. From a distance these fast-rushing waterfalls look solid and unvarying, like glaciers or wide vertical seams of quartz, yet I know they are moving.

Look out of your window towards the far distance. Chances are the backdrop looks much the same as ever – static, in other words – with maybe occasional changes, which in the context of the scale of the background range from unnoticeable to subtle, most of the time (unless something major happens, like a building is razed to the ground). Yet you know intellectually that hundreds, or more likely thousands, of lives are being played out in that backdrop: people, voices, movement, noises, cars/lorries/buses, animal, insect, plant life – in fact it is teeming with life, rather like the jar of stream water – though to your eye most of it looks motionless, fixed.

But in the foreground the picture is quite different, and the detail changes all the time. A window is opened. A dustbin appears; disappears. Some washing is pegged out. Someone walks by. Cars rumble past. A cat flicks its tail. The shadow from the wall opposite changes. A leaf moves in the breeze. A drink can is dropped and rolls away to the kerb. The shadow has shifted again. There is a constant stream of moments, of movement. That the stream will continue to flow is reasonably predictable; the content isn't. But if you shift perspective again and look back at the backdrop, you can see neither flow nor changing detail. No visible cat, let alone a flicking tail.

Then there is the issue of changing pace. How different, for example, is it writing descriptive prose from writing a love scene, or one depicting anger or jealousy? And what about the qualitative difference, for you, between the demands of poetry and the demands of prose? I know for me that prose is a relatively relaxing experience, one from which I can emerge, and into which I can re-enter, without too much disturbance; whereas the catching, shaping, drafting and redrafting of a poem is an activity which is a kind of heightened experience for me – I feel breathless and adrenalin-full and intensely, excitedly absorbed when I'm working a poem. And I hate being interrupted. This is the same when I am reading prose or poetry, too.

Without thinking about it, we shift modes all the time. We don't usually take the time to evaluate our experience; it's habitual. But what is it like, making the transition from, say, a run to a standstill? From sleep to waking? How different is it to walk along a beach just to stroll, from training on the road for the next London marathon? From looking at the sea to being in it? Without ever giving it a thought, we get into a car, drive ten or a hundred miles, arrive somewhere different, get out again. What happens to our bodies, our emotions, our psyches as we make these transitions? How does it affect our creativity?

The brief to participants on my courses is often to do with the movement between states: inner and outer; movement and stillness; past and present; memory and imagination; distance and close-up; the recorded prose-like stream of things passing, and the moments they choose to freeze in a tighter more focused form, a poem.

A writer is making shifts of attention all the time. She is also making choices all the time: what to put in? What to leave out?

In a way a writer – any writer – is lifting a jar of water out of the river for a reader. When we choose to write about a particular moment, experience, situation, we are in effect choosing to freeze the passage of time; we are lifting that glass of water. In a life of billion upon billion of moments, of experiences, of imaginings, what do we choose to freeze-frame? What are the things important enough to you for you to write about? Of course, if we think of choices like this, we might never write at all. But the moment, as it passes, touches us, marks us – and if we're paying attention everything is worth recording – a totally impossible task. So we 'pan' the passing experience – real or imagined – and alight on something – anything that we receive, through our senses or our imagination that makes some kind of an impact – to record. Some of these recorded moments will be banal, some will be inspired. That's the nature of it.

Starting points

Stills

1

This one works best outdoors, where you have a breadth to draw on.

a) Take the long view first. Pan the landscape around you and record its generalities. Think of this as just making the equivalent of a quick monochrome pencil sketch to fix contours and impressions. Don't be too 'precious' about this – just record it as it is, as notes.

b) When you have done this, choose to freeze elements, and examine them in vivid detail, minutely. Write to convey their uniqueness. Do this by alighting on a specific 'frame'. You might want to actually make a frame out of paper or card – just an inch or so square – and look through it; or between finger and thumb if you have to. Exclude everything that isn't in the frame from your 'picture'; and write about the interior, the 'still', in any way you like – you don't need to spell out what it is you're framing; the piece may be more interesting for being unexplained.

c) When you have completed one, quickly but vividly, frame another (though you may want to relax back into the broad view in between, just note-making).

d) Redraft, setting yourself a 'frame' in the response, too; say a poem of five or six brief lines per frame. (Experiment: draw a box and use only those words and spaces that will fill/fit the 'frame' exactly...)

Stills

You stand motionless
Back like a horizon
Outlined by leaf burst.
Sand form, hoof resting,
Blond tail flicks the dust,
Mane like rainfall.

Breeze vibrates the fence line
At random, scores the backdrop.
And here you gently tear at grass
Between the buttercups,
Tail like a sable brush, pointing,
Mane of sisal, bearded fetlocks.

*

It only matters
That the air is full with song
And the river, an inset
Like the pearl cloches on the hill,
Moves only because I know it moves,
Through the haze, nuzzling a shimmer,
Nurturing stillness.

Mary Gillett (from the above workshop exercise)

2

Philip Gross has a poem, or sequence, called 'Stills', in which he characterises people and situations in a few lines each.

If you were to apply the exercise above to people rather than surroundings (the frame will then be metaphorical), how would you portray people you know or encounter? What detail would you choose to 'lift' from what you know of their lives or can tell from looking at them?

3

Perspectives

This one's good for doing somewhere other than home, and preferably outside. Make notes on each of these perspectives:

a) Foreground
b) Middle distance
c) Horizon
d) Over the horizon
e) Very close up – inches. Your thumb, a daisy, an inch of soil, an inch of brick wall, the grain of, or marks on, your writing desk...

Keep your responses to each of these perspectives very brief, and in the present tense. You'll probably find that some are easier/more interesting than others, and need more time/words. Note that you are not necessarily asked to be literal... OR you might want to answer these questions first literally, physically, and second, metaphorically: to take the long view, then the short view, of your life. It can be more interesting to interleave the two, though, so that you're not labouring any point. Be imaginative!

Note the difference in your emotional responses to each of the perspectives... Which was hard, which easy? Which did you enjoy? And what was it about any that you enjoyed less?

Which was easier for you, the more rambling generalities' recording, or the more intense stills? Why?

One of my students interpreted this exercise imaginatively by giving each perspective to a fictional someone who exemplified in some way the qualities in question; for example a microbiologist, a visionary, and someone who was visually impaired.

4
Stepping back
Take a look at what you have done in the above exercises. Any surprises? Any connecting themes? Anything that doesn't fit the sequence? How might you tighten – or loosen – what you have done by excluding or including lines, sections or pieces? Which of the pieces want to relax into prose or contract into poetry?

TALES OF WONDER

from *What you should know to be a poet*

all you can about animals as persons
the names of trees, flowers and weeds
names of stars, and the movements of the planets and the moon

your own six senses...
Gary Snyder

As humans, we need mystery. As writers, we also need bottomless curiosity, the capacity to be astonished, a passion to carry on learning, and a sense of wonder. These all help to keep inspiration alive, and resuscitate a flagging imagination. This is also, clearly, quite a good recipe for life, too; and as a prescription it is as likely to be an inquiring mind which is both cause and consequence of a spirited old age as anything else...

As you'd expect, most writers I know love learning new things. I talk in 'Beachcombing' about our acquisitive nature, and how you never know which little bit of tinder will ignite a conflagration. What I do know is that my creativity is often born in the place where a detail excites me.

If I analyse what inspires me personally, much of it is probably universal: music, art, literature, friendship, love, walking, good conversation and new ideas. Human achievements and human acts of courage and compassion. Also for me colour, places, gardens, being outside, dramatic or wild landscape, the ocean, the winds, travel, and so on. Animals, plants, trees, stones. Esoterica, mythology, philosophy, mysticism. Old manuscripts: the Books of Hours; the Celtic holy books such as *Kells*; sources like the *Mabinogion*. Stories. Poetry, of course. Language and languages inspire me, and etymology – finding connections between things. (Connection is a very important one for me.)

What I've only realised recently is just how much scientific discovery inspires me, especially in the categories of cosmology and new physics, in addition to subjects I already knew inspired me: history, natural history, geology, archaeology and anthropology; and the way in which things are made – glass, for instance. I have only recently realised how fascinating *The New Scientist* is for non-scientists!

So I have started to keep yet another notebook – this one just for astonishing facts. I know, just know, that one day I'll use this snippet from Radio 4: in Italy, in what's known as the Botticelli Gorge, is a single stratum of clay just one centimetre thick in between layers of limestone. This layer has a much higher concentration of iridium than would be expected for such a thin layer of clay, even given that it has been compacted by successive layers of limestone. (At White Scar Cave in Yorkshire there is, apparently, a similar layer of clay in amongst limestone.) Physicists agree that this suggests extraterrestrial activity, such as the impact from an asteroid. So 65,000,000 years ago, apparently, that little seam of clay was laid down as a result of the meteor that, we think, took the dinosaurs. 'So looking up at the layers,' said one of the radio presenters, 'you can see and move through time...' I am astonished and excited. Inspired.

Looking back over what I've just written, I see that it's very simple. What inspires me is the universe, but especially the earth. The earth moves me to awe. 'In reality, the earth is the centre of mystery in our lives,' says artist Daniel De Angeli. 'Despite the thick layers of civilization and mobile phones, we are still not very far away from our origins, and nature has the power to take you back to the elemental, to a state of surprise and silence.'[1]

I'm at the Cotswold Water Park, one of a team of artists working on a project there. Today we're learning something of the history and prehistory of the park, which is, we're told, part of the old Thames floodplain. 'Wherever you go here, you're walking on water,' says Dr Simon Pickering, the Park Biodiversity Officer, a fact that is already inspiring me.

The Water Park contains probably the least known but one of the biggest and most exciting fossil sites in the country. Fossilised remains of crocodiles, giant squid, one of the world's largest sharks and of such creatures as woolly mammoths and woolly rhinos have all been found here.

Most of these fossil beds are being exposed – and destroyed – as they are excavated for aggregate from the limestone beds. The 'spoil' heaps (not accessible to the public, but we are accompanied by an 'official' geologist) contain ammonites bigger than a man's fist, cannonball-sized. We stumble over each other in our excitement. Then our guide, the geologist, lifts a large lump of ordinary-looking clay from a heap and gives it a sharp crack with his hammer. It splits, but he hands it to me without separating the two halves. I open it and gasp. The interior is solid with ammonites of varying sizes. The central one, larger than the others, has a hollow right at the heart of its spiral, and in the hollow is a drop of water. 'Taste it,' he says. 'That's seawater that's been locked away in darkness for 160 million years. No one's seen it before, ever.' I dip my finger and taste salt.

He's right.

I'm speechless (no mean feat).

That experience blew me away; and several years on I'm still overawed by it. 160 million years that secret drop of water has kept its salt taste! And needless to say I wrote about it; and wrote about it; and... And it has inspired me to new heights of enthusiasm for researching fossils, and the ages of the earth. The more I discover, the more I'm enthused, and the more I'm kicked sideways to write about new things.

The more I learn about the world the more astonished I am, and the more I want to know; and paradoxically, the more mysterious this whole thing – this being alive, this planet, this universe – seems to me. If I lose that ability to stand in awe, I will no longer be able to create.

It doesn't take much to light my day – and for that I'm thankful. Sometimes – as often as I remember – I set myself the task of seeing, hearing, learning, being aware of, noticing, at least one new thing each day. That's not much; but it keeps me 'tuned in'. I'm constantly learning to look, really look, and to listen properly. 'So much of listening is hearing what we expect and tuning out the rest,' said someone wise. 'The real voyage of discovery,' said Proust, 'consists not in seeking new landscapes but in having new eyes.' Henry Miller set himself this task in his strolls around Paris; so does essayist Jacques Réda, Phil Cousineau[2] tells us. As writers, part of our job is to draw attention to what others ignore, or miss, or simply take for granted.

Learn something. Little details stay with you. As the contributions to this book came in from other authors, phrases or details from all their pieces have lodged in my memory, where they sit and glimmer. Here are some: Jane Spiro's telling that in Arabic the word for amber is the same as that for electricity; Andy Brown teaching me that the word 'arena' comes from the Latin for sand, with all its implicit subtle shifts; Neil Gunn's phrase 'atoms of delight' from Kenneth Steven's piece; Stephen Parr giving me that wonderful line from Tomas Tranströmer: 'The heart went on leaping from second to second like the toad in the wet grass of an August night'; and (heart again) Keith Jafrate offering me Ken Smith's image of the heart as a fennel root. And a wonderful sentence in Keith's essay which sums up what is important in poetry for me: 'This is not an ideology, more a belief that the magic of poetry can make us better attuned to the universe, and that this tuning process will erode what might be cruel or exploitative or indifferent in us.' These have all inspired me.

I've always been interested in pigment, colour and minerals. It's July or August 2003 and I'm on a train to the north of Scotland for some work. I'm one of those travellers who doesn't like talking unless she has to; in fact if I'm honest I don't even like sitting beside someone else unless there's no choice (I blame it on lack of time to myself, but maybe I'm simply selfish).

Anyway, as we come up to a station – I forget which – in the north of England, an interesting-looking woman with a lovely smile comes up through the now-crowded carriage. I shan't mind if she sits beside me, so I move my bag and books to make space and smile back. She's reading a book with an intriguing cover, and I surreptitiously crane to try and read the title. She sees me looking and tilts the book to show me. Ah; one I'd seen reviewed and intended to buy: *The Colour of Heaven,* about the colour blue and lapis, by James Runcie. We talk. (As it turns out, we have mutual friends, but that's another story.) She is Victoria Finlay, author of a book called *Colour – travels through the paintbox.* She's on her way to speak with Runcie at the Edinburgh Festival. Her book is a record of her journeys in search of, amongst other things, lapis lazuli; and as she talks she takes from her bag and hands me (this seems to happen to me!) the biggest lump of rough lapis I have ever seen; a piece she was given on a trip into a lapis mine in Afghanistan.

Another of those moments. I had already read Alexander Theroux's books on primary and secondary colours; both very inspiring for a creative person; Victoria's company set me off again on a deeper search into the history and mystery of colour.

And here's a piece of colour serendipity: in writing this up from my notes I realised I'd forgotten Theroux's name, so searched for him on the internet. In the exploration, I discovered that the primary colours are not, in fact – wait for it – red, yellow and blue, as we are all taught (though if you paid attention to physics at school, you'll know this). In brief, it depends whether we are talking about *emitted* light or *reflected* light.

With emitted light, we have what we call the 'additive' primary colours: blue, red and green, which when mixed together at full intensity make white. The 'subtractive' primary colours (reflected light) are cyan, magenta and yellow – as used in printing, for example. These when mixed together make black. Well, there's my today's hit of new knowledge and inspiration...

So in honour of extending our knowledge, I encourage people on my courses to recognise the areas of expertise in their life – often fields of interest or experience which to them are so commonplace as to mean nothing, but to someone else will be completely new; a foreign language. Nothing is too small or too insignificant. What is ordinary to you may be completely extraordinary to someone else. And it doesn't have even to be useful, or to have a point – just learning for learning's sake, extending your boundaries (though of course there is also a point where knowledge needs to become wisdom).

It also expands our view of someone; learning about their specialities gives us insight into their deeper natures, their personal passions, quirks and abilities. I love this.

It's a wet evening. Three of us are playing Scrabble. I might be passionate about words but I'm useless at word games. I'm taking forever at my turn each time; I know I am. Ruth, who's the scorekeeper, is doodling away on the paper as she waits for me. Eventually I glance over to apologise. It doesn't surprise me that she's drawn a stave and filled in a musical score; she is a part-time musician. What does surprise me is that she's written a passage in Welsh, and a phrase in beautiful flowing Arabic. This is not showing off; it's simply how she doodles. I know that Ruth's modest; and I also think I know her very well (she's my sister). But because she doesn't use foreign languages in any way in her daily life I forget that she's also a self-taught polyglot.

I laugh admiringly. 'I don't know anyone else who would do that,' I say.

'What does the Arabic mean?'

She laughs too. '"Take the horse to the bridge," she tells me ruefully. 'It's the only phrase I know, virtually. Might be useful if they ever ask me to come and mediate...' (This was during the Iraq war.)

Paying this sort of attention to people can help us too in character creation: carefully drawn idiosyncrasies can really bring a character alive for a reader.

It seems to me that the creative writing process draws on five primary areas: one is what you know, the second is what you can observe, the third what you can find out, the fourth what you can imagine, and the fifth is the unquantifiable, what I call 'factor x' – inspiration.

The third is the one I want to talk about in the rest of this chapter: what you can find out. 'I like to read fiction with 'stuff' in it,' says Sara Maitland, 'new things I did not know before, references I can draw on and link to literary and other culture... I like quotation, intertextuality... If I like it as a reader, it has to become one of the things I work with as a writer.'[3]

One of the joys, and one of the requirements, for a writer, is finding stuff out. Asking questions. Why do planes stay in the air? What is dark matter? How can the arrow of time be forward, reversed, stationary and non-existent all at the same time? How do they cantilever bridges? Why do eels go to the Sargasso Sea? What makes glass a liquid? How do swallows navigate across oceans? Why do puffins look like they do? How many shellfish did it take to dye one sleeve purple, before we invented chemical dyes? (The answer to this one is a whole boatful of crushed murex and purpura, according to poet Michael Symmons Roberts[4].)

Often the information will take you off in a totally new creative direction.

Maitland talks about a novel she was working on which ostensibly focused on the nature of relationship between gay men and heterosexual women, and which also, incidentally, included on the periphery glassblowing (the book, not the relationship). However the more she found out about that art, or science, the more pivotal the glassblowing became, until finally it hijacked the plot.

Kate Grenville, whose book *The Idea of Perfection* won the Orange Prize, talks about researching bridge-building for her book, which she had intended to be about Sydney Harbour Bridge[5]. However, in the course of her research, the book metamorphosed into a book about 'two people haunted by the idea of perfection'; and the bridge took a backseat, but an informative one, as it happened, in as much as the idea of a bridge as a metaphor for human relationship underpins the novel. 'Douglas and Harley [...] discover that Leonardo da Vinci's description of a bridge is also a good guide for relationships: "An arch is two weaknesses that together make a strength."'

En route she discovered, she says, some 'fascinating [if] seemingly irrelevant' information. Did you know, for example, that concrete is actually a very thick liquid, which carries on flowing, or 'creeping', long after it's set? Or that, when water hits cement, the chemical reaction is so fast that we still don't know what goes on at a molecular level?

OK, so maybe that didn't inspire you especially. Does this: 'An Arctic tern, migrating from the Arctic to Antarctica and back, might fly 25,000 miles in a year – a distance roughly equivalent to the circumference of the earth'?[6] Or that a Manx Shearwater will have migrated the equivalent distance of *ten* trips to the moon and back in its lifetime? Isn't that astounding?

I set one group of my regular students the task of researching something that interested them, with a view to giving a very brief presentation, making it as inspiring as possible, to the rest of the group the next time we met. (Although I always hope that ideas so researched and presented will spark some creative expression in the researcher and/or their listeners, I didn't have any agenda as to 'what then'; this was purely to explore and present a new subject.) This is some of what we all learnt that session:

Over a period of about two days, a mushroom will release 40,000,000 spores per hour, of which only a few will grow into new mushrooms

A seasoned grower can tell each of 40 varieties of potato apart by their flowers

Indigo (which incidentally goes blue on exposure to light and air) was used to dye the cover for the Tabernacle of the Ark of the Covenant, long before it was used to dye Levi's jeans

In California 10,000 people make their living from harvesting sea urchins; the sea otters which eat the urchins are in decline; the urchins are devastating the kelp forests which are used as fertiliser, soil conditioner and for maintaining the frothy head on Irish stout!; but due to a kind of sea-urchin gold rush for their roe for sushi they themselves are now under threat

When bats return to roost in the loft after a winter hibernating in caves/tunnels/old mines, the mothers only have one baby each and only a quarter of them survive to the following autumn. They have to learn to fly at 3-4 weeks, and are weaned at 6-8 weeks and then have to find their own insects to eat. And all those droppings of theirs are very handy – collect them on newspaper and dump it on the compost heap or put a bit in the watering can.

Starting points

1

Well, clearly I'm going to ask you to think about something about which you know a lot: herb growing, scuba-diving, belly dance, crop circles, the Green Man, cooking, yoga, minimalist music, algorithms, Renaissance dance, child psychology, Gothic architecture – whatever it is. (If you're struggling with this, cast your mind back to adolescence. What inspired you then? And if you're *really* struggling, then your forfeit is to do the exercise below with *two* subjects...) Find a way to write about this that is both succinct and informative/entertaining (or both).

2

You guessed: choose a subject about which you know little or nothing, but which interests you. Research it and write it up; and while you're thinking about it, be aware of how many times that subject crops up in other contexts. It's uncanny how that happens, once you bring something into consciousness.

How do [...] wild salmon find their way back to their home stream after swimming thousands of miles out across the vast Pacific? We simply do not know.

By what kind of deep somatic attunement – feeling their way between faint electromagnetic anomalies, riding a particular angle of the sun as it filters down through the rippled surface above, dreaming their way through gradients of scent and taste toward the lost beloved – how do they find their way to that source, that particular place inseparable from their being?

David Abram

SHIFTING ARENAS
BY ANDY BROWN

I am fascinated by shorelines: both the real ones where I live in Devon, and the metaphorical shores of the poem or story. Years ago I took a degree in Ecology, studying co-existence strategies in British periwinkles. My deepening relationship with edges and shores grew out of science. But my passion goes back even further than that, of course, to childhood summers hunting for creatures in rock pools and the thrill of being tumbled by waves. That feeling persists. It is the same thrill I find in writing and reading a good poem or story – surrendering to the tidal pull of the language.

I love the wind; the salt spray; the shoals of fish and diving birds. The sight of a seal is always a thrill; that of a basking shark or dolphin makes for a moment of grace. The flora of a cliff walk and the scurrying of clandestine animals in bracken and heather pull me into wonderment. And walking (that most rhythmical and hence poetic activity) the shore or coast is a pleasure nearly always taken in company; on several levels it is a communion.

The poet in me starts to search for words. One I delight in is 'arena' derived from the Latin for sand. It opens a theme of scene-shifting – the shoreline is neither land nor sea but shifts between both. The word 'arena' also opens up the possibilities of *change*; the opportunity that we as writers must embrace: the metaphorical 'shifting sands' in the word 'arena' help to reinvent the shoreline; it becomes a place to welcome (and a metaphor for) change.

Poems and stories are formed from and informed by that most elusive and slippery of things: Language. The familiar feeling 'Words cannot express…', might have us believe that language itself is not always up to the task of grasping the essence of experience. But the poetry of our experiences paradoxically comes from somewhere. For the writer, it is language that sublimates experience into something new, turning one thing into another. Language is a shape-shifter. It creates its own reality. Language – like a tide – covers up just as it reveals and, thankfully, resists total explanation. Language signals what it may have left out, by suggesting the underlying silence beyond what has been written.

I like poetry and fiction that seems to be out for a walk itself – experiencing things; experiencing language; expecting the unexpected. But being 'out for a walk' necessitates a return 'home'. As global and local Ecology becomes increasingly important, its meaning (derived from the Greek, *ecos*, meaning 'home') heightens. Home is vital; the real home and the metaphoric home; the 'ecological home' and the ontological home of 'self', as well as the idea of the 'home' of language. When I am out for a walk along a coast path, or through the metaphoric landscape of a poem, I find myself asking how we might 'be' at home on the earth; how we should 'dwell' here. Ultimately, how does the language of a poem or story help us to realise that dwelling; to negotiate the space between the real world and the imagined; the real landscape and the landscape of the poem?

Landscape, poem and story each abound with gaps, borders and edges. Real borders and transitory zones (the cliff, the shore, the woodland edge and the suburb for example); real poetic gaps (line breaks, stanzas, paragraphs, chapters); as well as the more abstract gaps between the said and the unsaid; between experience and the language of experience; between types of language (poetic, scientific, spiritual); between personal identities (public and private) and the shifting arena that is the dialogue between memory and self. Through the interplay of the said and the unsaid, the known and the unknown, the expressible and the inexpressible, the poem or story writes itself into being.

Which brings me back from the tumble of the wave I began with, full circle, to standing again. At the literal, metaphoric, scientific and spiritual level, for me the shoreline embodies constancy and change; solidity and fluidity; gaps and boundaries. Poem and story can both be thought of as shoreline; a shifting tide that covers, reveals and negotiates the boundaries of the real and the imagined; the experienced and the written. The shore is a shifting zone; a mirror of the shifting nature of language, and vice versa. In *the written landscape*, the self looks out to sea – metaphorically looks out to memory, experience and imagination – and then looks back across the land; the real landscape and the ontological home. It may then jump, and I mean that both literally and metaphorically – jumping is an act of faith – with good humour *into language*.

Writers need to write and read themselves away from the edge of the known land; away from the edge of the known self; away from the edge of the known landscape and language into surprising new arenas. And in so doing, their writing may just become surprisingly readable; that is, it may come to hold readable surprises.

Shooting the Sun

The coastal path directs us like a telepath: our cross-staff and astrolabe.
Like apprentice mariners shooting the sun, it leads us out from sweet to
brackish; to ozone and salt-spray. From shoals in shining waters to the
intricate grain of the coast, everything happens with deceptive ease. On
shore, the fishing rods tremble; their quivers meaning bites.

Birds – I think they're fulmars aren't they? – bank on high winds, the shirr
of their wings in a soundless sky. Sea grasses flex. Waxen figures bob in a
boat with a sail. Old wooden cabins line the waterfront. High on the strand,
the dry remains of dogfish twist in piles of weed. Big and busy bugs skim over
meres behind the dunes, bothering cattle and sheep. A bird's song cascades
up-shore, carried by wind to the geese at rest on the reed banks. Buds of
poppies, mallow and clover; swallows plucking insects from the surface. Ducks
fan the ripples; waders stilt from foot to foot. A heron, motionless, startled
by apparent nothingness, sweeps into the stillness of the sky. Its sudden,
guttural cry. Slash of a sinuous fish sliding through dark waters. Clouds
sluice across the sky like tea in a Wedgwood cup.

A fish carcass draws a harrier down. It flies low, dipping feet into water;
the bobbing fish belly-up. Claws gaff and lift. Downstream, its flight path
gently curved, the hawk descends. A walker's dog disturbs the feed. The hawk
forgets its quarry. The dog moves in, licks the fish, then pulls off to the
walker's distant voice. Among alders and birch the morning takes place: the
leaps and bounds of foraging foxes; mute deer laying back their ears. Above,
clear space and enveloping light; the sea in our wings.

Celebration of an unseen bird.

Minutely, over the flats, the tide.

Starting points

Go for a walk along the coast or a river. Find a space and sit alone. Observe closely. Write down specific names of things around you. Be alive to all of your senses, including your imagination, which is also a sense; a way of perceiving. Find this space and moment alive with active detail. Begin to sketch them together with active vocabulary. Be light with it; don't try to draft your poem or prose here and now. Back at home, concentrate on selecting details in the following ways:

1

Write a poem/prose passage as a composite of your images. Use them as collaged snapshots – 'this thing, then that thing, then this thing, then that'. Use colour and contrast, or one of the other senses, to move from one image to another.

Or

2

Find the images that combine to create a mood. Focus on the sensory. Don't include too much – be selective and prepared to pare it back. Look for something that would be unseen by others. Again look for colour and contrast, or one other of the senses. Introducing something from an alien/other landscape, go from 'the natural' to introduce the 'unnatural' or the 'man-made'. How does this change the written world of your poem/prose?

CATCHING THE WAVE

...the way I'd always worked was, for all its appearance of disorder, a kind of system. Knowing in advance what you will discover is certainly neater and more reassuring than walking forward into the dark. But the imagination is not a neat creature, and it has a mind of its own. The perfect process for writing (and probably for other creative acts as well...) is to find a way of working that balances the need for chaos and the need for structure. The imagination needs the freedom to improvise. Guess, follow absurdities and give the impossible a hearing.
Kate Grenville

Writing, like any other creative endeavour (including life), requires a willingness to jump off the cliff, or throw oneself in front of the wave – not once, but many times – with no knowledge of where one is going to land, only the faith that one *will* land, eventually. What you parachute, or surf, on is the slenderest glimmer of a spark of inspiration – or sometimes just the hope that if you jump, there will *be* one.

Constantly as writers we come up against the hard place of not knowing what or how to write or continue writing, as I explore in 'Begin Anywhere, Begin Somewhere'. Or maybe you've had an idea that seems promising, but after a tantalising start it is in danger of fizzling out, and you can't see how to resuscitate it – or even if it's worth it.

A hard time for many writers is immediately after the successful completion of a piece, and before a new creative project has properly announced itself: the fear that one's wells have dried up forever, and inspiration was last seen legging it over someone else's horizon; we may feel we have nothing useful or original to say. You come up against the foot of the cliff: is this it, now, then? Will I ever write again? Was the last piece simply a fluke? Am I a fake?

The trouble with writing is that – even when you have an idea in mind – it is potentially so formless, so *baggy*. It's not like cabinet-making, where the brief is to make a cupboard to fit into the space of *x* by *y;* nor like dentistry, where you have Mrs P's appointment followed by Mr H's; nor like gardening, where you can see that you have just finished hoeing the row of carrots, or dead-heading the flowers.

Orange prizewinner Kate Grenville says: 'We all have an image of the writer in his or her book-lined study, knowing just what their book is going to be about, starting at page one and calmly writing until they reach the end.'[1] I don't know any writer who works like that. The process is a great deal more shambolic, full of attempts and refusals. Each time you begin a new project, you feel like a complete beginner; each time, you feel as if – in her words – you have to reinvent the wheel. There's always the fear that, this time, it won't work.

It's also elusive. You get up one day, and it's there; you get up the next and it's not.

Even if you do have hold of a thread in your hands, it proves to be both alive and slippery. Rarely does it move predictably; it proceeds, in my experience anyway, in a series of leaps and bounds; some forwards, some backwards. Often you lose sight of it altogether, after a promising start.

I almost never know where the end will come (and often it's only in retrospect that I recognise the beginning). Knowing when to stop is just as hard as knowing where to begin.

But this is just how it should be. The imagination can't be marshalled, or planned into being (though the results might be). It shows up, or it doesn't. All you can do is put yourself in its way, and when it does show up be prepared to follow where it leads. It's like tracking a hare by the light of a dim moon.

As I've got older I've occasionally wondered whether maybe I should have lived my life differently. Perhaps I should have learnt to *plan*, for instance. When you plan, you have a goal, and you work out the necessary steps to get there. Then you follow them. With a good rudder, a single-minded focus and a following wind, you end up where you had planned to, more-or-less.

OK, I confess: the more dominant part of me says: *Let's hope you want to be there when you get there!* Another way is simply to allow the wind to take you; and to want to be wherever it blows you. Not a very secure way of living; and probably very frustrating to other, different, people. I've always felt vaguely guilty about the fact that this has been my way; and admiring of, and slightly intimidated by, people who seem to have defined goals and a fixed focus. My way is much more chaotic; and it makes me feel less than grown-up around such people. Increasingly, though, I'm beginning to realise that I'm not alone: this is so often how it is for creative types.

But there is a certain virtue in chaos, at least creatively speaking. It's to do with letting things unfold when they're ready to, rather than imposing our ego-

or fear-driven schedules on a process that is not mediated and regulated by the intellect.

I love what Adam Nicolson has to say in his book *Sea Room*[2]: 'I never think things through. I never have. I never envisage the end before I plunge into the beginning. I never clarify the whole... I bank on instinct, allowing my nose to sniff its way into the vacuum, trusting that somewhere or other, soon enough, out of the murk, something is bound to turn up.

'I'm wedded to this plunging-off form of thought, and to the acceptance of muddle, which it implies. Something that is not preordained, that hasn't even envisaged the far wall before it has started building the near one, has the possibility, at least, of arriving somewhere unexpected.'

And this, of course – this possibility of arriving somewhere unexpected – and by implication marvellous – is why writers tend to resist the straitjacket of too much planning. If you let it, the imagination can be a cornucopia; a bottomless Lucky Dip. Each time, there's a surprise; and eventually you might find there have been enough of them for you to have created something of substance almost without being aware you were doing it.

Grenville says of her book *The Idea of Perfection* that it was a hopelessly unpromising first draft. There was no clear plot line, she felt; just a series of 'unconnected vignettes'. Reading these fragments, she was tempted just to toss it all in the bin, and go and get 'a proper job'. But what kept her going was the memory of the fact that her other books had started the same way, and eventually each of them had taken shape. 'This forward-in-the-dark way of writing seemed chaotic, but it was actually a system – just one that I hadn't ever articulated.

'Many drafts later, the fragments had joined up into longer scenes....'[3]

Years ago I was learning to surf. I love water, but my preference is to be on or near it. Being *in* it, though exciting, holds a bucketful of fear for me if it's deep and wild water (which, it being the North Devon Atlantic coast on which I was brought up, it was). I also love waves; but being tossed and thrown by big breakers a long way out of my depth, with my head continuously thrust underwater, is a terrifying experience.

So since surfing involves – in my experience! – a great deal more immersion than buoyancy, you can imagine how I was pushing my fear threshold every time I carried the seven feet of fibreglass which represented my notional *terra firma* down over the sands. And, though the exhilaration of catching a wave is unlike anything else, and worth all the duckings, I found it quite hard to get myself to the stage where I could let go into it. I'd shiver on the shoreline, dig my toes into the sand, allow myself to be distracted by shells and pebbles – anything rather than notice how the undertow pulled at my ankles, and just how many hundreds of miles and billions of gallons of water swayed deeply and horribly between me and America, with only the three miles of Lundy Island to break it... (The procrastinations, of course, were a precursor of my life as a writer.)

Slowly then you edge towards the water, wading until the surf is beginning to break against your knees, then creeping up your thighs, and you're raising yourself on tiptoe or jumping to avoid that first cold slam of water against your lower belly. By this time you're far enough out to launch yourself belly-down on your board and paddle out past the waves. Then you meet the first serious breakers roaring towards you, enormous as you're lying prone, mountainous glassy walls about to crash; and either you breast them into a moment's stillness the other side before the next one towers, or they pour their icy weight over you. And you paddle and duck, paddle and duck until finally, eyes stinging, arms tired, you turn, pausing in the quieter waters, keeping an eye out over your shoulder for a promising swell. It's tempting to stay here, where it's calm. This is where the waves are born, first as gentle undulations, then rollers, then the fearsome elemental breakers, which charge the shore and dissolve, before sliding back home to start the cycle again.

The aim is to catch a wave just before it breaks. As a likely looking swell rolls towards you, you paddle like crazy towards the shore to be travelling at the right velocity to catch the wave just as it peaks. If your timing's off, you will be thrown, tossed under like flotsam, separated from your board and tumbled, flailing in cubits of opaque choppy water; of no more note than the bladderwrack with which you might share this tumultuous break of water. You're trying to catch your breath and the board before the latter catches you; ribs can be broken, temples smashed, eyes taken out, even, by the sharp hooked fin that stabilises and steers the board. You wonder – in between fighting for air and desperately struggling to get your head above water – why you ever thought this might be fun. You wonder whether you'll drown.

But if you catch it, you're borne in like a *bona fide* part of this watery world towards the shore, sweeping in like a sea god(dess) on this flimsy piece of board. And – like after childbirth – you forget the terror.

Writing's like that. Every time it's an assault on the unknown, a venture into exciting and potentially terrifying territory. You may float; you may get knocked back; you may catch a wave; you may not. You may lose your board. You may go under. You may not come up. You'll fall off the board over and over. You may only catch damp squibs: little waves that break up just as you are about to stand up. You may catch one and live, briefly, in another world. Sometimes you break through into a calm, still place with the ocean rippling beneath you. All the time it's just you and the sea.

And as long as you're prepared to launch yourself in, *something* will happen. It may not be what you'd intended, or hoped for, or planned; or even what you thought you wanted. But it happens; one moment you're becalmed, with the blank page of the ocean below you; the next you're immersed, tossed and wet and surfing.

Or to return to my original image of the cliff: 'Writing's like paragliding,' said Viv, in one of my workshops. 'You can't imagine how it's going to happen; but you just run and run and suddenly it happens and your legs are running in mid-air and you're flying.'

The key is to believe, to trust; to act 'as if': as if you knew what to say, as if there were no doubt that you'd catch the wave. As if there would be another hundred perfectly catchable waves behind it. As if you can surf; as if you can fly; as if you've a story/poem/passage to write. Just do it. Get words down, let them make their own shape, add a few more; and suddenly there's a piece of writing.

The journey of a thousand miles begins with the first step.

COMMITMENT

...[T]o write is to feel your way step by step along a thread of beauty. Along the thread of a poem, or of a story unfolding on a sheet of silk. For the poet, like the tightrope walker, must go forward, word by word, page after page, along the path of a book. And the most difficult thing is not that you must keep your footing on the rope of language, with only a pen for balance; nor to keep going straight ahead, when the way is blocked by the sudden drop of a comma, or the obstacle of a full stop. No, the difficulty for the poet is to stay on the rope that is writing, to live every moment without losing sight of his dream, and to never come down, not even for a second, from the rope of his imagination.
Maxence Fermine, tr. Chris Mulhern

From time-to-time, when someone asks me what I do, I say: 'I write.' And then, now and then, I hear myself answer instead: 'I'm a writer.'

The latter's a response that makes me feel slightly ambivalent. On the one hand, I ask my students to declare out loud 'I am a writer'; to claim that, and the power of that statement; to take themselves seriously.

On the other, there's an edge of ego and inflation in that phrase that makes me feel slightly uncomfortable. There's a certain notion of glamour attached to the idea of 'being a writer' – though goodness knows why; most of the writing life requires a lot of self-discipline, passing up on more 'fun' activities and social events, hard slog for little recognition and little financial reward. The headliners whose lives are transformed by fame and recognition are a very tiny fraction-of-a-percentage.

Writing also requires the kind of dedication that means that you spend a lot of time in solitude, resisting the pulls towards easier, less demanding and more sociable pastimes with friends and family. It also means writing whether you feel like it or not – especially when you don't.

What I'm getting at is that there may come a time in every writer's life when they need to recognise the gulf between wanting to be a writer, and writing. I have any number of students on courses who declare a passionate engagement with, and commitment to, their writing; but time after time they also declare with varying degrees of sheepishness that no, they haven't 'had a chance' to do any writing since we last met. If I'm feeling gentle, or guilty because I've hardly done any writing 'since we last met' either, I'll nod and say, 'It's hard always to make time, isn't it?' But if I'm feeling stroppy, or bold, or simply smug, I'll say in one-way or another, 'Why not? Do you want to write, or do you just want to be A Writer?'

It's true there are easier things than being a writer. Climbing mountains, for instance. Getting, and staying, married. Crossing the Sahara on foot. Running a marathon.

I'm being only partly facetious. I've already said that writers write. As someone else has remarked, that's what we do; as writers there is no way around it. You show up, as Natalie Goldberg (I think) says, you sit down, and you find a way to let, or make, the words shape themselves on the page. If it's not flowing, you act 'as if'. You find a way to make footprints on the blank sand of the page even if you don't know where you're going. Whatever, you *do* it. There is no one else holding you to it. There's no one to let down if you don't show up. There may be no one else who knows or cares whether you put down some words or whether you don't. And you do it even if no one else likes your writing, reads your writing, or pays you for it. Your contract is with yourself, and the blank page, or screen. Does that make it harder? Probably. You have to be immensely motivated, self-disciplined and pigheaded.

I don't mean to sound harsh. I'm as guilty of avoidance as anyone else – and it may be worse in my case because I have made more of an overt commitment to writing than most of my other course participants, as writing and writing-related subjects and events form my working life, a greater part of how I spend my days.

But ultimately you write because you *have* to. Any other reason, you're probably not a writer; you might write, but that's a different thing. That's OK, too.

It's true there are any number of other things that get in the way; many of them legitimate. Maybe you don't spend enough time with your family. Maybe writing's too intense. Maybe you're scared you have nothing to say; or that you won't possibly be able to do it justice, to find an authentic and strong way of saying it. Maybe you really do have something important to say, and the task feels so huge you're terrified. (It's when I feel I'm really on to something that my resistances come up big time.) Maybe the house really *does* need cleaning (when I go for the oven, I know I'm *really* in trouble). Maybe you're feeling lazy; you need a rest; you need a walk. The dog really does need walking.

All these things, of course, can come in the way of your extending yourself; and writing requires that of you all the way. You need to be wide open with the process, being OK about being intimate with yourself, and the world, and the page.

Debbie Taylor, editor of *Mslexia* magazine, used an image that I find helpful to remember. You have a bucket, she says, and each day you will fill it with rocks and sand and pebbles. If you put the rocks in first, there's room for the pebbles and then the sand. But if you put the sand in first, it's hard to squeeze anything else in. If your writing is the rocks, make sure you put those in *first*.

So do I want to write, or do I want to 'be a writer'? The contract with your writing – with my writing – if you are seriously committed to it is as sober a commitment as any other you make; it is also a commitment to your inner life, and to creativity. It is a relationship: it requires engagement, and patience, and self-belief, and belief in the process itself; it requires the kind of struggle and doubt and questioning that any other relationship requires. It requires wanting to do this thing at times more than you want to do anything else. Nothing other than wholeheartedness will do, or you will simply fall off at the first fence.

Starting point

If you are one of those people who truly never have a problem with resisting the process, skip this. Otherwise, try closing your eyes a minute and allow an image to arise that signifies your resistance. Take a good look at it. What's its name? Does it suggest fear, to you? (And don't forget that fear can masquerade as anything: bravado, cockiness, avoidance, boredom and so on.) Enter into a conversation with it! Then write down everything that comes to you in relation to all this.

After that: take a few minutes for thinking about – and answering! – these questions. And be honest with yourself!

> When did you last sit down and write?
> How long did you stick with it?
> What determined when you stopped?
> How typical was this?

There are one hundred and sixty-eight hours in a week. Knock off say a third, for sleeping, which leaves one hundred and thirteen hours. Of these, how many do you truthfully spend writing?

Is that total OK?

If not, what *really* stops you spending more time writing?

How could you change this?

What would you need to say no to?

How do you sabotage yourself?

Are you willing to commit yourself to changing what needs changing – or at least to start to?

In very practical terms, what can you realistically expect of yourself?

Make a contract with your writing self. Note this down in real terms: 'I will write in my journal for ten minutes a day every weekday; and on Sunday mornings I will write between ten and midday. Once a fortnight, I'll clear the whole of Thursday as well. I will say 'no' to the easier option of staying in bed with the papers on Sunday, and ask someone else to cook Thursday's supper. I will tell the family that I am not to be interrupted except in the case of fire, flood and death...'

And finally, what does the writer in you need? Do you know which times are the most creative for you, and under what circumstances you write best? How can you maximise these things in your life? Be aware of your 'style': when you're feeling creative, what do you do about it? Drop everything and act on it? Stuff the feeling? Notice but don't act? Procrastinate? Find something more 'useful' to do? Raid the fridge?

CAR MECHANICS
BY DAVID KEEFE

Yesterday someone backed into my car. No one was injured and not too much damage was done. Still my initial relief was followed by what can best be described as dismay – woven through with an underlying panic. 'Oh no', I kept thinking to myself, 'Yet another thing to be sorted out that will keep me away from writing' – writing this as it happens.

This was hardly a useful response. It's true that writers need what Robert Bly has called 'cunning' – rearranging their life in ways that keep them in touch with the inner experiences which cause them to write. Bly compares Walt Whitman, whose cunning was to be surrounded by other human-beings – riding Manhattan street cars, crossing the Brooklyn Ferry etc – with Rilke, whose poetry required him to find long periods of solitude – a need so deep that he willingly endured years of loneliness.

Cunning however is not the same as control-freakery. The first stems from abundance, a sense that our inner world is full of riches that are worth nurturing and protecting. OK, they may be vulnerable to theft, but at least we have faith in their continuing value. But when this becomes an obsessive need to control everything that happens to us it is a form of impoverishment, if not imprisonment. Not only will we screen out all sorts of interesting encounters that could actually enrich our work, it also suggests we believe our ideas so feeble they will wither and die if we don't capture them immediately. We are snatching at the things we write about when we should be caressing them – desperation, we might say, being the near enemy of commitment. As always it is our motivation that makes the distinction.

William Stafford, for example, worked on his poetry early each morning – a chance to 'let things happen', as he described it – a discipline he maintained for over forty years. Yet asked how he felt if circumstances prevented him from writing, he replied, 'I forgive myself for those days, it's not a fetish.' Writing was not a fixation or a mania, it was something that he simply loved to do. But he could also do without it. Hold your tricks lightly, as a magician friend once told me. If our motive is more neurotic – writing to seek approval, to try and justify our place on the planet – then too much is at stake. It will be scary to stop doing the one thing that we hope answers our needs. We have begun to confuse writing for life.

In contrast, notice that Stafford is able to say he 'forgives' himself when he cannot find the time for poetry. This is of a piece with his whole philosophy of non-violence, Stafford having been a lifelong pacifist. How absurd it would be to try and spread love to the world and not include himself. Yet isn't this what so many of us do? It's a problem of compartmentalisation, believing that the ideals that hold in one part of our life can be put to one side when it comes to another part.

Our tendency should be towards wholeness – we must keep bringing the wolf to the door. Which means that in our writing we should seek unification with, not denial of, the life (our life) that supports it. Sangharakshita uses the example of work, 'Unless your work is your meditation, your meditation is not meditation.' Any good developed in meditation will quickly be undone if our daily actions are not in accord with the kindness and awareness that underlies our meditation. Which means we need to make more balanced effort in everything we do.

Part of the problem is that we tend to view writers from the Hollywood perspective: the solitary genius, starving in their garret, misunderstood and pilloried by the society around them; even feeling something is wrong if creativity comes too easily. This is going to be a dead end for most of us – I say 'most of us' because there is always that matter of 'cunning'. Gary Snyder, who supported his writing and early studies of Zen Buddhism by working as a forestry labourer and in the engine rooms of ships, has said that if you want to become a poet apprentice yourself to a craftsman such as a carpenter or a car mechanic. This is clearly meant to be provocative to our romantic notions of the artist, but it also makes a lot of sense. He's reminding us that teachers and teachings are everywhere; and that what you do is not so important as the way that you do it. In the same way, although we have no control over where the next accident will come from, we can choose where it takes us.

The mechanics at my local garage – there's only three of them to do everything – are geniuses at multitasking; at improvising in order to save their customer's money; and at how to keep focused whilst at the same time constantly being interrupted. (Contrast this with my precarious attitude to writing.) When I took my car round to them yesterday, I noticed for the first time in their tiny little office, where the whole operation is run so efficiently, an oil-stained poster with the following inscription:

I've been Beaten, Choked, Kicked, Lied to, Swindled, Taken advantage of, and Laughed at ... The only reason I hang around is to see what happens next.

BEGIN ANYWHERE, BEGIN SOMEWHERE

For a long time, I stated – *ad nauseam* – to my students that there was no such thing as writers' block. I quoted Peter de Vries' words when asked whether he waited for inspiration before writing: 'Yes, and I make sure that I am inspired at nine o'clock every morning.'

I really believed that such a phenomenon as writer's block was a delusion, a failure of confidence, something that could be willed away. *Mind over matter and get on with it – stop being such a prima donna.* (I don't actually *say* this, but it has been my attitude.) *Just sit down and write the first sentence. Then another; and another.*

Over the years of course I have written probably billions of sentences in articles, stories, poems and reviews and a number of published and unpublished full-length manuscripts, with never a moment's hesitation. I'd never found myself unable to write.

Now I understand. I'm no longer quite so cavalier. Partway through my second novel I hit Block. Big block. For weeks, even months, I felt as if my tongue and my hands were tied. The worst of it was that that book had become so 'forefront' I couldn't do anything else either.

I don't know how it is for others – you – but maybe it's always the same: it wasn't that I didn't like what I wrote; it wasn't even that I didn't know what to write next. I had the plot all worked out in my head, and a chapter-by-chapter breakdown (sort of) on paper. It was just that I couldn't actually make myself get the words down.

I am learning, now, to be gentle on myself (I'm much harder on myself than I am on my students).

The truth is, there are times when I simply can't write. That's how it is. There may be any number of reasons: times of personal crisis or change; times when the ideas are not 'ripe' enough, when you need to write something else, something different; times when you're too tired, or distracted, or stressed; times when what you really need is a treat, or a rest, or a walk or some input from something or someone else. Or when something else is more pressing than writing. Maybe, as Hemingway (was it?) said, the well needs to be filled up again before you can draw anything off. Maybe – as I explore elsewhere in this book – you are simply still somewhere else in the creative process, incubating.

And sometimes you have to just sit and do it anyway. The wisdom, of course, lies in differentiating between states.

It's a bright December morning, and I've cleared a day to write (this year, this has been a relatively rare occurrence). Because I need space to think, away from admin, phone and family, I treat myself to breakfast in the local wholefood café by the church, where I can see trees and sky and jackdaws. The café's warm and the coffee's good and the light slanting in is of just the right quality and intensity, and the lunchtime quiches and cheese scones are steaming temptingly and my folder is sitting weighty and promising on the table beside me. There was a stimulating programme on the radio as I drove in – Melvyn Bragg's *In Our Time,* exploring the connections between language and thought and identity, something which interests me greatly. So as I sit down my head is full of ideas and I can't wait to get back to the next piece for this book, which is today's agenda.

I'll just have a look at the newspaper, I think; I don't get much time to read papers at the moment. Just five minutes with my coffee.

But the paper – of course – is back-to-back disasters: too many to process. It seems to be worse even than usual at the moment: an unmitigated picture of grotesque murders and senseless cruelties. And five minutes in and already I've lost it, unable to wrench my mind away from the news, and unconvinced that anything we can do, even anything creative, can stand between us and some of the grimmer aspects of life. How can writing do *anything* to tackle unnameable pain and fear and torture and injustice? And if it can't, then is it just a comfortable bourgeois indulgence? And if that's the case, where does that leave me? I'm full of fear and dread suddenly for this world we live in; for all of us, all our fragile lives; for another young local girl who's gone missing so soon after the last tragedy; for my own daughter; for Iraq and Palestine and Israel and numerous other countries; for what today seems like an insuperable excess of the clashes of violence and powerlessness in our species; for my own helplessness.

Right now, once again where it leaves me is with my hands tied and my mouth stopped. There. That's how it is. So after an hour of not writing, I get up and go out; look at the bare trees, the Christmas lights, people's faces, the traffic, the moors just visible beyond the town. And I drive home: east wind, mud on the lanes, cattle in the dunny winter fields.

And I can't write a word.

Q: *Do I let it go, or push on through?*

A: *Today I really want to write.*

OK. So how to find a way in?

Peter Redgrove's essay on 'Work and Incubation' that a friend has sent me sits in my folder. I scanned it through again just now; and here is Rodin, answering a younger artist's question: 'What do I do when I can't work?' 'Work at something else.' Anything, actually, will do. Keep a folder of 'rainy day ideas' that you can pick up and put down. Edit yesterday's work. Wash the dishes. Bake some bread. Make or play some music. Go for a walk. Go for a run. Be gentle with yourself. Go look at the bare winter trees. Write about them. There's always more to observe in this world than you will have energy or time to write about. Remember you're a writer. Write something. Write anything. Begin somewhere. Write about what's stopping you. Write yourself through it.

Begin somewhere.

As I think this I think about the many times I've said (perhaps not so brutally, but the gist is there): 'I don't care if you don't feel like writing. You say you're a writer. Sit down and do it anyway.' Easy words.

Time for my own medicine. *Write yourself through it.* And there's my gap. Instead of 'forcing' myself to write the chapter for the book, I write to a friend of how distressed I was at this morning's news, how it's affected the rest of my day. (So often the problem and the solution arise in the same place – reading words 'blocked' me; writing words about not feeling able to write, and about those read words, frees me.)

And now, here I am: writing something; writing about what's stopping me, about that whole process. And – see – here's what I needed for the book.

For the truth is writers write. It's what we do; it's how we make sense of the world; it's how the world speaks to us; it's how we answer, and how we question. It needs no justification and maybe value judgements are anathema. We may not stop the world or change the world or even speak to one other person. But still we write. 'The real writer is one / who really writes,' says Marge Piercy. 'Work is its own cure. You have to / like it better than being loved.'[1]

Starting points

1

Well, no prizes for guessing this one. Yes, save it for when you're struggling...

Pan your life – the foreground of your life
How is it for you today? What's the feeling tone of the day? The colour? If it were an animal, your life today?

What is it that is hard in your life today? (You might want to write about your immediate situation or circumstances, which is fine; but I'm asking you to look behind those things and look at your attitude: what is it in you that is making your life hard today? What are you having a hard time accepting about how it is?)

Just write it all out. (Don't worry about analysing it.)

Then take a sideways leap:
Either take yourself back into that last piece but now turn the circumstances and feelings into metaphor, and if you wish

Lift a poem from the notes and metaphors; or

Give that story to someone else. In other words, tell it in the third person, and invent, elaborate, exaggerate... and keep writing.

Most important: don't set yourself up to fail by giving yourself an agenda, or an expected creative outcome. Just write; and follow the words. William Stafford said that if he hit writer's block he allowed himself to lower his standards. During one of these phases, it is enough simply to be *writing*.

2

Another way in for when imagination fails:

Being here:

Write about how it is to be here now; the presences of this moment. Start in this room: these things I see, these sounds I hear. Allow your mind to wander away at will and alight on images, memories, dreams, fragments; record all these glimpses. Then bring yourself back to here, now, this room, this moment. Keep it concrete, and keep the notes brief.

Then go outside and do the same thing – just collecting images, notes and fragments.

Then copy all these – or some of these – fragments out legibly, in individual lines or phrases. Cut them up, scatter them on the table, and then recombine – collage into short 'glimpse' poems or one longer piece. Don't worry about sense so much as surprise.

GOING TO THE COAL FACE
BY ANDIE LEWENSTEIN

I have in my mind an ill woman who never leaves her house. She has been there so long, she says, that it is part of her body. It is in a cul-de-sac and seems to be in permanent winter. Even in the summer, the back room where she lies is dark with the shade of poplar trees that press around the house. The light hurts her eyes. Near her is a loom on which she weaves an abstract woollen picture – grey, green and blue – but she can only sit for fifteen minutes at a stretch before she has to lie flat again. Reading makes her dizzy and she doesn't watch TV or listen to the radio. She looks out of the window at a patch of sky between two trees.

'I look at cloud shapes,' she says. 'There's always something new. Yesterday a camel came. Today a giant with a rucksack on his back and he turned and looked at me. The clouds speak to me, the rain too. I look at the drops on the windowpane. I listen to them.'

Brian Keenan, held hostage in Beirut, in filth and darkness, is unexpectedly given a bowl of fruit and finds 'the world recreated in that broken bowl', his soul restored and named by the colour orange.

Where all systems fail, poetry begins. Is essential.

I have in my mind a scene from the film 'American Beauty'. A teenage boy has filmed a white plastic bag on a stretch of asphalt by a brick wall. It is caught by the wind and begins to dance. Looking at the image caught on film, the boy says, 'that's the day I realised that there was this entire life behind things and this incredibly benevolent force that wanted me to know that there was no reason to be afraid'. In the spaces, in the margins where we think that nothing happens, such epiphanies occur.

New writers are often encouraged to keep a notebook in which they regularly 'free-write', covering as many pages as they can with whatever words come onto the page. I have noticed that my students are often enthusiastic about this practice at the beginning, encouraged by the flow of words that come like water from a tap from who knows where. Then the doubts come, along with a disabling self-consciousness because so much notebook-writing is 'just about me and my boring life and complaints' – about how the car broke down, the child was off school with a cold, there was a queue at the supermarket and the library books are overdue. No epiphanies here.

But words on paper are the *sine qua non* of the working writer and whoever you are – seasoned author, beginner, teacher of creative writing – you have to go to the coal face, inspired or not. You present yourself, as a priest does when saying the Office, whether or not there is a congregation and with no knowing how, or if, the Spirit will move, to write, perhaps, something like this:

'Today all I can think of is that when I looked into the mirror this morning, I saw that my eyes were the melancholy sloping down at the side kind of eyes and I had never noticed before how much they slope. Had a headache and more lines on my forehead and wished I had eyes that turn up at the ends, then I would look happy and people I don't know wouldn't tell me to cheer up. I lifted up the corners of my eyes with my hands to see how it would look, then I pulled back the skin on my face.'

As I pushed the words out an image came to me of a woman about to give herself a facelift, and I wrote, 'A face like a new canvas, ready to begin afresh and telling no one anything,' and then the title of a Jeanette Winterson novel: *Written on the Body*. I looked at what I had written, underlined the words I wanted to use and began again:

'This morning I lifted up the corners of my eyes. I had a brand new face, like a new canvas, ready to begin afresh. This morning I took a scalpel to the loose skin around my eyes and the fallen flesh around my mouth and underneath my chin. I cut neat lines around my face as though preparing a piece of fabric for the making of a new garment and I pulled and pulled at the fabric of my soon-to-be-new skin until it tightened around my eyes and nose and mouth and shone with a new possibility.'

As I worked on, there she stood: a woman, Lady Macbeth-like in her resolve, on the verge of a facelift, a breakdown or a breakthrough. The end result was a poem I called 'Facelift':

Today I lifted up my face.
I took a scalpel to the skin around my eyes
and the fallen folds around my mouth.

I cut a line around my jaw as though preparing
a piece of fabric for the making of a new garment
and I pulled and pulled until it tightened and shone.

I sewed it into place with needle and flesh-coloured thread.
I cut away the old skin.
It fell away without fuss, there was no trace of blood.

With my tight new skin I am clean and strong as a virgin
who has never been scorned by a lover, nor given birth
to blood and membrane or looked at the sky night after night

and watched her hopes grow pale with the shrinking of the moon.
It is morning, and my new face is a canvas on which I will write
the only story that will ever be told.

I have buried the old skin deep in the earth.
It is not connected to anything
and has no mouth to speak with.

BEACHCOMBING – BITS OF BLUE PLASTIC

Crow spraddled head-down in the beach-garbage,
    guzzling a dropped ice-cream.
Ted Hughes

Every writer I know has a bulging tinderbox of one sort or another stored away somewhere in their imagination. In here are crammed tiny pieces of flammable or fissile material that we've collected over a lifetime. These scraps are sparks-in-waiting.

The imagination is like a magpie, and every writer is a kleptomaniac. We gobble things up, or squirrel them away; nothing is too dull, or too difficult, or too sacred, to save for a day when we need a little fire – because we're arsonists, too.

I talk elsewhere in this book about the fact that the writer inhabits a kind of twilight or threshold zone much of the time; that territory which sits between conscious and unconscious processes. Norman Jope speaks of the writer as a kind of psychopomp, whose task it is to move, and mediate, between different realms. This is, amongst other things, the realm of the imagination.

I think of this threshold zone as a tideline. (Like Andy Brown in his chapter 'Shifting Arenas', I find shorelines, real and metaphorical, endlessly intriguing.) On a beach, even a privately owned one, I believe that the area known as the 'no man's land' between high and low water is recognised as being beyond human ownership. It's a shadow zone; marked at its (changing) upper limit by the tideline, repository of all manner of flotsam and jetsam.

Just as the tideline itself changes on a daily basis according to the moon and the varying heights of tidal ebb and flow, so do the deposits on it: some objects are reclaimed by the sea, new ones wash up. Haphazard amongst the bits of rope, single flip-flops, ring pulls, condoms, Coke cans, rubber gloves, washing-up bottles and garish bits of plastic are sea-glass, mussel shells, cuttlefish, limpets, gulls' corpses, sea urchins, winkles, dead fish, faded driftwood, spars from boats, kelp, bladderwrack, mermaids' purses of empty egg-cases (whelk? Dogfish? Whichever I want them to be.). On my childhood beach in North Devon we would occasionally meet with a whole storm of spider-crab shells, or a fleet of jellyfish, thrown up after wild weather; both species inviting, curious and slightly menacing in their quantity and unfamiliarity, as well as their spines in the case of one and stingers in the case of the other. My elderly and eccentric childhood-next-door-neighbour was a connoisseur of tidelines: he and his wife spent most of their days beachcombing, and their house (and garden) was an Aladdin's Cave of detritus. As a child I was fascinated in a slightly ghoulish way by the sheer quantity of unexploded mines, left over from WW2 that he found. (Although these didn't end up in his garden, the bomb disposal people practically lived in his house.)

The tideline is unchoosy; and so, to some extent, is the writer. There's nothing we like better than to pick through disparate fragments in the jumble sale of the mind. I suppose we are looking both for harmony and for the means of disrupting it; for order and chaos; for patterns, contrasts and random felicities.

The imagination is caught more by juxtapositions than by the expected. This is what sets light to the tinder: the roughness created by difference rather than the smoothness of the predictable.

Though, as a lifelong country dweller, my own imagination turns most easily on the natural world, everything in a tideline holds my interest. I think it's important, when you're beachcombing, whether that's literal or, as in this case, metaphorical, to sift through without too many preconceptions about what makes beauty, what has potential. So although I might be more discriminating about what I bring home – or work up into a piece of writing – initially I try to let everything have a voice.

Friend and student Julie-Ann Rowell writes lucid, sinuous, delicate poetry that runs through my veins like whisky. She has a strong innate sense of the power of imagery; the magic that 'ordinary' objects hold. Coupled with this, I think, is the awareness – conscious or otherwise – that too much harmony may be aesthetically pleasing but does not, in the end, hold a reader's attention in the way that something that jars that harmony a little might do.

She has two instincts in particular I admire: one is the willingness to bring together light and dark; the other her assured use of concrete detail. In her poem 'Crossing The Dart', you will see the undercurrents and transitions of which she is speaking; the movement, apart from anything else, away from the world of childhood towards the darker waters of the adult world.

Crossing The Dart

The black tongue of the river
lured, and we tumbled to it
losing our blue beaker in the gorse.
The wind scalped, we plunged on,
a rabble of dirty-faced kids
blind to the zinc-white sky, down
to the lip of the rapids that gorged
through granite. We attempted to cross
roped together by our hands
and we might have been lost
but achieved the virgin side
we wanted to trample, conquer,
raise our flag, plant our emblem.
It was me, the youngest,
who stumbled upon the dead lamb –
my first carcass, ribs extant,
eyeless, splayed, wool rotted,
fly ridden. I was nudged to turn
its skull with my toe, a trophy
on the dead side of the river
I wished we hadn't crossed.

This poem has many things to say, and all of them skilfully handled; but for me, somehow, that 'blue beaker', with all that it *doesn't* say, makes the poem; and is the image I remembered for months after Julie-Ann first read the poem out in a workshop – even more than the felt shock of the dead lamb, which is somehow more expected, given the geographical and emotional territory.

I'm also thinking about an afternoon I spent with a group of writers with whom I was working on Port Ban, a wonderful crescent of white shell-sand on the Hebridean island of Iona. Port Ban is known for its swarms of miniature shells – tiny cowries and mussels, minuscule yellow periwinkles (or are they whelks?), miniature flakes of lacy coral.

As a break from writing, we were playing. Actively working with the other senses nourishes a writer's creativity, so we were collecting and assembling these minute shells, and backing them onto double-sided sticky tape on strips of card – a neat way of making patterns as well as a record of a place and a time (an activity I think originally devised by Earth Education as a 'learning about nature' creative tool for children).

Most of the group members were sitting patiently and obediently collecting the most beautiful shells and sticking them, completely immersed. Maggie, however, who is a champion of the art of irreverence, was wandering alone at the tide's edge. When she eventually joined us, she said (being Maggie), 'I can't be bothered with that kind of arsing about' – and simply dunked her cardboard strip upside down in the sand, then plonked a shard of bright blue plastic at random about a third of the way along the strip. Well, while Maggie's was not the most beautiful strip, it had a vigour and vitality that none of the others had, due not so much to the lack of patterning but rather to her instinct for the surprising, the unexpected: the incongruity of the juxtaposition of that small acid-blue jagged bit of plastic with the natural objects.

So allowing oneself to be surprised, to be nudged or thrown into unexpected directions by allowing those disparate objects from the tideline in your imagination to rub up against one another seems to be a good prescription for creativity.

And let's not forget Crow in all this. We're scavengers. We may love things of beauty, but we don't mind riffling through rubbish bins, either, getting our hands dirty, mixing ice cream drips and beach-tar. We're not fussy. Everything's pepper to our grinders; and we'll feed our imaginations in any way we can. Ted Hughes has us down pat: after the majesty of the eagle, and the delicacy of the song of the curlew, and the grace of the swallow, and the shyness of the bullfinch, and etc etc, comes crow, spraddling, scavenging.

Starting point

Assemble:

    A well-used household object, such as a mug, soap-dish or teapot
    Something 'natural' – a stone, or shell, or feather, or lump of coal, a twig
    Something very ordinary that you would normally throw away: a used

postage stamp, a tin lid, a plastic carton

Something belonging to/originating from someone else: an item of clothing, or a letter they wrote you

Something you associate with yourself in some way: your toothbrush or pen or reading glasses, even a shopping list

Something at random: something you had forgotten or to which you pay no attention

A phrase that you like, or that moves you – yours, or someone else's. Don't be afraid to lift it from a song, a book or a newspaper (but do remember to credit it if used in the final draft).

Write:

A couple of lines on each: follow your imagination and its first promptings, no matter how apparently absurd and disconnected; and do allow in specific associations or memories.

Now:

Find ways of interleaving some of these lines and ideas, looking less for smoothness of 'fit' than for things that will throw others into relief, and offer surprise

Then, adding and subtracting as necessary, work this into a new draft, with no agenda for the outcome. Allow the subject and associations/relationships to suggest themselves and the writing to be bizarre if that's what happens.

What is this piece of writing really about? Find a way to title this obliquely rather than face-on.

'SPOON' – HOW DO YOU SPELL IT?

BY PAUL MATTHEWS

A permission of language is always a permission of consciousness: this is my starting point for all the group-work that I do in Creative Writing. It means the craft exercises that I come up with are also 'spells' to carry people across (if they are willing) into that place of Imagination from which all true language comes.

Noun and Adjective and Verb, for instance, where do they come from? What three stances to the world do they embody? What is it in our human nature that is seeking utterance through them? In my exploration of such things I might ask those who are working with me to stand like a noun, an adjective, a verb. I invite them to parties where only nouns are made welcome. Only adjectives. Only verbs. Silly games… to reveal the serious presences and dynamics of these three Spirits that inhabit our language.

Then, bringing it back to words, I say: please indulge one of these modes as you write in response to what is around you. Or (because the value of something is often realized through its absence) I restrict their employment. To describe the room without using nouns, I mean – what state of mind does that invite us into?

Much of this I pointed towards in my Creative Writing workbook, *Sing Me The Creation*,[1] but since then I have tried to take it further:

Go out into the world in groups of three and, when you have found one human-made object (preferably not a work of art), spend some time in its presence, observing it through your various senses and taking note of its particular physical and human environment. Having done this, let one member of the group write about IT; another address it as a YOU; and the third lend it a voice and speak for it as I. Or you could try all these modes in turn, starting with the most external.

e.g. A SPOON:

> IT: *Here is a spoon. It is lying outside on a picnic table. It has been out all night. I know this because a drop of rain has gathered in its upturned hollow. Rainwater flecked with milk. A soup-spoon. Colour of silver. This spoon only*

touches the table at two points – at the tip of its handle and at the underside of the deepest point of its bowl. The handle slants diagonally towards the edge of the picnic table. A yellow leaf is lying beside it at the same angle – its stem pointing the same way, its concave face turned upwards. Both spoon and leaf reflect the sun. A spoon filled with morning sunlight after a night of rain.

What a 'boring' task, some people sigh, and certainly the danger is that we define the thing to death; that it dies into *noun*. Yet this initial sacrifice of standing back from the world, not imposing our emotions or symbolisms upon things but respecting their otherness, is essential if we are ever to know them truly. Often the one who takes this role in the task will describe the object as 'lonely', when actually it is their own separate identity that they are experiencing. This is the pain, but also the gift it gives. It seems, at first, to be a renunciation of any poetic engagement with the world, but the strange thing is that if we do manage to let a spoon be just a spoon then, when the time is ripe, it will the more readily make itself available as unsentimental interpreter of our deepest feelings.

YOU: *It is already warm here in the sunshine, yet how cold you feel against the back of my hand! Some spoons turn my face upside down when I look into them. But you…you are just too dirty to reflect anything! Except the sun! Who left you out all night? What dish ran away with you, and then abandoned you at just this angle? You are not just a spoon, Spoon. You are a whole story – though the two words printed on your side tell only a small part of it. 'Taiwan' is one of them. 'Stainless' is the other. This large milky fingerprint on your inside surface is all that prevents you from betraying the stains on my face this bright morning.*

This permission to address the world as 'you' allows our life of feeling (and its lively servant, the *adjective*) to come flooding in. It is important, I think, to keep the task linked to the details of external observation, but to add now a further attention – to our relationship to the object, to the feelings that arise as we stand in its presence. It takes practice to sift what belongs to me (that, too, can be named) from the qualities that belong to the object, but with perseverance 'the heart's affections' (as John Keats called them) can be trained to perceive the meanings and magics that reside even in humble things. 'Imagination' is another word for this faculty.

I: *I am all spoon. Others may prod or slice if they wish. My work is to scoop and serve. To lift food to your mouth. To lift grace to your eye. For, yes, long before you took me by the handle, the wink of my silver caught your attention. Cut no lip, curve yourself round, serve sippers and gulpers alike, are the laws I was born with. Night long I mirrored the Milky Way. Then the clouds came. This drop of rain is all I can serve you this morning.*

To lend a voice so that seemingly inarticulate things can find utterance is no mere 'literary device' but, potentially, one of the deepest human acts. It implies Intuition – the ability to know something from the inside out. Is that impossible? It certainly is, unless love is involved in the act of knowing. But if love is present…then we can begin to stand within the *verb* of the thing, the creative intention involved in its forging.

In summary: something like this, maybe, though I don't insist on it –

Noun	Adjective	Verb
It	You	I
Thinking	Feeling	Doing

It has long been a question for me how close up to the world can we get, and do the things we write about really accept our language? Here, three simple steps of grammar (from *it* to *you* to *I*) show us a path towards such a participation. My own experience is that if you do the task faithfully, without trying too hard to be literary, then the common objects of the household become charged once again with the wonder that we knew in childhood, enhanced within our loving attention and through the words we touch them with.

And here, beyond exercise, is a fine sonnet by Andie Lewenstein, in which the spoon, finding a voice, interprets our own condition:

Silver Spoon

Mornings I stir the coffee with skimmed milk.
She licks me clean and I reflect the sun
Of a naked lightbulb. I feel empty – she's begun
To starve herself again. Too weak to walk,
She feeds herself on magazines and talk
Shows on TV. The politics of skin and bone
Have reduced me to base metal. I have done
My best for her. I was her treasure, wrapped in silk,
I used to feed her well, I knew her mouth,
Soft rose that opened for me night and morning,
I was aeroplane and flying fish,
She held me in her fist, she pressed her teeth
Into my hollow, I was meant for bringing
Sweet delight, I was not made for this.

FEATHER SLIPPERS

Humans have known forever the power of objects: maybe as tools or utensils useful or necessary to survival; maybe as ritual symbols; maybe as currency; maybe as all three.

Even the most apparently simple or domestic objects have their own life and mystery quite apart from us; and they also have whatever power with which we invest them. Even across the centuries we feel that potency: the Roman coin, or piece of mosaic, dug up in a back garden, the flint arrowhead stumbled upon, the cave drawings in Lascaux or Altamira, the Bronze Age stone circles on Dartmoor, the Pictish symbols engraved on menhirs in Scotland, even fragments of blue and white pottery or the stopper from an old glass bottle may hold our fascination in varying degrees.

This attraction is rarely to do with monetary value and only partly connected with rarity. Sometimes it's to do with its age, and history; but it's also to do with origins and ontology, and the passing of time. There's something exciting and profoundly mysterious about the whole concept of the numerous human lives that have passed across the surface of that object, or created it; and the layers of emotional, practical or magical energy with which it has been invested.

Then there's a whole category of individual domestic objects which symbolise something to us personally: the jug that was your mother's, the brooch that belonged to your grandmother, or an old enamel bowl; a book given by a lover, a set of chisels or a torch from your father.

Natural objects too fascinate us, of course – we're all magpies at heart.

In terms of writing, objects can provide powerful starting points, allowing us to write not only about the thing in front of us but also to let fall a story or a history which may obliquely address personal issues that we may find hard to write about otherwise. Sometimes this happens not only because it may be intrinsically difficult to write about deeply personal or emotional matters, but because we don't always know *how* to write about them. An object, working here as an image or symbol, might enable a passage right to the heart of something by bypassing the intellect. There is also the physicality of the object, which, in involving our body through the senses, allows us to broaden our perception and our perspectives.

I have what I think of as a spellbox that I use in workshops. Most of the objects in it have been gifts, brought back by family or friends from travels: a coconut flower from my daughter from Costa Rica, a 'donkey's eye' seedpod from Tobago, a shell from the Maldives, a pre-Christian clay jug handle from the Syrian desert ('get a handle on it', said my friend Anne), a little glass cube ('a writer's block so that you don't have to have one' – Judy), a Guatemalan gourd shaker painted like a tortoise, a buzzard's feather, a pilgrim's scallop shell, a patterned piece of twisted gorse root, a Native American flint arrowhead, a few strands of white buffalo hair, a slender plait of chestnut mane hair from a much-loved horse I used to ride over Dartmoor, a geode, a small fossil which looks to me like a petrified comet-plus-tail, and one or two other objects.

Each of these objects has meaning for me, and a history of which I only know a tiny fraction. But in a workshop I say nothing of any of this; merely put them out in a circle and ask people to choose something, then watch with interest.

Starting points

1

In 'Beachcombing' I suggested an exercise involving various objects. This exercise takes it further.

> Again, choose an object – domestic or natural. It doesn't, by the way, have to be either 'special' or unusual – a piece of coal has produced a quirky and powerful piece of writing in a workshop; a cup is fruitful, or a zip or button.

> I begin by asking people to closely observe, with as many of their senses as possible, the object they have chosen, and to make notes. This part of the exercise is an objective study.

> *2x1 inches: a warm shade of mud yet hard as glass: a small triangular tongue of stone, sharp-sided, its sharper end smoother, darker, perhaps dirtier.*

> I ask them to consider how it might move; and whether it would be solitary or occur in pairs, groups or flocks... What company it would keep.

A peninsula in miniature, slopes eroded into shallow ravines down to cutting-edge shores. Cliffs in places. But the landscape is the same below as above: turn one over in the hand and there's its twin, its echo, its subterranean self.

If, I say to them, inviting in the imaginative faculty now, you had never seen one of these before, what might it be? What might its purpose be? Then I ask for a short piece of writing circling the object with imagination, without ever actually naming it, extending their observational notes creatively.

Give this object an 'I' voice, I say; write its story in the first person.

I lived four lives.

Darkness, pressure, heat, noise: millennia to stasis, silence.
Indistinguishable from my bedrock, weight and comfort of companionable tons around not-yet-me.

Struck into solitude by catastrophe, sundered, separate in air yet undefined.
A pause.

Chosen, handled, percussive blows shaped me for something. (I don't believe in God.)

Bound to a shaft I fly the bowstring twang, bury myself in flesh. Something dies. I may not be recovered.

(With thanks to Avril; the object was a flint arrowhead)

Later, you might want to find the poem by Craig Raine: 'A Martian Sends A Postcard Home'.

You might also want to consider what of you is reflected in those observations and imaginings…

2
Feather slippers
This great title comes from Becky, one of my workshop participants.

a) Here I'm going to offer you the subject of 'shoes' as a starting point, employing the usual stream-of-consciousness technique for a timed piece of writing. You'll be surprised what emerges once you start, so I suggest you allow twenty minutes. Of course, the 'shoes' may be a pair you had as a child or a teenager, or they may be a pair belonging to someone else. Do use a personal memory though so as to avoid moving into conceptualising.

b) Stand back. Look again. What do you notice? Any surprises? And how does this piece of writing make you feel? (N.B. I'm not asking whether you think it's any good or not, but what it triggers in you reading it back.)

c) Consider how your piece of writing might change as the footwear changes. How would it be – how different would it be – if you wore jackboots, thigh boots, velvet and sequin slippers, slippers made out of feathers? Purple stilettos?

d) OK, so what are you *really* writing about? What's the subtext? Your marriage, your anger at your restrictive working life, your mother, being a teenager, your first love affair, your dead grandmother, the bunions and calluses on your life? Where does your life pinch? Whose shoes do you walk in?

Write about what you were *really* writing about now, in the same way, for a few minutes.

e) And finally shape a short poem, or longer piece of prose (a short story?) out of this or these somehow.

ONE FOOT IN FRONT OF THE OTHER

The miracle is not to walk on water.
The miracle is to walk on the green earth,
dwelling deeply in the present moment
and feeling truly alive.
Thich Nhat Hanh

Both as a writer and as a workshop facilitator, there are three interlinked practices that I increasingly consider crucial to the practice of writing.

The first is the cultivation of *mindfulness*; the second, the practice of *living more deeply*; and the third, *walking*.

Mindfulness, in the way in which I have used it here, means the practice of paying attention, of noticing, of awareness; of being with the whole of oneself in the present moment: alive to how it – everything – is, and also alive to all the undercurrents, invisible qualities and imaginative possibilities of which 'now' consists. It's a constant movement and exchange between inner and outer worlds.

Mindfulness is an end in itself: to me, the practice and the process are more important than any notion of 'arriving' somewhere – although for a writer the chances are that the more this quality is cultivated the better the creative 'product' will be.

It is also a vehicle for writing more deeply. This, in turn, will reflect our willingness to engage with, and courage in, living deeply – our emotional capacity for being with every aspect of how things are; our acceptance of shadow as well as light, loss as well as love; the cycles of things, their ebb and flow; what Clarissa Pinkola Estes[1] has called the life/death/life nature.

There's something here about being fully human requiring us to embrace all the paradoxes and pairs of opposites in our lives and the world around us. When you are in the rain, can you fully stand in the rain without sacrificing your ability to recall sun? When you are in summer, are you willing to remember winter without that thought shaking you out of yourself, out of your life, out of the present moment? In the middle of an argument, can you be with your anger without losing love? Can you love without looking ahead to its potential loss?

It seems to me that both these qualities – of mindfulness and of deep living – are brought together in the act of walking.

Walking is a very direct way of reminding ourselves of our immediate and tangible connection with the earth, and with the elemental. (This is hugely augmented when walking barefoot – when was the last time you did that, outside? Try it; and not just on dry manicured lawns or tarmac – go uninsulated!) Walking can be a kind of meditation – indeed it is used as such in Buddhist practice – and can create a particular quality of stillness in the three spheres of body, mind and heart, which allows other things to come through – purity of perception (perception without the judging and interfering mind interpreting), intuition, attentiveness, renewal. And inspiration. Artist Daniel de Angeli says: 'There is a visual power to walking which I have never experienced in any other way. I think inside each person there is the possibility of living in a tangible but contemplative dimension... walking – the act of putting one foot in front of another and continually moving – brings me closer to that state.'[2]

I've always instinctively used walking as a way of solving the problems of both living and writing, and as a way, too, of healing. There's something about the repetitive action (more of that in 'The Creative Process' section) and the rhythm. Whatever the issue, the act of moving through a landscape, across the land, on the earth, both enables and restores something in me. This is not a conscious process; it's not that I set out to 'think' something through, or to resolve anything; it's something that simply happens in the course of a walk regardless of what actually goes on in my conscious mind – which is often nothing to do with the matter that's pressing on me. When I get back, invariably things have changed in me: either I know what to do about an issue – even if the answer is 'nothing'; or things have become clear enough for me to be able to let it be.

I also, slightly more consciously but without any planning or forethought, use this process when I know I'm incubating a piece of writing. (What I mean is I'm aware that it happens to me but it's not something I 'do'.) It is, for me, at a certain stage in the creative journey, a freeing process that comes prior to sitting at the table putting pen to paper or cursor to screen. It happens when I've 'gone into labour', so to speak: when an idea is pushing below the surface but has still to emerge. Suddenly I find myself standing up abruptly and turning away from writing implements at just the point where words are starting to form themselves. It's as if something in me turns away, paradoxically, from language and into the body to free the words.

Today is a wild April day with torrential rain storming at the window, and a wind that has more than a bite to it – clawed and fanged. I'm in a remote spot on a Hebridean island, and it's been cold enough throughout the day for me not to want to wander far beyond the front door. Besides, I'm up here to work on this book, so I'm quite pleased that the weather isn't especially seductive. Yesterday in sunshine I had an especially inspiring day in the lochs – otter-watching – and mountains, finishing with a visit to a gallery, a sculpture garden and the green waters of the local bay, so I should be well fuelled-up. I need to make the most of that store of inspiration.

However, at the edges of my consciousness there is the glimmer of an impending poem. I have been pushing it away, as there are only a few days here and I have much other writing to do. I am also aware that it is time I found a new poetic voice – the old one is becoming husky with repetition. This poem promises to deliver more of the same – landscape and landscape. And landscape alone – even this wild dramatic landscape with its Neolithic sites, its bardic overtones and its rugged and tumultuous history of Clearances – is not enough in itself to make the threatening poem interesting. So I resist it.

But I need to go out. Just before dusk there's a small break in the clouds; a scrap, too small to make even a patch on the Dutchperson's trousers, but just enough to remind me how immense the sky is here over the ocean; immense and purple and black and indigo, save for a small brilliance blazing away in the west.

So I huddle into jumpers and scarves and waterproofs and squelch up the track, setting a flock of redwings up from the mud, and a single buzzard. A hooded crow on a fence post eyes me. I can hear the sea crashing on the point ahead of me; below at the foot of the cliffs to my right the breakers churn. It feels good to be upright and moving, the rhythm of walking.

I stand at the point and do nothing. I'm not thinking – for once; just watching, paying attention, looking at the land, and the sea, and the sky.

Walking the mile or so back I'm thinking about supper; realising it's hours since I ate – a good sign. I've been immersed – a satisfying feeling.

As I've been walking I've occasionally let my mind dwell on the next chapter, in between watching the wheatears and hawks, and the way the light is winking on wet rocky outcrops on the hillside or catching the water fanning out on the boulders in the burn. As far as I know I haven't thought about the poem that's pushing at the door. However, as I turn the corner to the front of the cottage two lines suddenly spring complete into the forefront of my awareness. And they're two lines that will lift the poem – whatever it is – out of the 'landscape groove'. As I walk in through the door the rest of the poem slides into view – rather like a ship entering harbour stern-first and turning out to be fully-rigged and ready to go. Five minutes later I have the first draft down.

It's the walking that released it; and while my conscious mind was busy with what I was experiencing outside, and the material for the book, my unconscious was being primed by the physical rhythm and mental freewheeling of walking.

Starting points

The walk

The exercises below are interconnected, and lend themselves to being practised over and over – even in the same place, month-by-month or season-by-season – even day-by-day. They are a way of seeing more deeply, and practising moving between inner and outer. All three, by the way, require that you actually walk – rather than imagining a walk! – and that you write 'on the hoof'. If you walk with someone else, make an agreement that you will walk in silence.

These are some of my favourite exercises, and for many of my course participants too. Don't be fooled by the apparent simplicity – like so much else, the doing of it offers a profundity that mere words don't.

1
Beads

Take a short circular walk, and as you go note in simple stanzas of 3 to 5 lines at a number of different random points the details of the changing land around you. Start and end with the same place, but make the opening and closing stanzas subtly different. Aim for between 7 and 12 little pieces, recording the external world with all your senses. For this one, keep yourself out of the picture.

Don't worry about poetic devices – go for simplicity and pithiness of expression, brevity and vividness. (This works best if you stick with the same stanzaic pattern throughout and keep each line brief.)

Here's a 'closing bead' from a sequence I wrote in Gascony:

> thunder speaking in tongues
> and the buzzard's high mew
> the voice of the bell
> and then only silence
> dropping like petals

2

Waymarkers

This is probably a longer walk; or at least needs more time. It should be approached in a contemplative spirit. It differs from the previous exercise in that it is not simply an observational piece: you are moving between your inner perceptions and feelings and a specific chosen outer place each time, including yourself in the written picture. Aim for fewer pieces.

You will be stopping and writing tiny poems in a handful of places that suggest themselves to you as 'waymarkers' or 'stations' – be aware of the quality of the place and why it 'pulls' you. What is its essence? How do you feel there? How would you name this place? I suggest that you spend some time in each place immersing yourself in it, saturating yourself, before trying to write.

Whether you set yourself a pattern or not is up to you. It may be that each place will need a different shape, perhaps echoing its own physical, geographical/topological or atmospheric 'language' – for some a couple of gentle long lines; for another a short chunky poem. Think about the words you choose too – how might they echo the feel of the place? Long soft words with plenty of vowels conjure a totally different feel from short sharp words with plosive consonants.

I first created this exercise for a literary festival with an outdoor component that I used to organise on and around Dartmoor. I added the 'naming' bit after the first course I co-tutored on the Isle of Iona, where an old map shows wonderful place names such as: The Bay at the Back of the Ocean; Cornfield of the Meadow; Hill of the Crows; Little Fairy Mound; Plain of the Wine; Pasture of the Geese; Place of Red Flowers; Lochan of the Lapwings' Meadow; Well of the North Wind; Raven's Peak; Hollow of the Thistles; Hill of the Angels; Eithne's Fold, etc.

3

The string

This one's lovely, and pulls together the other two.

This time, rather than stopping and writing, you are writing as you go – stream-of-consciousness, moving all the while between sensory perceptions/ observed detail and simply noting them as they come, in a long string. But every so often you stop, take a breath, and put yourself in the picture in a little intense 'bead', where you move from outer to inner and back out again. Your thoughts and feelings too will change – maybe perceptibly, maybe almost imperceptibly, as the scenery changes along the way; so as well as capturing the essence of each passing moment in each passing place, you will be capturing something of the quality of your moments, too. Stay sensitive and stay open, and allow whatever comes – memory, thought, feeling, imagining, image, whatever.

Bear in mind that beads can be strung on a string in any way: they don't need to be regularly sized or spaced, or the same colour. Sometimes the 'bead' might be a knot of two or three words; sometimes it may be so fine that it is only faintly discernible above the fabric of the string; sometimes it might be a great chunky lump of a bead. Sometimes there's a lot of string and few beads; sometimes, even on the same string, it's mostly bead. Find your own pattern.

Boscastle

Driving down the last hairpin I'm in thin hot blue air, despite the earliness of the day. Below me, strangely, the sea is downy – fat cushions of mist thickly covering the water.

I park under the sycamores by the little brook. As always, the meadowy way to St Juliot's Church across the valley sirens, but today – as always – I need the cliffs.

I walk this place because I love it; but also sometimes as a rite of passage, at transitions. Beginnings, endings.

I'm adrift in fog, lost to myself.

Trekking back up the hairpins
the narrow track along the hill's shoulders
avoiding the crowds already thickening the harbour walls.
The path's been scythed; mowings and meadowsweet scent the air

clouds of pollen rise
above the summer mist –
the dogs' brushing past

Heading up towards Willapark. Reverberating against the cliffs and through the sea mist the voices of gulls and oystercatchers net the bay. Pairs of kittiwakes squat on narrow ledges. Further out on the apex of The Meachard above the scarves of mist, black smudges might be razorbill or guillemot, even puffins

spilling down the cliffs
                              thrift and trefoil

                                             late tatters of bluebells

Lundy Island swallowed up.

Lundy high, weather dry.
OR
Lundy clear, rain is near.

And if it's totally obscured? Here on the cliffs it's hot, hot

          pyramidal orchids
                    bladder campion
                              sheep's bit scabious

and then Forrabury Stitches with its ancient strip-farmed uplands

          corn marigold
                    restharrow
                              yellow rattle

I'm alone and the land around me sings.

A sky you could vaporise into. I stop to look at stonecrop and pennywort, tilt my neck for skylarks, watch pipits flit from rock to rock. Meadow cranesbill breaks through dock and hogweed. Chiffchaff and stonechats in the gorse and elder.

The slate wall here by the quarry is honeycombed – nests or holes for winches? Underfoot the slate spoil tinkles like wind chimes. Steep drop to deep green water – even from here I can see the bottom, and swirling weed. This coast is hazed with the ghosts of wrecks.

Emerging from mist a fishing boat ploughs a dark vee; the sea to each side ruched

the
steps
down
are
steep
edged
glossy
with
worn
blue
slate

and the puppy, huge and clumsy, rabbit-hops awkwardly down. At the bottom the wooden slatted walkway spans the brook, choked now with hemlock water dropwort. The dogs wriggle through the thicket of it to slurp and belly in the shallows. Scent of bruised mint saturates the morning

sky blue speedwell
pale forget-me-nots
pink-flowered thyme

up the other side

Squat Trevalga Church, and a sweep of meadow the horse in me wants to gallop across. Ahead chevronning the horizon the beautiful 'curzy way' herringbone stone wall, protruding slate slabs for steps. Ash scrabbles and whines, and I heave her over. We pass

people who like dogs
people who do not like their knees licked
people who divert into the bracken to avoid us

then a bench by a bent thorn tree high above the water. The dogs flop into shade, panting

two huge hairy caterpillars
guts extruded
by unseeing passing feet

On the headland the blowhole's boom is a bass note below the continuo of sea and gulls. I lie on a platter of warm slate and stare at cirrus clouds, feel the sun and the sea burn me away out of my self. Left, the hillside's custard with swathes of trefoil. The air's honey

if time is a palimpsest maybe you're still here
stretched to the sun
beside me

On the point the slate arch of the Ladies' Window leans out high above the rocks and water, vertiginous doorway
I find
my hands clasped
at my chest
like a pilgrim

this will be a new start

close your eyes
step through
trust your feet to find the way
back to some kind
of faith

Then the height and the drop make me giddy – and the dogs playing on the edge. I lean back against the stone shoulders – pocked, chipped, wind-shaped; call the dogs, feel my way back through with my hands

suddenly I'm scared

confetti-edged leaves of slate, worn almost hair-thin

I breathe
> through
>> and round
>>> and through again

Cornering the hillside the other side of the valley suddenly the sea-song stops; only the stream, skylarks, my heart – slowed to the speed of this day – my own day. I am not – bliss! – thinking.

>>>>> *this will be a new start*

The past burning away to a thin silt

and now again the slope down to the sea, mist lifted

toadflax
> snapdragons
>> cuckoo spit everywhere

Finding a way back.

4

Shaping

Consider the element of surprise. Think about the shape – the physical visual shape – that the finished pieces might take. Do they have to be on paper, or on screen? What about on sand, in earth, made of shells or stones, bones, feathers, twigs? Check out the work of land artists who also use text, like Richard Long, Hamish Fulton and Ian Hamilton Finlay.

Mindfulness means paying attention in a particular way: on purpose, in the present moment, and non-judgmentally... our lives only unfold in moments. If we are not fully present for many of those moments, we may not only miss what is most valuable in our lives but also fail to realize the richness and the depth of our possibilities...
Jon Kabat-Zinn

Writing is like crossing the road: stop, look and listen.
Elisabeth Rowe

It matters little how quickly I reach the end; what counts is what I discover along the way.
William Peers

THE WRITER & THRESHOLD CONSCIOUSNESS
BY STEPHEN PARR

An Irish monk, on the sacred mountain of Craigpatrick, was talking about the effects of September 11th 2001. He said: 'At the start of that day, there were many tourists around the world; at its close, there were many pilgrims.'

That statement startled me into thinking about the nature of journeys, especially long journeys; about why we make them; about what we get from making them; and about the change (or otherwise) that journeys make in our consciousness, our deep attitudes to ourselves and to each other; and also about the ideas of the pilgrim – what differentiates the common tourist from the relatively uncommon pilgrim, and why it might take a catastrophe to change one into the other.

There are two other ideas that have been bothering me for quite some time, on more or less the same topic; they both concern the poet Coleridge, who was born in 1772 (two years after Wordsworth and Beethoven, and three years before the start of the American War of Independence).

The first is the meaning of Coleridge's great poem 'The Rime of the Ancient Mariner', first conceived, according to Dorothy Wordsworth, 'on a long winter walk over Quantoxhead to Watchet and Dulverton, beginning on 13 November 1797 at about 4 o'clock, when the sun was just setting over Longstone Hill'.

The second item preceded this in Coleridge's life by about eighteen years, in 1779. After a quarrel with his older brother, he fled the family house and hid all night long by the river Otter, about a mile from his home. He watched the cows in the field beyond the river, and at last went to sleep under a mass of old thorn-bush cuttings, within a few yards of the water's edge. He was eventually discovered by some villagers, part of a search party that had been looking for him all night. Much later Coleridge remarked that he would never forget the tears of joy streaming down his father's face when he was finally handed back to his parents. This experience coloured his entire subsequent life and writing.

What is the import of these two events – one from real life, one from Coleridge's imagination? Of course they both involve a journey: one very small, the other very large. They both involve danger: danger of loss of life, relationship with society, even sanity. They also both involve transgression and redemption, and ideas of justice and punishment. The seven-year-old Coleridge attacked his brother and fled through the fields to the river, spent a night in exile from human society, and was 'redeemed' by the expressed love of his grieving parents. The ancient mariner undergoes a remarkably similar path: his ship is blown off course, is lost and becalmed; the mariner then – for some reason never explained – shoots an albatross – a sacred and entirely benign creature that has been following the ship – and in so doing incurs the wrath of Nature. After undergoing a prolonged period of nightmare and terror in which a kind of initiation into the non-human world takes place, he repents of his deed, is 'blessed' by the spirits of the air and sea, and 'blesses' them in return. Transformed by this experience he returns to the human world, and is then consumed by the need to wander endlessly from place to place and communicate what he has seen to anyone who will listen. In Coleridge's myth the essence of the Mariner's message may be summed up in the words 'love everything unconditionally without discriminating or judging what is worthy of love'.

We may also note that the 'message' in the running away from home episode is very similar: 'love me unconditionally – not only when I behave well and abide by your rules'. From the standpoint of the poet what is of great interest in these two myths – or two versions of one myth – is that *a crucial change of consciousness takes place* as a result of what happens on the journey. We could say that the Mariner starts his journey as a tourist (if a hard-working one) and ends it as a pilgrim. His experiences of other worlds as a result of his shooting of the albatross result in a permanent change to his subsequent actions and beliefs. In Buddhist terms you might say that insight had arisen in his mind as a result of what happened on that journey.

So how exactly does the tourist turn into the pilgrim? And how do these two states relate to the journey of the poet?

The American critic Edward Dahlberg wrote 'There is no place to go – so we travel.' Having just come back from a very long journey I think I have a sense of what he meant. The more you travel, the more everywhere looks the same: the same shops, the same streets, the same preoccupations, the same anxieties, the same pervasive images; you begin to realize that what makes a place interesting is not the scenery, or the official sights – but the quality of consciousness of its people. I think there's a lot to be said for the view that 'travel broadens the prejudices'. One can travel to grab more experiences, to accumulate external knowledge, to tick places off in one's diary, to be distracted from pain, to ameliorate an inner restlessness at the heart of one's life – or one can travel for self-knowledge, to become open to the genuinely new way of seeing – developing insight – that constitutes spiritual growth. But of course this isn't guaranteed: the poet Rimbaud travelled compulsively out of self-disgust and boredom, and at the end of his life was left with exactly that; D H Lawrence travelled incessantly to find the ideal place where he could write – but the moment he found somewhere to his liking he discovered something wrong with it, and had to move on: he became the eternally disconsolate wanderer.

The truth is, I suspect, that often physical travel is a substitute for something we do really need: change of consciousness, from 'central' to 'liminal' – edge or threshold consciousness. The American poet Jane Hirshfield:

'More is changed during this 'threshold' period than simply the understanding of self: free of all usual roles, a person experiences community differently as well. The liminal is not opposed to, but the necessary companion of, identity and particularity – a person who steps outside her usual position falls away from any singular relationship to others and into oneness with the community as a whole. Within the separateness of liminality, connectedness itself is remade.' [1]

Hirshfield quotes Czeslaw Milosz's poem 'Ars Poetica?':

The purpose of poetry is to remind us
How difficult it is to remain just one person,
For our house is open, there are no keys in the doors,
And invisible guests come in and out at will.[2]
(translated by Czeslaw Milosz and Lillian Vallee)

For the writer to be of value to society he must be hospitable to every kind of image and energy. The great film director Werner Herzog once said: 'If you put light into every dark corner of a human being he will become uninhabitable. I have seen too many uninhabitable men.'

You might say the urge to travel – to be a tourist – to accumulate places – is akin to shining a light into these dark corners which are essential to us to be habitable: we're running away from our uncomfortable ignorance, our contradictions and mysteries. To be habitable – open to all these creative energies – we need to stay still and allow them to find us. The culture of the west today – essentially characterised by anxiety and restlessness – frightens me, because it can't bear contradictions and mysteries, which are the food of the soul, and of the poet. Now all our guests have to be interrogated before they are allowed in: and who knows how many turn away rather than be subject to such interrogation?

A writer cannot function fully behind locked doors: security, a recognised role in society, even – dare one say it? – a salary. The truth is, the poet has to stand outside all roles if he is to produce work that is of any real value to society. He has to let go of the very idea of a career, because a career represents a closing down of that liminal consciousness, that state of not belonging to any group, group-mentality, status-group, even pressure group or political group.

For the same reason I think it's a danger-point when writers are awarded huge prizes and the consequent fame (I know this may sound like a classic case of sour grapes!) and media exposure that generally go with them, because the pressures of such 'success' inevitably would tend to pull the 'victim' into the central consciousness and away from the liminal. The two states are mutually destructive: all too often the selfsame hand that offers the bounty dictates the text.

So what Hirshfield calls 'threshold life' is essentially a state of non-belonging, non-alignment; not dancing to anyone's tune. There have been many poets who have become adepts of the threshold life. We may start perhaps with Han Shan who wrote a famous collection called *Cold Mountain Poems*.

Han Shan ('Cold Mountain') had been an army general in the 7th century in T'ien T'ai province of China. In 621 he became a Buddhist monk and retired to live in a small hut in a dark, wild and remote wood on the slope of Ts'ui-p'ing mountain. He is famous for writing poems inspired by Buddhism on rocks and trees, and eschewing human society.

> I chose a dwelling place on the mountain with many crags,
> Inaccessible to humans, there are just the birds.
> What is left in the courtyard?
> A white cloud embracing a lonely stone.
> I have lived there for many years
> And saw winter repeatedly transform itself into spring.
> Please tell the ruling families
> That vanity is without recompense.
> (*translation by Wu Chi-yu*)

And there is William Blake, who said 'a man must create his own system or be enslaved by another man's'. Almost totally ignored in his lifetime, he was the ultimate nonconformist, the man who carved his own path out of the mountainside. But since his death his name has become a beacon to all those wishing to follow the path of art – almost a byword for inspired creation.

Since Blake we have had Baudelaire, who has given us the image of the hero-rebel outsider in search of truth and true beauty in the figure of the Dandy; and Rimbaud, who began as an adolescent haunter of cafes in provincial France, and ended up trading guns in Abyssinia, having exorcised from his mind the conventional preoccupations of poetry in the process. His great poem 'Le Bateau Ivre' describes the journey of a boat cast free of its moorings from the cold rational European seas to the sensuous, life-affirming tropics:

> Iridescent waters, glaciers, suns of silver, flagrant skies,
> And dark creeks' secret ledges, horror-strewn,
> Where giant reptiles, pullulant with lice,
> Lapse with dark perfumes from the writhing trees.[3]

It is the journey of a poet from conventional timeserver to visionary outcast; and emphasises the need for the poet to break social taboos and follow his heart where it leads if he is to receive fully the gift of the gods of poetry.

And in our own time we have the American Beats: Kerouac, Burroughs, Ginsberg, who were drawn together perhaps more by their dislike of American mores of the '50s than by any conscious pursuit of the liminal; nevertheless they were undoubtedly voices at a tangent to the consumerist ethos of that society.

There is an apparent polarity here, if not a contradiction, between writers who follow a path of 'commitment' to social criticism, open rebellion against mass values, and those such as Machado, Tranströmer and Gunnar Ekelof who appear to eschew visibility and overt involvement in the struggle for change. Both Wordsworth and Coleridge in their youth appeared set on a path of open social opposition, and were both active in bringing pressure to bear on the inequitable institutions of their day. Yet both withdrew from such activity to lead lives of isolation and solitude, to different degrees and for different reasons. But through this deliberate act of withdrawal it is possible for the poet to become far more deeply engaged with human life, because he is able to drop all social roles and commitments – even drop the idea of being a writer or artist – and become simply a wanderer, or perhaps an explorer of his own mind. This role-less engagement eventually produces its own fruits.

For the writer who chooses to stay 'visible', as it were, it's useful to remember that in England there is a circle of Hell specially set aside for poets who have the gall to swerve from accepted norms. When Coleridge published *Cristabel*

– even after a delay of 16 years – he was excoriated – not for its sexual content, which would have been understandable at that time – but for its departures from strict metrical observance. So any writer who depends on critical approval will be unable even to hear his own 'inner music' – let alone publish it. It seems significant that in order to write 'Kubla Khan', with its hypnotic chant-like rhythms, Coleridge had to be in an opium-induced trance – for without it his conscious brain would have silenced him.

The poet Rilke was given by Rodin, the sculptor, a practice of 'seeing exercises'. Rodin brought to bear on his sculpture a concentration so great that the energy that had gone into its making became visible to him; its intensity of aliveness made it into a source of insight: 'There is no place that is not looking at you. You must change your life.' It's as though he's saying: we are not separate from things; our dividing up the world into living and inanimate things is nothing but habit; to really see an object is to see the reality beyond such divisions, and the result of such clear seeing is that we must bring our behaviour into line with this new insight.

Rilke worked intensively at these exercises for several months, and they were to profoundly affect his work.

Moving now into the twentieth century, the New Zealand poet James K Baxter wrote extensively about the nature of the poet's relationship with modern society. Born in Dunedin in the South Island in 1926, he became a Catholic in 1958, and spent most of his remaining life writing poetry which has an increasingly powerful spiritual dimension; but he is to my mind essentially a poet of the Threshold consciousness: he was always writing from an awareness that human life is a precarious and precious state – and of how easy it is to lose our essential humanity by too much concern for security, comfort, social status, money and possessions. In 1951 he wrote: 'The typical dilemma of the modern poet is one of divided aims. A man who is working as a schoolteacher, a tradesman, or a government official in a society which he knows to be unjust, cannot dare to think clearly on moral issues; for the society is part of his physical and even psychological security.' [4]

This passage seems to me crucial in understanding the poet of the threshold: if a poet can't think clearly on moral issues he can't be a poet; therefore he mustn't be dependent for his livelihood or his position in society upon those who have made investments in the inequities of society. Society needs the truth that the poet can tell: and if the poets don't tell the truth for fear of their living (or their reputation) being threatened, then how is the truth to *be* told? Who else is going to tell it? We can't rely on anyone who has a position to defend. Baxter saw all this very clearly, and decided to 'drop out' of conventional employment and live in a commune with others of like mind – if not of like vision. This choice involved him in much dispute with authority, much poverty and much discomfort – even though he knew that for him it was a voluntary condition.

Modern society has produced affluence and comfort, but it comes at a price that the threshold poet isn't prepared to pay: isolation, lack of community, emotional deadness, a state of spiritual sleep. In order to become of use to his community, in order to acquire 'knowledge' the poet has to experience *nothing*: no role, no position, no identity – not as a theoretical possibility but as a lived experience, a state of being. Not that he stays in that state, but it must become part of his total experience, so that he never loses that perspective. Only then can he produce work that will be of lasting value to others.

I can't finish without mentioning the Swedish poet Tomas Tranströmer. He has been described as one of the great 'religious' poets of the 20th century – yet the religious element is always implicit – held far in the background. To me his great value lies in his ability to bring all the different subjective worlds we inhabit together in one image, so that we're forced to question the tacit conventional assumption that the worlds of everyday experience and the spiritual *are* separate.

There's also another quality in his writing that I value highly: freedom. The freedom to tell the truth. The freedom to find one's own voice. The freedom to write what is shocking, dangerous or uncomfortable. The freedom to bring two facts together which may detonate our assumptions. And the freedom to question everything, by the form he chooses as much as by the content.

Because I've led a few workshops I sometimes catch myself thinking I know what a poem is – and to think that, for a poet, is death. In reality no one knows what a poem is, because a real poem is unique: it has never existed before. So how can we recognise something that is completely new? If we can't recognise it by its subject or form, all we can do is be open to what it actually does, what effect it produces, what changes it brings about within us – and such changes are very often impeded by the invisible conditioning of our society and times.

A good example of this is Wordworth's publication in 1807 of his life-defining collection *Poems in Two Volumes*. The reviews of this collection were consistently devastating. Byron dismissed most of the poems as 'common-place ideas clothed in language not simple, but puerile… namby-pamby'. The *Critical Review* entreated him 'to spend more time in his library and less in company with the moods of his own mind'. The *Edinburgh Review* used phrases like 'a very paradigm of silliness and affectation'; The *Eclectic Review* in 1808 declared the Ode 'a wilderness of sublimity, tenderness, bombast and absurdity'… and so on. Yet by 1835 he was being fêted not only throughout Britain but all over Europe and even in America as a genius and leading poet of the age. The wheel of literary consciousness had turned. It took 25 years for his poetry – the unique product of his vision of the relationship between man and nature – to become visible to the mass of educated society whose minds were the product of 18th century rationalist models.

And so back to Tranströmer, who has described his poems as 'meeting-places' which 'make a sudden connection between aspects of reality that conventional languages and outlooks keep apart'. In 'Answers to Letters' there is a meeting-place of different times, different weathers, different personalities, different states of mind: 'In the bottom drawer of my desk I come across a letter that first arrived twenty-six years ago. A letter in panic, and it's still breathing when it arrives a second time…'[5]

To describe a letter as 'still breathing' opens up for me a sense of infinity, of limitlessness; of the barriers between mind and the physical world dissolving; and in doing that, it changes me, not just for that moment, but for the future.

So liminality can occur when conventional linear language gives way to images that present us with spatial or temporal contradiction. In the above example, someone stands at a window and sees black sky, while from the others can be seen bright daylight; to normal consciousness this is impossible, so to imagine it we are forced to change our consciousness a little, to bring imagination to bear on the scene. In doing this, we change the way we are able to relate to the world generally, as we become able to hold opposites simultaneously in our mind. Similarly, the poet talks of hearing one's own steps walking on the other side of a wall; this makes us question who we think we are; we have to ask, 'how can I exist in two places at once?'; forces us to bring the imagination in to deal with the contradiction. In reading this piece, we have to make a small, temporary excursion from normality to take on board this new world that is presented to us.

To return to our metaphor of the journey. It is possible to regard each moment of our lives as a journey – which as we saw at the beginning, may be either a tour or a pilgrimage. And what determines which it is will be the kind of change – the quality of change – that takes place in our attitudes and perceptions.

The journey of the creative artist has to be a pilgrimage, because the mentality of tourism is entirely antithetical to that of art. In the classical Noh play, the smallest inclination of the head, the flicker of an eye, a nearly invisible hand gesture, can have (we're told) cataclysmic effects on a sensitive observer. Similarly in a poem the precise placing of the absolutely right word or image can change a competent verse into great art, and evince a gasp of recognition – even a determination to change the direction of one's life – in a reader hundreds or maybe thousands of years distant.

But in order for such a miraculous equation to work, the artist has to have the right energy at his disposal, and such energy can only come from a total lack of division of his mind: a complete flowing-together of his deepest energies into the work. And how can this be if he is, with part of his mind, thinking about not upsetting the selection committee of the Arts Council, or whatever respected body of opinion-formers happens to prevail? Although the artist may be aiming at the trans-human, the reality is that he is still very much human, and by no means free from all the needs and beguilements that go with that state. To quote Baxter again: 'Poverty, even tiredness and lack of leisure, are not the greatest checks to good writing; rather a too-complete surrender to the local climate of opinion.'

Coleridge's Mariner, with his 'long grey beard & glittering eye' was doubtless thought a crank by that hurrying, salivating wedding-guest; but he had come from a different world, and was the bearer of genuine 'news': experience unique and original; in other words, something that society needs for its renewal – and therefore for its survival.

This is what the greatest poetry offers: the genuinely new, the unique, the blessing from another world. And to be the bearer of such a blessing, the poet has to abandon willingly every other resort: he has to be utterly himself, true to his experience, even to the point of becoming invisible to the normal world.

SAUNTERING

No journey is too long when you are coming home.
John O'Donohue

I want to follow on from what I wrote about in the walking chapter ('One Foot in Front of the Other') by taking the concept of journeys a little deeper.

Phil Cousineau, in his beautiful book *The Art of Pilgrimage*[1], tells us that the verb 'saunter' derives from the idea of making a journey on foot to 'la sainte terre' – to the sacred, or holy, land, whatever that means to the one making the journey, or the pilgrimage – which of course is what such a journey is. I love that idea – to saunter towards that which pulls you, that which has you by the heart. So that's what I want to write about here.

It's difficult to talk about 'pilgrimage' in a culture which is primarily both secular and materialistic, and which sees itself as culturally and intellectually sophisticated, and therefore 'beyond' such 'superstitious' rites. However, exactly because of that – our cultural spiritual anorexia – it feels very important. But I need to say immediately that by 'pilgrimage' I don't necessarily mean a journey undertaken with piety and religious affiliations – or at least, not in the traditional orthodox sense.

At the risk of my sounding patronising, would you take a moment here to note down your associations with the word 'pilgrimage'?

It's one of those words, like 'religion', that tends to conjure a strong response in people; sometimes one of attraction, sometimes one of aversion. Often we bring our habitual reactions to such words: 'Oh, I don't do religion'; or 'Pilgrimage is a Christian concept'. It's true that pilgrim routes, at least in Europe, are most often Christian; however, many of them are older processional tracks. And Christianity does not have a monopoly on the need to tend one's soul and redefine one's sense of meaning, which are central to the idea of pilgrimage. So forgetting dogma, what else might pilgrimage be about?

For me, these are some of the definitions:

A journey undertaken with conscious intent
A way of reconnecting (this has within it some of the true etymological meaning of the word 'religion')

A way of stepping back out of the glare of ego into the subtler light of soul

A way of getting out of my own light

A way of stopping, looking and listening

A way of remembering (re-membering, as they say, irritatingly but accurately, in New Age circles); drawing together the fragments, rediscovering my true nature

Time out to *be*, consciously

A way of effecting healing

A way of soul retrieval

A rite of passage, making a transition between life phases

A way of moving on from somewhere in which I have become stuck

A way of bringing myself back into the heart of things, the centre, when I have drifted too far off course

A way of reminding myself of priorities

A way of shaking off the demands of an outer-driven materialistic way of life

A way of moving away from being caught up in the trivial dramas of my own life

A way of remembering humility

A way of remembering compassion

A way of being still and silent

A way of slowing down

A way of attempting to make sense, find meaning and purpose

A way of bringing together in me the instinctual and the transcendent, the human and the divine, heaven and earth – not to mention doing and being

A way of restoring balance

A way of accessing creativity when I have spun too far away

A way of remembering that humans operate in many different worlds at once, which seems to be *de rigueur* for a writer

Looking back at that list, I suppose it could be summarised in that word 'reconnecting' – though I don't really want to specify with what I am reconnecting; except in as much as to say 'everything', maybe. Stephen Parr in the previous chapter talks about being changed by an event such as a pilgrimage; experiencing a shift in consciousness.

So pilgrimage – and both concept and action predate Christianity – is a way of travelling mindfully: perhaps for the destination, perhaps simply to travel purposefully. Symbolically, it is also the journey from ignorance to wisdom. Like writing, like any creative act, it's a journey from the known to the unknown. (I am writing here, you will have realised, about journey in the metaphorical sense as well as the literal.)

It's easy to have romantic notions about the idea of pilgrimage. But the truth is that pilgrimage is neither easy, nor synonymous with rest and recreation. That's a holiday (interesting how that word has devolved from 'holy day', with all its connotations). I think it's important to mention that anything that qualifies for the title involves a degree of arduousness and also some significant length of time away from your familiar surroundings and 'everyday reality'. It needs conscious *intent*. It requires discipline, persistence and courage. It will, even if only in moments, take you into dark places and shake your assumptions and certainties. It will bring you face to face with yourself; bring you up against your own raw, rough and often painful edges, unmediated by the usual 'drugs' of familiar routines and comforts. Pilgrimage is pilgrimage *because* of the potential for discomfort, confusion, change.

Mindful travel in the spirit of pilgrimage involves bringing the whole of one's self to the journey; meeting the challenges; being aware of all the surface details of the place or places through which or to which we travel, but also looking below the surface, looking for the deeper meaning, listening for what Ralph Waldo Emerson called 'the undersong', being aware of the connectedness of everything, despite apparent outer disparities.

Always, it seems to me, it's about trying to see how things actually are, devoid of our imaginings and projections and judgements. And it's about making time for soul in a world that generally doesn't. For the Celts, always aware of the presence of the Otherworld, pilgrimage opens a passage between the two worlds – the material and that of the spirit.

It would be easy here to digress into a discussion of what is secular and what is spiritual. For the purposes of this book, though, that would be irrelevant; and for the writer, too. What matters is the truth you bring – your own truth – to the journey, whatever it is or wherever it goes; and you can, of course, make a pilgrimage out of walking (travelling) *anywhere* – what matters is the spirit in which you undertake the journey.

Nonetheless, there are some places that somehow make this process easier. Certain places hold a remarkable ability to soothe, to reorder turmoil, confusion and chaos. Some of these places will be personal, particular to you; others are places where, in the words of the Celts, the 'veil is thin', and whether by virtue of their geographical location and attributes, or whether as a cumulative result of centuries or more of people travelling to them in such a spirit – or both – their atmosphere is almost palpable. Some would say these places are nodes of energy; power centres or earth chakras. There are many: Chartres, Santiago de Compostella, Holy Island, Lindisfarne, Macchu Picchu, Avebury, Rome, Canterbury, Uluru (Ayers Rock), Lourdes, Assisi, Newgrange, Castlerigg, Callanish, Stonehenge, Glastonbury, Jerusalem, Mecca, Bodh Gaya, Carnac, the Pyramids, St Michael's Mount and Mont St Michel, the Alhambra, the Taj Mahal, Iona, to name a few.

French existentialist writer Albert Camus said: 'We travel for years without much idea of what we are seeking. We wander in the tumult, entangled in desires and regrets. Then suddenly we arrive at one of those two or three places that are waiting for each of us patiently in the world. We arrive there and the heart is at last at peace – we discover that we have arrived.'

A place of pilgrimage is a place where we can bring ourselves home – even if paradoxically, the place that facilitates this is thousands of miles from 'home' (though equally paradoxically it may not even actually require going out – ancient Eastern sacred texts talk of knowing the whole world without even going out of one's own door). It's a resting place where we can gather together the scattered parts of ourselves and our lives, return to the hub.

Each year, with my friend author and poet Kenneth Steven, I lead a writing retreat on the Isle of Iona in the Hebrides. We call it 'Into Blue Silence' – and for anyone who knows Iona, it will be clear how apt that title is. Unlike a traditional pilgrimage, I can't truthfully say that we approach it with austerity and frugality – the hotel in which we base it is right at the water's edge; all that sealight and saltwind and shell-sand and the sound of the waves which create the island's pulse all constitute the most sumptuous of banquets for the senses; and since the hotel is noted for its food we hardly deprive the body, either.

Nonetheless, it's quite a journey for most of the participants, involving hundreds of miles and at least two sea crossings. (For myself, travelling from Devon, it's two days' travel. I generally take the train; for a number of reasons, including the environmental, I choose not to fly, despite – in fact partly because of – the speed of air travel. I'm firmly with the Sherpas, who take time out on the mountain after a certain amount of hiking to allow their souls to catch up. So when I arrive after up to four changes of train – plus my journey to the station in the first place, a night at a B & B, a bus journey and two ferries – I truly feel I've travelled.)

It's also, for many of the people who attend the week, another country – a vast distance away from the substance of their daily environment and routine.

These ingredients can be, first, disorientating; and, second, the catalyst for profound experience.

We include in the week a daily period of silence, and some of our walks on the island are conducted either in silence or in solitude – or maybe both. What emerges from the week is a great deal more than writing; the experience is often deeply transformative for people.

This is partly of course to do with Iona, which has been for many centuries a place of pilgrimage. Yet many of the people who come, either to the island or to our course, do not share Kenneth's Christian faith – myself included. And still the place works its magic.

There is something, too, about making a shared journey, even if you choose to keep yourself partly apart. The companions on such a journey are integral to the experience. When I arrive on Iona, my companions will be those who have chosen to make this particular week's journey with Ken and me.

I'm thinking about companionship on the train on the way up – my friend Mario has mentioned to me recently that it comes from the Latin – 'com pane' – those with whom you break bread. In pilgrimage you cast yourself upon life, and your companions are not always of your choosing. So:

> *April 2003*
> On the train. My companions on this the first part of my journey:
> 1 *The Guardian*. I read it virtually word for word – maybe three hours
> – such a rare luxury. And therefore another companion:
> 2 The war on Iraq. All that annihilation: people, buildings, a culture
> – destruction in the name of democracy. I'm frightened. It's impossible
> not to be terrified – for the people of Iraq, for the future, for all of us.
> How can a 'war on terror' do anything other than perpetuate it?
> 3 A gorgeous young Asian guy with two hearing aids. He mimes that he'd

like to borrow the discarded bits of my paper, and roars with laughter at the cartoon: Muslims walking in and out of Baghdad airport, under the huge new sign: 'George W Bush Airport'

4 Four Germans, who spend all their time in our carriage shouting with laughter and drinking, just when I was enjoying the quiet. Besides, I'm tired after a very early start and a crisis with one of the animals whose care I was passing to someone else for ten days. My initial irritation soon subsides at their good-natured smiles, however. The Germans wear blue neckerchiefs and identical red sweatshirts with train logos. They're here, they tell me and anyone else who'll listen, to make their twelfth entry into the *Guinness Book of Records* for the fastest crossing of a country south to north by zigzagging across it east to west... Presumably breaking their own previous record, because I can't imagine who else would have dreamed up such a venture (although maybe there are whole clubs of people worldwide doing this in their spare time). They offer me some *wurst*, but I decline. I wouldn't mind breaking bread with them, but as a vegetarian meat's not on. In the spirit of a true pilgrim, though (accepting what is offered on the journey – unless it's meat) I do share their bottle of very good Schwarzwald wine with them, readily repressing my inner critic who says one shouldn't start drinking at ten in the morning, especially not on pilgrimage... I'm sad when they're displaced from their seats by

5 The official reservees: a couple in their early 60s who initially look like they're not going to be any fun at all. I immediately have them down as sourpusses (my initial name was a ruder title). It seems to me they will be disapproving, conservative and humourless. Ah, the follies of the judging mind! They turn out to be delightful, entertaining, well read, thoughtful and very attentive, not only to each other but also to me. Eventually they too leave and their place is taken by

6 An RAF pilot. Well, I'm a peace campaigner; but I'm also a human being, and besides this is a pilgrimage. I think ruefully of how I judged the previous occupant of his seat. So I (peacefully) smack my Inner Judge down into silence and open to a conversation with the guy, and for an hour or two we share our mutual interest in wild places – Dartmoor, Cumbria, Scotland – and border collies; then

7 He leaves and the train crosses the river into Glasgow in the evening

sun. (I reflect how fond I have become of these Glaswegian bridges.) Since my very early departure from Plymouth this morning, I've had to change trains unexpectedly twice, in addition to the scheduled – already tight – changes, due to breakdowns (of the trains, I mean). It's been one of those smooth days, though, when miraculously – due to the knock-on effects of other hold-ups elsewhere and unconnected – I've been able to make the original connections as they too have been delayed. And astonishingly we arrive into Glasgow only 50 minutes late, the first 12-hour leg of the journey nearly complete – and there's Kenneth, my 'planned' pilgrim companion, and a hug, and one kind of homecoming.

Every journey, in its own way, echoes the archetypal Hero's Journey spoken of by that great mythologian Joseph Campbell: that is, every journey contains separation from the known, initiation into a new way – with all the attendant ordeals – and return, bringing what we've learnt[2].

The person who arrives home will be slightly, or even greatly, different from the person who left; and after a journey we bring with us the capacity to re-vision our home, to know it 'for the first time', to paraphrase T S Eliot.

If, then, I can make the journey/s of my life as mindful as possible I begin to get a clearer idea of where, or what, home is; and of course it is not always a place. Sometimes it's a person, or a group of people. Sometimes it's something like learning to live more deeply in your own skin; living more intimately connected to the landscape or landscapes in which you find yourself, and all the mineral, plant and animal life; living more closely connected with the people who surround you. For some, it has to do with making a connection with whatever they perceive as being larger than themselves: 'God' is the usual shorthand for this in our culture, but It has many names – and none.

So there's a sense when, even if you are travelling alone, both home and pilgrimage are to do with coming into an awareness of the interconnectedness of everything. At this level, it's also about intimacy. We will be as intimate with the world only as we are able to be intimate with ourselves.

So living more mindfully might bring us closer to home, wherever we find ourselves. If a pilgrimage is a journey taken mindfully, consciously, then every moment is important; and every step is both the beginning and the end of the journey; the departure and the destination. Every step becomes home.

This, then, is part of the point: we are taken deeply into each moment. As a human being, and as a writer, this is what we work with – even when that moment is dark, is full of loss, or pain, or shame, or discomfort, or fear, or memories, or dreams, or hopes, or longing. Or, of course, laughter, or joy, or love, or belonging. Blisters, kisses.

There are dark times on a journey, just as there are wonderful times. It happens on a pilgrimage that you are sometimes plunged into despair; taken out of your habits of being, other things arise, things from which we have become adept at turning away in our distracted and distracting modern lives. Then just as we think we are moving forward suddenly we have a memory that tugs us into the past, into something unresolved. We journey into what we have been, what we haven't been, what we might have been as much as forward into who we might yet be.

Sometimes it's so hard we don't want to know. This is the raw material of which we make our lives; and our writing. We take a step, we get knocked sideways, we stumble to our knees, get up again and walk on. Our feet hurt. We weep. We sing. We're still alive. 'We are always on a journey from darkness into light', says John O'Donohue. How it is. As you travel, you watch – you watch the world out there, the world in here, and you watch yourself and the way you relate to it. This is what mindfulness means. This is how we learn who we are – and who we are not.

And if we get lucky we finally remember how to really *dwell* in each moment – remember how it was to be a child, to be completely immersed in something?

Then the healing starts. Though often traditionally pilgrimages were and are taken to places that are known for their healing power, something subtly unfolds in the act of travelling mindfully; and we discover it is the journey itself that brings the healing. Lindsay Clarke says that the Quest for the Holy Grail is not about the achievement, the attainment of the end event, but about the *process*, the quest itself. All journeys, if undertaken consciously, can be journeys to the stillpoint, the centre, the heart of things. And, paradoxically, in that movement, in the journey itself, can be found stillness, just as in stillness we can find the dance, to paraphrase Eliot again. And then we are connected to the interplay of everything.

If we can bring the same spirit of mindfulness to our writing as to our pilgrimage, paying attention to this moment means we bring a certain depth to our writing. And we're making a space where our stories and poems can sprout and grow.

But, at least as importantly, writing is a connecting thread; and, more, it can also be a 'hotline' to the invisible worlds of which we become aware when we journey in this kind of spirit – the similarities behind the differences, the enduring behind the apparent transience of things, the universal behind the personal or particular, the significant in the small, the extraordinary in the ordinary. Was it Lawrence Durrell who said something along the lines of the writer being a kind of conduit who passes a current from one world to another? Hermes/Mercury, the magician messenger of the gods, was both the god of language and communication, and also the psychopomp, who accompanied souls between realms. Language is a powerful tool: it makes spells, it changes lives, it finds lost worlds and creates new ones, it can both tap into and trigger, says Phil Cousineau, divine events.

In the beginning was the Word.

Language is a way of bringing it all back home – retaining the thread which connects us to where we have been when this moment, as it will, dissolves into the next.

how many miles
and how many journeys
just to be with   ourselves

Starting points

1

The journey – 'snapshots'
The next time you make a longish journey – by car, bike, horse or public transport – as soon after it as possible record some of the moments you recall. They don't need to be significant – or maybe every moment is significant; so simply close your eyes and allow 5 or 6 moments on the journey to arise in your memory and imagination.

Aim to write a few sentences, or a short paragraph at most, for each and keep it vivid and focused. Find a way to capture the individual essence of each moment as it passes. This is prose, but heightened tightened prose. Start with your departure and end with your arrival; include snippets of dialogue if appropriate, and anything at all that suggests itself. Include, too, yourself and your passing thoughts and feelings. But stay *brief*.

2

Stepping stone moments

Close your eyes and allow some moments in your life to emerge that were in some way significant, even transformative. These won't be the big obvious moments like leaving home, getting a job, marriage, birth of child (we work with these elsewhere in the book); rather they'll be moments of transcendence that arrived out of the blue, or maybe they were apparently small decisions or choices which turned out, in hindsight, to have huge consequences in your subsequent life, maybe changing your direction completely: meeting someone, hearing something, arriving somewhere, seeing something, a realisation.

Note these down.

Now choose a few to write about; briefly, in the present tense. Keep them rooted in concrete detail, and try to pinpoint what was extraordinary about them, or different. Did you know at the time that they were significant? What was the emotional tone of each one? Think about them, too, as points on a continuum: how do or did they connect with other events?

3

Spirit of place

Imagine that you are wanting to tell someone you love, who will never be able to go there, about a place that is very important to you. Write a thumbnail portrait of that place, using all the senses, in such a way as to convey not only the physical presence but the spirit of that place; why it moves you as it does.

4

Home

I think of this as the hub and wheel exercise.

a) Without thinking, and without mentioning an actual house in which you've lived, write stream-of-consciousness piece about 'home'.
When you've done this, look back over it and pick out – or add – a keyword that epitomises what 'home' means to you.

Find a large sheet of plain paper – as big as possible – and some coloured pens. Choose a colour to represent home. In the middle of the sheet of paper write your 'home' keyword in large letters. This is the hub.

b) Make a circle around the periphery of the paper by noting down, in single words – nouns – or short phrases, everything tangible you associate with that word that means home. It may be people or animals; it may be objects, furniture, garden plants or aspects of landscape; it may be the immediate surroundings; it may be something you do ('playing the piano') or all of these things. Use colours as and when.

c) Now for/from each of these things draw a spoke connecting it to the hub, and write along that spoke a keyword representing a feeling quality or adjective that represents that thing. For instance, you might feel being in your garden gives you a sense of peace, so that word would make the spoke for 'garden'. Maybe a 'warm bed' is on the rim of your wheel; perhaps 'comfort' or 'security' would be the keyword. Perhaps it's a particular coat: why? Or perhaps an important aspect of 'home' for you is your lover: what is the particular quality he or she brings to your life?

d) If you wish to, write a short poem that takes an interesting or oblique angle on the whole concept of home, maybe using something on your wheel as a starting point.

Where we had thought to travel outward, we will come to the centre of our own existence. And where we had thought to be alone, we will be with all the world.
Joseph Campbell

All our journeys are rhapsodies on the theme of discovery.
Phil Cousineau

The real traveller finds sustenance in equivocation, he is torn between embracing and letting go, and the wrench of disengagement is the essence of his existence, he belongs nowhere. The anywhere he finds himself is always lacking in some particular, he is the eternal pilgrim of absence, of loss, and like the real pilgrims in this city [Santiago] he is looking for something beyond the grave of an apostle or the coast of Finisterre, something that beckons and remains invisible, the impossible...
Cees Nooteboom

One needs cross neither ocean nor land to journey. One needs merely to travel beyond what one knows. Even then, the destination will only ever be a familiar place.
Natalie Savona

SILENCE

Ben Okri talks about words being a kind of silence; I like that idea.

And there is a point beyond which language cannot go. I wonder whether, just as eyes have been called the windows of the soul, language might be thought of as the window into the great silence beyond?

When I first introduced a few minutes of silence – I'm talking about four or five minutes, that's all – into the start of one of my regular writing groups several people were uneasy. Maybe they felt there might be some sort of connotation – perhaps they ought to adopt a particular *quality* to their silence; maybe I expected a religious kind of observance. Or maybe it's hard for us living in the West to shake off the kind of Calvinism that suggests we 'ought not' to sit still, in silence, at ten on a weekday morning. More likely, in a secular society that is wedded to action and achievement and stimulus, it is simply very hard for many people to just sit still, with nothing they should be doing and nothing they should be thinking or feeling.

The interesting thing is that, as time went on, if ever I skipped my few minutes' silence at the start of a session, people clamoured for it.

Now I kick off my regular poetry group with half an hour's silence, during which people can sit, or meditate, or free write, as they like. It is an integral part of the retreat-type courses, such as the one I lead with Kenneth Steven on Iona ('Into Blue Silence'). We introduced the half hour silent bit in 2003, and noticed that it made a significant difference, not only to the day, but to the quality of the whole week, and people's experience of the course and the island. In 2004, we extended it to an hour. Now, silence plays a bigger part in many of my courses.

It is not possible to be fully mindful of the quality of each moment without being able to be fully present in that moment, and what we could call 'active' thinking, and certainly talking, can take us right out of the moment and our indwelling. There are, of course, times for both; but it is a rare life – outside of the contemplative's – that has any kind of balance of this nature in it.

Like solitude, it is initially frightening for people; and it can be almost embarrassing, too, to be around other people and not to talk. It requires a different kind of intimacy, which is, after you have experienced it, astonishingly rich and full, and compelling. To share a meal with friends while talking 'properly' – that is, in a reasonably profound way – is a tremendous gift; to share a meal with others in silence is at least as powerful, if you bring the whole of yourself to the whole of the occasion. Eye contact becomes more important. Facial expression. Touch, too. But the biggest gift is the opportunity for awareness – without the space being continually filled with words, one becomes so much more aware of body language, levels of comfort and discomfort, tensions and harmonies, the way in which we approach or avoid others, the quality of presence and attention we are able to bring to each moment and our fellow participants.

Clearly, as I mentioned in the last chapter, we will be as intimate and comfortable with the others with whom we share this silence as we are able to be with ourselves. This is hard for contemporary people in our culture. So much of our time is filled with distracting ourselves from our lives that it is very difficult, initially, to simply be with who one is, and know that that is enough, both for oneself and for one's companions. At first we tend to lose ourselves in self-consciousness – looking outwards, feeling silly; then gradually little by little we let go into it, and come back to ourselves. Having remade the connection with ourselves, remembering to sit at the centre of our own lives, we are then freed to reconnect with others and the world from a deeper, and slower, place.

Silence has a particular quality of its own. The state of silence is more than a mere absence of sound, just as darkness is more than merely an absence of light (metaphorically if not literally).

But total silence, of course, doesn't exist. Writer, composer and philosopher John Cage speaks of going into the anechoic chamber at Harvard, where he expected to be enveloped in utter silence; and being shocked into a new creative direction by hearing, instead, the high song of his nervous system, and the lower hum of his blood. So we are talking about relative silence; more specifically a withdrawing from language.

In Buddhist tradition there is monkey mind, or chatterbox mind – Natalie Goldberg writes of this – and there is the Buddhist/Beat generation concept of 'big sky mind'.[1] Stepping from one into the other requires an effort like that of navigating outer space – it's like making the journey from one planet to another. This is part of the purpose of meditation, of course; it's a way of stilling the spinning world. We live surrounded, taken over, by continual internal and external noise and chatter, and few of us have the ability, knowledge or even desire to switch it off, even for a few minutes, without practice.

Words can take us towards silence. 'Words,' said T S Eliot, 'after speech, reach / into the silence.' But once they have taken us there, they have to leave us: words cannot make the journey alongside us. So there is the flood-tide of words carrying us to the shores of silence, then the turning point, then the ebbing where the wet sand shows the passage of language at our backs but the words have receded.

It's in the silence that the things you most need to hear become apparent. This is the place where your writing may start.

Many people think that creativity starts with an idea. I don't think that it does. It seems to me that, before the idea, in a pre-verbal, pre-conceptual place, arises an image, and before that a feeling (Robert Frost talked about poetry beginning with a lump in the throat, a feeling of homesickness).

Before that again flares a wild spark of fire, a starburst, that sets its seed in a rich and fertile place, where all these things are latent. Somewhere out there in the great silence.

Starting point

Try introducing into your daily rhythm a time of complete wordlessness. This may be as brief as fifteen minutes daily; or it may be an hour at a weekend. Involve your family; prepare or eat a meal in silence, or wash the dishes together.

Clearly this also means no word-based stimulus: radio, TV, music, books. If you can, try and use the time to be still, physically; and simply listen. Pay attention to the passing moment. If writing comes, that's a bonus; but let that be afterwards.

Dawn points, and another day
Prepares for heat and silence. Out at sea the dawn wind
Wrinkles and slides. I am here
Or there, or elsewhere. In my beginning.
T S Eliot

There are times when memories are not enough
and neither are poems, even when the words,
having come so close to what we cannot say,
gather themselves slowly around the silence.
Neil Curry

THE STILL SMALL VOICES

I went out to the hazel wood
Because a fire was in my head...
W B Yeats

This chapter is actually about being alone – something that is not really culturally sanctioned in the West. Many of us have issues about it, too: it seems selfish, or weird, or an admission of social failure; or involves 'rejecting' another person; or maybe we're scared of it. We have so little time for solitude, so few places where we can go to really be alone, to fast from people and stimuli. Culturally there is no structure for this kind of experience, though in the past of our own and the present of some other cultures, there has been the mechanism of 'vision' or 'wilderness quest' as a way of being still, looking for answers and/or healing, and marking a rite-of-passage; and then there was the original 'quarantine': an almost unthinkably strenuous period, to our contemporary minds, of forty days alone.

But how else, without this time alone, will we listen to the 'still small voices'?

And the truth is, no matter how we attempt to fill the void, avoid the question or cram our minutes full, we are all, ultimately, alone. We come into this world alone and we leave it, too, on our own. This is the truth of it. This is of course not to deny friendship, intimacy, deep connection; nor to dismiss religious and philosophical traditions – not to mention the new paradigms thrown up by sciences such as quantum physics and chaos theory – which remind us that an equally valid truth is that we are all interconnected.

So we are solitary and we are also each part of a greater whole. We have an effect on the world around us, as it has an effect on us.

But the fact of our fundamental solitude is not something over which we have any power; there is no choice. The poet Rilke talks about this: 'We *are* solitary. We may delude ourselves and act as though this were not so. That is all. But how much better it is to realize that we are so, yes, even to begin by assuming it. Naturally we will turn giddy.'

I guess the reason for my addressing this is obvious – writers have to spend large periods of time in self-imposed solitary confinement. No choice about that, either. I wonder whether sometimes when we say we 'don't have time' to write, we are actually afraid of the solitude?

It's a very wet March day on Dartmoor. There's a force 9 gale haranguing the trees; everything looks sodden and winter-black. I have my waterproofs and a rucksack, in which is my sleeping bag, minimal shelter (the flysheet for a tent and its poles – rickety, to put it mildly), some water, a notebook and pen, and an emergency stash of dried fruit and nuts. I have no book, no mobile phone (and besides there would be no signal) and no 'proper' food. I'm walking into a wild-ish patch of woodland under one of the tors; beside me is my friend and guide Jeremy Thres (see his piece in this book).

I'm about to enter a short period of fasting – from food, words, people and my normal distractions, like phone, books and music – time alone in the 'wilderness'. Jeremy and I have spent some time preparing, and we will spend this day together at 'base camp', too. After that I'll go off a little way on my own, and my agreement will be to be there on my own for thirty-six hours. There will be a day of re-acclimatising afterwards.

In the general run of things thirty-six hours is nothing for a wilderness, or vision, quest. Usually the time out alone, fasting, is a minimum of three days, often longer (and I was 'allowed' more shelter – the flysheet – than the usual basic tarp). Later, when I co-lead a quest with Jeremy, the whole thing will take a week: two days to prepare, three days out, two days to 'come back to the world'; and the participants will go farther from base camp than I, coward that I'm being, choose to.

The point of it all of course is mindfulness: the unadulterated meeting with World; and the meeting with our selves, without the usual distractions with which we fill up our lives, and therefore avoid meeting life face-to-face. It's a time to let all the little voices – normally rushed away before we can catch them, like leaves on a river - have their say.

I'm used to relatively untamed and/or remote places, having grown up in rural coastal Devon and spent almost all of my adult life living on or near Dartmoor, as well as having spent quite a lot of time in my early twenties in the high Pyrenees, on the border between France and Spain. I spend a lot of my time, on a regular/daily basis, walking alone with the dogs. When I travel, as I do for my courses, I have also always tended to be in wild-ish places, such as the Hebridean islands. I really love solitude, especially outdoors; it's also when I am at my most calm and my most creative. Solutions, ideas and inspiration all arise during my time outdoors. I'm also very interested in natural history, in animal, bird and plant habits and habitats. And in my habitual adult life, I don't get anything like enough 'free' time to do what I love – time to think, and to be, and to hang out in wild places.

So of course I was looking forward to it; and not really expecting any deep fears to arise. I have, after all, I think, spent a lot of time 'looking at my stuff', as they say.

The first few hours were great. I had been relishing the prospect of no interruptions: no phone, no work, no chores.

I wandered a bit. I sat on a wet and mossy rock and thought. I wandered a bit more. I got out my notebook.

I sat.

I tried not to think.

I wished I had a book.

I wished I had a dog.

I wished the sun would come out.

I sat a bit more.

I put my now-damp entirely-word-free notebook away.

I wished I could hear more birds – there seemed an unhealthy absence of bird-life.

I resented the mud and the rain and the ragged grey sky.

I heard my own voice talking.

I wondered about the current reports of another Black Beast of Dartmoor – a puma-like creature roaming the uplands of the moor, apparently spotted on a number of occasions not too far from where I was. I wondered how timid they were. I wondered how close they would come to humans. I remembered a recent case in the States of a woman jogger mauled and killed close to a town by a wild puma.

A fire. That's what I needed, a fire. But there was no hope of dry tinder, and I wasn't supposed to be drawing attention to myself anyway.

I was wet and cold.

I was – already! – tired of the inside of my own head. I couldn't hear any 'still small voices' for the drumming of my own rampaging fears.

Well, it was a tough thirty-six hours, when I faced my own fears of boredom – I, who longed, in a very full life, to be able to experience the space to be bored! I experienced the fear of meaninglessness; and of oblivion. I thought about mortality and immortality. I felt frightened by both. I realised for the first time how much I use the stimulus of reading and music, for instance, as a way of not being still and utterly alone with myself – and the world as it is, and the Void.

Time stretched.

Then two little things happened to break the surge of panic and desolation I was feeling. One was my noticing how, just as the light was ebbing at dusk, the rooks and jackdaws somewhere on the verges of the wood all took to the wind cawing and clacking in a wild mingled swooping flypast, before finally settling. Somehow that lifted my spirits, took me out of my spinning head and dropped me firmly into the life of this particular wood at this particular moment; made me smile. Then, at dawn, after a damp, headachy and very restless night of almost no sleep and fleeting but disturbing dreams when I did manage to doze, I opened my eyes into more rain and wind – and somewhere close by thrush-song. Back into the moment, and a tuning-in to the waking sounds of the wood, the smell of sodden peaty soil, the spikes of bluebell shoots.

And now I could and did write – about my observations of my immediate environment, and then about my fears, and about what they triggered: about my realisations to do with the very real and basic fact of our aloneness; about my own spectres of loneliness and boredom.

Suddenly then too I realised how short my time out there alone really was, where yesterday it had seemed painfully endless; and of course by extension how short all our time 'here' really is.

There's nothing like the shock of realising how you're 'wasting' something as precious as unstructured time in a life that is continuously overfull and unrestful to focus your mind. Still small voices? Boy, did I start listening. And the rest of my very short period of time out there on the moor proved to be extraordinarily fruitful as an extremely intense spell of total immersion in everything around me; to the extent where, for a brief spell – and I use that word deliberately – I lost awareness of myself as a being separate from the rest of the universe. And, several years on, the small amount of writing I did during that time, and the awareness I brought back from it, is still influencing my life.

So, times like this morning when I hear the song thrush start up at 6.45 from the copper beech tree near my window, I'm jolted back into that time, and then into giving my full attention to listening, just listening, for a few minutes.

There's an enormous energy loose in the world and it passes through all of us. And some people who end up being writers or photographers or painters try to shape that energy through the techniques they have mastered or apprenticed themselves to. And make out of that energy a story. And so they stay attuned in their lives to that movement of energy through them. And for most artists that attunement requires some degree of solitariness – either in the reception or the creation...

Barry Lopez

TONGUES OF THE EARTH
BY JEREMY THRES

We are the weavers of the fabric of modern society.
We can weave love, truthfulness and peace
Or we can weave hatred, mistrust and war.
We will have to wear whatever fabric we weave.
Vimala Thakar

'WHY HAVE YOU COME HERE?' demands Baba Yaga, the fearsome Russian Witch of the fairy tales. The fence surrounding her home is decorated with the heads of previous visitors from whom she hasn't liked the answer, so it is important to answer her well.

Yaga represents Dame Nature in her full and potent form, and though in the stories she takes the heads of those who approach her shallowly or without heart, if approached well she is a generous bestower of gifts.

I ask that same question – her question – of those I am preparing for a journey into the wilds in my role as midwife, standing at a doorway marked 'wilderness rites of passage'. Work of this nature, as well as being a way to confirm and move into new stages of life, is also renowned for its potential gifts of vision and inspiration.

As a consequence it attracts creative people, and a writer might come seeking the Muse. During or following the experience participants may well receive a fresh outpouring of language and creativity, of poetry and prose. It's heady, seductive stuff, but, as I have learned from the elders to whom I was apprenticed to support this work, the question is a good one to engage with for those who come: *What is your intent? Why are you here? Why do you want vision at this time? And, say the Muse or some other gift comes your way, what will you do with what you receive?*

This emphasis on intent in the necessary preparation phase of such a rite is the same whether the formal preparatory threshold time is to be just a few hours or several days. *Why are you here? What brings you to this passage at this time? Who are your people? And what do you dream of?*

This questioning is not so much for the interest of those supporting the work, though certainly there is genuine interest in what people choose to dream; it's important to recognise that everyone's dream, and the depth of it, has an effect collectively on all of our lives. But through the listening and sharing process – from their own stories, from what feels appropriate from myth and story of 'others who've gone there before' – participants are supported in going deeper, 'to jump as high as they are able', as one story tells it.

The support also involves helping participants in remembering the wider context and continuity of which they're a part, so they can be more awake in their relationship to life around them. In a way any increase in power is dangerous unless it also goes hand in hand with a similar increase in awareness and responsibility.

There are any number of stories that teach us the attitude we need. There's something here about not directing everything to the service of our own 'little' selves, our egos. 'Many people are looking for their dogs to serve them, rather than something greater to serve,' writes scholar and elder Hyemeyohsts Storm in *Seven Arrows*. In the Grail Quest stories Parsifal can only achieve the Grail by moving away from the 'little' world of the ego by asking the bigger question: 'Whom does it serve?' Our stories, particularly at this time, need to expand beyond the merely self-serving, or self-centred.

As in the 'everyday' world, but in a heightened way, the attitude with which we go out on such a journey makes a huge difference to our experience. Go out 'like Prometheus looking to steal fire from the sacred altar of vision, and what you steal will probably die in your heart. Go out hoping to take a recreational dance through a phantasmagoria of altered states, and you will probably be unable to find a comfortable place to sit.'[1] Move too fast and your clothes will get caught in the briars. Go out with arrogance and you will probably put your foot down a rabbit hole or in something else you'd rather not tread in. In the wilds life reflects us back onto our selves more clearly than in the surrogate-cushioned worlds we create within it.

So it's important you go out looking for your fire, your vision, your dream, your Muse, for the right reasons, and with the right attitude: with some measure of humility, openness and courage, and a willingness to learn, to see with new eyes. And go out with love. (George Washington Carver said 'If we love something enough it will reveal itself to us.') Then jump – as high as you are able.

So that is what we are doing in my field of work, supporting people to consider deeply their reasons for engaging with this work, knowing that not only they, but also the greater world of which we are all a part, will benefit from their honesty and their 'jumping as high as they are able'. Supporting them to engage with some measure of humility, openness and courage, a willingness to learn and see with new eyes. Preparing them particularly for when they cross the threshold into the second phase of the passage and come face-to-face with Baba Yaga, in her wilderness domain – whether inner or outer; the wilderness from which our stories and poems spring. *Why have you come here?* Yaga asks; as do the many other eyes that are upon you.

Participants can tell as many lies as they like to those who are preparing them, or to themselves, but here in the wilderness (as it perhaps really is always) it is just themselves relating to the greater field of Life.

And in this greater field the stories we bring back matter. Where do our stories position us? What is their central truth? Are they healing stories or stories of destruction and dominance?

Humanity, as we all know, is at a crux point in relation to Dame Nature right now. Our lifestyles have exceeded her limits, pierced the protective atmosphere of the planet, radically altered the carbon cycle, and poisoned the rivers and seas. Yet our bodies and those of our children depend on the wellbeing of the Earth's body. If we are not wiser in our approach, Baba Yaga will recycle us all and our children sooner rather than later, for though she is a great provider of gifts she is certainly not all fluffy bunnies.

I ask the question: what stories have we been fed and living to enable us to be so destructive to our only home? For the stories we hear influence our thinking and our attitudes, and how we perceive ourselves and proceed in relationship to the world.

One thing we will benefit from is more writers willing to get to know the earth…We need some writers to speak for Our Greater Body. To be, as an aboriginal elder remarked, 'tongues of the Earth'. Our relationship with the earth needs to be one of intimacy. Maybe it's the job of the poet, the storyteller, to listen, to listen intimately and wisely, to listen with humility, and to bring back these gifts to the whole.

They say the pen is mightier than the sword, and there is a rite of passage saying I have heard both attributed to African and European origin: 'Never give a man a weapon until he has learned to appreciate beauty.' As writers I trust you are all soon to pick up your weapon, your pen, so I wonder 'where are *you* writing from?'

And as storytellers and weavers of the imagination, I ask you not to forget our current context, to get to know well this beautiful world of which we are a part, to bring awareness to the seeds you plant, for as William Stafford said it is important that awake people remain awake, 'for the darkness around us is deep'.

DARK MATTER

Seek for the depths of things...
Rainer Maria Rilke

If you bring forth what is within you, what you bring forth will save you. If you do not bring forth what is within you, what you do not bring forth will destroy you.
Jesus Christ

...out of blood and love I carved my poems.
Pablo Neruda

Anger and tenderness: my selves.
And now I can believe they breathe in me
as angels, not polarities.
Adrienne Rich

In the chapter on solitude ('The Still Small Voices') I mention how time alone can bring up issues of loneliness and vulnerability. In a time-hungry world, people with a reflective bent who spend their lives surrounded by others often long for solitude. Paradoxically, though, when that time arrives, it can be less the imagined unmitigated bliss than a time of struggle and confusion. It is as likely to bring demons as it is angels; despair as epiphany.

For a writer, this is not all bad news, however.

For writing to have the power and passion to touch people it needs to go down as well as up: into the dark, mysterious and sometimes painful places of the human heart and the body. It is not enough to write about light, and angels, and flowers.

Writing needs to have what the Spanish call *duende*: a wild force, a passion, a recognition of the inevitable intertwining of the life cycles of pain and loss and death with those of joy and harvest and birth.

Federico García Lorca, whose name is synonymous with the concept of *duende*, calls *duende* a power rather than a method, a struggle rather than a thought. It needs, he continues, to rise up through the soles of one's feet; it is not a matter of ability or aptitude but rather the way one approaches one's life, an 'authentic living style... [which is] the spirit of the earth... of blood... culture... creation'. It needs, he says, to come through the body, so although it can be found in all art forms its natural domain is dance, song or spoken poetry. The arrival of *duende*, according to Lorca, 'always presupposes a radical transformation on every plane'.[1] Jason Webster defines *duende* as 'the intense emotional state – part ecstasy, part desperation – that is the essence of flamenco'.[2] This doesn't sit as easily with the Anglo-Saxon soul as with the Mediterranean, or Celtic; turbulence, (metaphorical) blood and fire are not easy companions of subtlety and restraint. *Duende* is dark fire; the dark face of the angel – and is as necessary as night is to day to the soul. *Duende* is not safe; but then, neither is life, nor art.

There's the famous saying – I've seen it attributed to both Rilke and Nietzsche – repudiating analysis: his fear that if he were to get rid of his demons, he might also lose his angels.

This bears examining. We are, in our culture, somewhat terrified by demons; and it's part of being human that, rather than turning and facing our own dark aspects, we find someone else on whom to project them. When this happens to an individual, fear is often followed by enmity and hatred; when this happens collectively, another culture or society becomes The Enemy, and war breaks out. So it seems important to find new ways of dealing with what we see as the demonic. (It is interesting to note that, in Buddhism, for instance, which in some branches incorporates the demonic in its pantheon, the primary duality is not 'good' and 'evil', but 'ignorance' and 'wisdom'.)

There is an important connection between demons and angels – I emphasise 'connection' rather than 'opposition', the more traditional way of portraying this relationship; and, more, there is a link between this relationship and creativity.

We are creatures of light and dark; we are full of angels and we are full of demons. If they – these warring forces within us – are made conscious, we can use the creative tension between the two to fuel our vitality, our lives and our work; and, more, take some steps towards healing our pain.

What I am interested in in this chapter is the fact that as writers we already have one of the most potent tools available to humans for processing difficult aspects of human experience; one which can aid the cathartic release of deep feeling, and go some way towards healing any associated anger and grief. Michael Mackmin, in his editorial in *Rialto* 55, puts it succinctly: 'Poetry is a formidable tool for dealing with difficult thoughts and feelings, for tempering pain and celebrating the dance of life lived with awareness.' There is much literature on this subject of the therapeutic benefits of writing, and a great deal of research has gone into the matter.

'Poets need to live,' says Ben Okri, 'where others don't care to look, and they need to do this because if they don't they can't sing to us of all the secret and public domains of our lives.'[3] (I am using the term 'poet' throughout to signify 'writer'; a poetic consciousness is the key.)

Writing that comes from the intellect alone may communicate to the head, but will probably lack passion, as well as emotional or psychological depth. Of course this kind of writing has its own necessary place – in report or academic writing, for instance, where what is required is marshalling of thought and factual information for clarity of conveyance, passion is likely to be completely irrelevant or inappropriate. But here, we are talking about creativity and imagination.

'Most of the methods of training the conscious side of the writer – the craftsman and critic in him – are actually hostile to the good of the unconscious, the artist's side,' said Dorothea Brande. Stephen Nachmanovitch[4] says something similar: 'One of the many Catch-22s in the business of creativity is that you can't express inspiration without skill, but if you are too wrapped up in the professionalism of skill you obviate the surrender to accident that is essential to inspiration.'

It's my belief that strong writing, like strong living, emerges from the conjunction of conscious and unconscious, as well as from a meeting of light and dark. We need both. When these two processes, or states, are severed from each other trouble starts – in writing and in life. (We'll look later, briefly, at how our myths and folk tales are pointers to ways of bringing the conscious and unconscious minds together; the subject is so huge as to be beyond the scope of this book, though I address it in an earlier book.[5])

In Jungian and archetypal thinking, the unconscious came to be known as 'the shadow' – that part of us which is largely unknown but makes itself felt in dreams, in moods, in extreme feeling states; it is commonly experienced in passions, impulses and instincts. It's the part of you which, the harder you try to 'behave', to be a 'good person', will torment you with dreams of wickedness and wild misbehaviour; the part of you, often childish and tricksterish, which will suggest that, rather than stand around making polite conversation, you'd like to make trouble, dance on the tables, take your own – or someone else's! – clothes off, say what you're *really* feeling instead of 'fine, thanks'; the part of you that screeches 'My God what the hell have you done to your hair? It looks terrible!' when what you had intended to say was 'Goodness, you look different with that new haircut!'

The shadow is in part formed from the aspects of ourselves that other people – parents, teachers, our religion, culture or society, or when we're older our ego/inner critic/conscience, have condemned as 'bad': our rage, hurt, selfishness, jealousy, envy, possessiveness, shame, guilt, blame, anguish, our sense of failure, fear (which may be the root of them all), and often our instinctual nature, our childish self and playfulness, our mild wickednesses, our clumsy or forbidden humour, and our sensual and sexual selves too. Then there's our fear of loneliness, stasis, 'is this it'-ness; and too the emergence of the demons from our past – losses, 'mistakes', paths and decisions we have or haven't taken.

The ultimate demon, of course, is death: the fact of it.

The shadow, though, is not all darkness. In the shadow, too, also live aspects of the beautiful, the loving, the kind, the compassionate, in inverse proportion to how we recognise in ourselves and live out these things in our conscious life. A rule of thumb for recognising shadow material, light or dark, is by the strength of our feeling response to these qualities in others. If something about another person makes you mad, or envious, or engulfed with admiration, chances are you need to acknowledge and work on that quality in yourself.

The shadow has enormous vitality. Our impulse to change comes from the shadow. Our instinct to survive dwells here, along with all the parts of us, as above, which are repressed and in exile.

'Civilisation' tends to squeeze the vital life out of human beings. Inasmuch as we learn not to act out our homicidal or suicidal or promiscuous instincts this is just as well; but in keeping the lid on these we also make access to our juicy creative life harder; and ironically the transmutation of these impulses into creativity (as opposed to acting on them) is a fruitful and healthy way of processing shadow material; so we lose out twice.

Just so long as we don't get 'stuck' in the shadow, our acquaintance with it rounds out our lives, makes us wholer, more creative, more compassionate, wiser. It makes our lives solid. 'My being would be a skeleton, a shell, / If this dark passion... / Did not forever feed me vital blood,' said Claude McKay.

What's more, we know from much research that writing about emotionally-charged issues can reduce their debilitating effects on the psyche; and the physiological effects of this kind of writing are well-documented: it can help decrease blood pressure and heart rate, improve immune function – white blood cell count – and reduce rates of minor illnesses![6]

All of us fear at times, and maybe many of us all the time, looking our demons in the eye. I guess this is because we are afraid we may not be able to handle it; and maybe we fear their unleashing. Is this why our Western life is so addicted to busyness, one of the reasons why we avoid solitude and silence?

I think it's important not to be afraid of the dark matter of the heart. We need to be willing to approach our feelings. As one of my course participants, Terry Glover, put it:

> Space to bleed. For me,
> I think, a necessity
> in forging my (he)art.

We think of dark as evil, and we use the word 'demonic' to mean 'diabolic'. But 'daimonic' in its archaic sense was closer to the notion of 'genius', or presiding spirit. To the Greeks, daimon (or daemon) meant 'divine power', 'fate' or 'god'; the daimon was also seen as spiritual advisor or mediator between humans and the gods. Psychologist Rollo May suggests that in their concept of the daimon the Greeks achieved a union of good and evil; one in which personal consciousness integrates the daimonic.

Whether we like it or not, it is a truism that 'the deeper pain carves into our being the more joy we can contain'. We all have places within us where the scars of past hurt, loss, grief, rage still itch, or throb, or ache. Our survival instincts might wish us to keep apart from these feelings; and there are times when this self-protectiveness is entirely appropriate for healing. But if you turn away, consistently, from the 'dark' stuff, your soul will suffer; and so will your life; and your writing. There will be a deadening where there should be something quick and vital.

In Western culture, where we so often think in polarities, we can tend to relate to our personal demons, our difficult feelings, in one of two ways. Either we repress those feelings, because we're 'nice people'; or we indulge in them by letting rip at whoever 'caused' them. Much of the time, we veer between the two.

In fact, neither of these two ways is about 'relating' – to feelings or anything else. What is hard for most of us is to recognise, honour and then find a good way, a healthy way, to relate to our feelings and our instinctual nature; a way which doesn't involve the projection of our darkness onto others by exploiting, manipulating or blowing other people out of the water, and doesn't involve simply shoving these difficult aspects of our nature back under the lid again.

There is an enormous amount of energy stored in these feelings. When we 'blow' at other people, we dissipate it. When we suppress or repress our negative thoughts and feelings, the effort involved in holding them down, even – or maybe especially – when it becomes a *modus vivendi*, uses up so much emotional and psychic energy that little is left for living creatively: our life-energy, our libido, too is repressed.

I also think that sometimes when we hit 'writers' block' we may be on the cusp of uncovering, or recovering, something shadowy but important. At times like this our obvious fear, clearly, is of the blank page and the sometimes-overwhelming sense of our responsibility for filling it, for finding the 'right' words to do the subject justice. And it is often also about where we have to go in the process of uncovering it.

Writing can offer a container, a safe – harmless – way of expressing this material, which will also allow us to process it. This shadow material can then be used to fuel our creative writing – look at the work produced by writers such as Plath, Solzhenitsyn, Neruda, Dylan Thomas, Wallace Stevens, Yeats, D H Lawrence, Lorca: shadow writers all of them; sometimes uncomfortable but always authentic. You can see the taproots of their writing dripping with mud and blood.

Robert Bly, in his *A Little Book on the Human Shadow*[7], suggests that all literature 'can be thought of as creations by the "dark side" to enable it to rise up from the earth and join the sunlit consciousness again.' He tells us that unless the shadow informs a piece of writing that work will remain lifeless. Living with our spiritual and intellectual lives split off from our physical soulful lives can breed nothing other than schism.

'If the poet begins to speak only of narrow things,' says Ben Okri, 'of things that we can effortlessly digest and recognise, of things that do not disturb, frighten, stir or annoy us, or make us restless for more, make us cry for greater justice, make us want to set sail and explore inklings murdered in our youths, if the poet sings only of our restricted angles and in restricted terms and restricted language, then what hope is there for any of us in this world?'[8]

It is not the case, of course, that any piece of writing that is simply a raw expression of passion, a shapeless mass of chaotic feelings of rage, grief, fear, lust, love is also a creative work; or at least, not without a great deal of redrafting, preferably some time after the initial burst of writing. Yet strong writing, and the passion in a piece of writing, are often directly linked to these potent, difficult and frequently unconscious feelings, even though the end result may seem to bear no particular resemblance to the 'trigger' feeling or incident. It's often in these private dark places that we find soul, and a sensitive reader has infallible antennae for the scent and music – or stink and dissonance – of soul. Literature has many faces and many functions; one of these is a doorway into the depths of feeling and of soul.

What does this mean for the writer? It means listening to the promptings of impulse, dream, feeling; it means being willing to just sit with difficult emotions and then to write about them, from within them. It may mean revisiting old pain and grief and rage in your writing. I've said that the things we turn away from often have great creative power, and lock up much emotional and psychic energy. It means to allow mud, and blood, and dirt into your writing – even if that writing is not ever shown to anyone else. It means to be aware of using things to distract us from discomfort: eating, drinking, drugs, chattering, sleeping, sex, television, music, books – whatever your avoidance mechanism is. ('Stick at the business of being alive,' says writer and creative writing tutor Graham Mort.) It means writing that's centred in the body. It means not turning away from difficulty but using it as the grit in the oyster, gradually surrounding it with awareness until it gleams.

Bly strongly advises our paying attention to reawakening the senses, and activities which encourage and support this: visiting museums and art galleries, walking, and activities which also support the senses of hearing and smelling – these senses are all too often sidelined in favour of sight; and we all know the impact and immediacy of smell as evocation of another time and place. Our senses, he says, form a bridge to our animal nature, and therefore also to the shadow. 'The senses of smell, shades of light and dark, the awareness of color and sound, so alive in the primitive man, for whom they can mean life or death, are still alive in us, but numbed... by safety, and by years inside schoolrooms.'

Bly talks of William James' warning that 'a certain kind of mind-set was approaching the West – it could hardly be called a way of thought – in which no physical details are noticed. Fingernails are not noticed, trees in the plural are mentioned, but no particular tree is ever loved, nor where it stands; the hair in the ear is not noticed... Since the immense range of color belongs to physical detail – the thatness – of the universe, it is the inability to see color.'

It should be obvious by now that we are talking about a turning away from wildness (as in Bly's definition, which is *not* to do with brutality and the savage or hostile), from physicality, from the natural world and ultimately from feelings.

There are many clues, giveaways, that the shadow is present in a piece of writing. One is that the passage or poem will have an 'edge' to it. Another, that the poem will be rooted in the world of the senses. And there's a third: that the poem is resonant with feeling; and that's *feeling*, not sentimentality; authentic lived experience. You will sense this in a poem that has a tone of mystery to it, maybe; some substance behind the words, something enormous hiding in its creases; and you will sense that it hooks your own feeling nature. This kind of poem is a doorway.

Any poem that leaps off the page with life contains this shadow. (It doesn't have to be serious, by the way; playfulness is especially good for drawing attention to the presence of shadow.)

It seems to me now still, as it seemed to Bly in 1988, that we are seeing at the moment in the West a great desiccation in the world of poetry: thin language cut off from its roots of blood and sex and love and longing and nature and childbirth and death and the senses. What are these poets doing with their shadows? What does it say of their lives? 'What has no shadow has no strength to live,' said Czeslaw Milosz.

So the shadow is the Dark Fire, the other face of the angel; as necessary to the life of the soul as night is to day. Working with shadow-material in our writing has two strong pluses.

Writing is a way of integrating the shadow into your life. '[T]he person who has eaten his shadow,' says Bly, 'spreads calmness, and shows more grief than anger. If the ancients were right that darkness contains intelligence and nourishment and information, then the person who has eaten some of his or her shadow is more energetic as well as more intelligent.' Dr Jung before him argued for the embracing of the opposites. A certain amount of creative tension is probably necessary for survival, full psychological health and certainly for creative productivity. This is how we come to wholeness.

The second is that it may make us a better writer: better able to pay attention, to notice the detail in things, to write in a more rounded way that includes the feelings, the senses and soul, to sustain a piece of writing through difficulties.

Writing that includes the shadow is not something that you can force; but you can practise it. Neither is it 'too negative' or necessarily 'too self-indulgent' as a practice, as I often hear people say – often those same people who are most afraid of their feeling nature. In fact, it may be an act of the utmost compassion, and of supreme responsibility: if you are willing to acknowledge your demons, you are less likely to unleash them, in their unconscious intensity, on the world.

It is also a way of acknowledging the existence of worlds beyond the surface, and of bringing yourself back to life. The cost of not doing so in writing terms may be uni-dimensional work. In your life, the price may be fragmentation, or the sleep of ignorance. Remember Sleeping Beauty? Her hundred-year sleep was the price she paid for her parents' fear of inviting the Wicked Fairy to the birth feast. Who do you think the Wicked Fairy is?

So here's the solid bit. You have to be willing to be changed by your own creations, says Bly. You have to eat the shadow, once you've recognised it; it is not enough to bring the shadow into your art; you have to change the way you live.

The alternative may be to keep your own work, your own creativity, split off from the rest of you.

Think of the darkness as potentially healing. It may even be the appearance of what Spanish poet Frederico Garcia Lorca called *duende* – the 'dark sounds' in music, dancing, poetry, [ritual]... the roots of all art. Goethe described duende as 'a mysterious power that everyone feels but that no philosopher has ever explained'. It is the 'dark and quivering' companion to the muse and the angel, the other two sources of inspiration and mysterious gift-giving to human beings... For Lorca, the dark sounds portend the tenderness that emerges after a brush with mortality. It is deeper than the melancholy of the muse, the wistfulness of angels.

Phil Cousineau

...[D]emonism and creativity are psychologically very close to each other. Nothing in the human psyche is more destructive than unrealized, unconscious creative impulses...

Marie-Louise von Franz

From so much loving and so much journeying, books emerge.
And if they don't contain kisses and landscapes,
if they don't contain a man with his hands full,
if they don't contain a woman in every drop,
hunger, desire, anger, roads,
they are no use...

Pablo Neruda

The Leaving

They've clear-felled the woods –
the eerie stretch where I hated to walk alone
and the two great oaks are gone, though their roots
still writhe in the sodden earth.

Even at night now light is everywhere.
Nowhere to hide – for It, for mystery, for owls –
even for me. You can have
too much light.

Under the moon the village is silent.
                                        Ebb tide.
Out on the mudflats the curlews' calls
          whistle up unimaginable distances.

Roselle Angwin

In Defence of the Raven

And it came to pass at the end of forty days that Noah opened the window of the ark which he had made: and he sent forth a raven, which went forth to and fro, until the waters were dried up from off the earth. Also he sent forth a dove.

Genesis Ch.8 v.6–8

It did not leave at once. For two hours
Or more it perched on the ark,
Eyeing the waves and the slanting horizon:
A dark witness under storm clouds.

Nor, when it finally left, did it go lightly.
At first, unsure of direction, it flew
Without grace. An equivocation of wings,
A mere inch above drowning water.

By all means cherish the dove. It returned
Loyally with good news in its beak.
So make it your icon on banners of peace
And hang them over the warring cities.

But, at night, as you try to sleep, remember
Far horizons, black holes, exploded nova stars;
Remember the curved edge of God's
Incommensurable mind – where the raven flies.

Peter Abbs[9]

PERSPECTIVE, PERCEPTION AND PRECONCEPTIONS
SHAPE-SHIFTING FOR THE WRITER

Does the world we inhabit have any true intrinsic objective reality, or is what we *think* we see – individually or collectively – in any way responsible for this 'reality'? This question has, of course, occupied philosophers for centuries. People have been excommunicated, exiled, tortured and burned alive for challenging collective conventions or upsetting the orthodox status quo, and suggesting that what we think we see may not be the true picture. This is still the case: society and its rulers are threatened by original thinkers and the potential for anarchy that comes with them.

Words can be dangerous. Words can be subversive. We're relatively lucky currently in Britain; we deal on the whole quite tolerantly with divergent views, and free speech is still an accepted part of our culture. Nonetheless, as a society we are culturally pragmatic, and tend to be suspicious of ideas that are too wacky, and people who promote them may experience a subtle suppression.

But writers, of all people, need to be free thinkers if what they say is to be of any interest or use. They need to be iconoclasts, or at least to be able to imagine different ways. 'The great tidal crowds of everyday events pour in one direction, sometimes the poet has to move in the other – often moving directly against them, at other times cutting tangentially across,'[1] say Ben Okri.

Events in the world of science are, however, slowly or at times swiftly, changing our collective view. It's not so easy to pretend any more that we inhabit a world of separate, static, lifeless objects whose movements we control. Quantum physics, for instance, posits what mystics and poets have always known – that life is a dynamic, and therefore infinitely variable, interaction between observer and observed. It may take a while for science to catch up with the view that at some level *everything* is alive, albeit operating at different levels of consciousness, energy and wavelength; but poets know this. We've always known it. It's part of our job. Everything that we know is made of the same stuff. We consist of cells, atoms, molecules, all of which move, change, vibrate, migrate. It's all a continuum. The difference between the rabbit and the toad and the toad and the stone is simply a matter of speed – energy and matter being slowed to what seems a standstill in the stone.

I'll come to the point, which is to draw your attention back to those two little words in the first sentence: 'we think'. Thinking is a subjective process, the contents of which can be altered at any moment. Since we know that the thoughts we think, and the resulting feelings, can have a direct and measurable impact on the body and our physiology – the connection between psyche and soma – it's important to be aware of this fact.

For the writer, our thinking needs to be able to be both as broad, and as deep, as possible. How many worlds can we encompass? – and as focused as possible, so as to bring back detailed news of these worlds. If we do our job properly, a reader should be able see that the messenger birds of the imagination have a heart that beats and mud on their feet. 'I am always astounded that poems are willing to lie down and sleep inside the flat, closed pages of books,' says John O'Donohue.[2] 'If poems behaved according to their essence, they would be out dancing on the seashore or flying to the heavens or trying to rinse out the secrets of the mountains.'

That's what we need to aim for in our writing.

Peter Porter, in his preface to the Carcanet edition of Rilke's *Duino Elegies*, suggests that the act of conjuring poetry down on the page is the job of the shaman; a view I share, and a view that Keith Jafrate also mentions in his piece in this book. It seems to me that a writer needs to be able to embody some of the skills of the shaman, who is a walker-between-the-worlds, shape-shifting at will to perceive what is, what was, what might be, what could be – to create for a reader other realities, 'to extend the boundaries of the possible... [and to] reinvent existence,' to quote Okri again. This is where the boundaries between reality and imagination blur. 'Reality' is fluid, is always in a state of flux. Nothing remains the same.

It's one of those writing truisms that the most helpful question a writer can ask of him or herself – or rather of his or her imagination – is 'what if'? (For a poet, an equally fruitful question is 'what's it like?') This is the key to any kind of storytelling. What if the world is not as we normally perceive it to be? We offer this possibility to our reader, and if they trust us, and we have engaged them sufficiently, they will ride along with us as co-creator while we remake the world. Psychologically speaking, we're all doing this, all the time, anyway. A writer puts this into the public domain, building on this tendency, exaggerating, extending. Writers are insatiable creatures, always wanting to open closed doors, see beneath the clothes, look under stones, walk through the witchwood, peer over the edges of things, ask questions, try new ways of doing things. Cultivate this!

Part of this art is choosing to shift perspective: moving between viewpoints (human or otherwise), time schemes, landscapes; walking in others' shoes.

Shifting between far and close vision – speaking both literally and metaphorically – is also good writing practice, selectively bringing different realities into the foreground, and focusing on them, as if through binoculars. It will help vary both texture and pace in your writing.

I mentioned earlier in this book that I think of 'far vision' in a writer as being that of an eagle or buzzard. This perspective allows us to place things *in relation* to each other, to contextualise; and gives us the broad picture of how things are interconnected (this seems like a crucial, if undervalued, useful life-skill, too). In juxtaposing in this way, it also allows us to gauge the relative importance, or otherwise, of things, situations, events.

Near vision, in converse, allows us to see things *in isolation*. How different from the hawk's eye view would be that of a mouse, or toad, or beetle, scurrying or creeping very close to the ground, where your reality – your whole world horizon – is bounded and defined by the immediacy of things right at hand, where your environment is a jungle of grass blades, and an inch of soil may offer a hundred possibilities; where your focus is on the horizontal rather than the vertical plane. In each case survival depends on your vision; so sight, though used differently, is fine-tuned, and in both cases detail is important. In far vision, you are selective: you choose your focus – that one (or two or three) microscopic dot(s) on a vast plain, but these selected points cannot be known in depth. The world is objectified. In close vision, everything is detail; not having the ability to 'pan', you do not have the same freedom of selectivity.

Humans are unique, as far as we know, in being able, physically and psychologically, to enjoy both fields – to see 'the wood and the trees': the vertical and the horizontal, the near and the far, and to draw conclusions from switching between both.

It's like the difference between painting a still life and a landscape. In a novel, or film, we move between the scenes, or set pieces, in close-up intensity, which takes us into dramatic or significant moments, turning points, the characters' lives; and the long-focus broad-screen panning that gives us the necessary background narrative, the 'filling in'.

A writer needs both skills, though of course one may predominate through habit, or temperament, or preference, or of course the demands of a particular piece. It seems to me that the poet may make more use of the close vision focus, with observation and use of detail being fundamental to the art. A fiction writer, on the other hand, will need to be able to use detail to support the narrative, whilst holding in mind the overall picture.

We could think of perspective, too, as exemplifying, in the novel, the differences between omniscient third-person narration from a multitude of viewpoints – as if from a distance – and a first-person viewpoint, where everything is immediate and 'in your face'.

Similarly, a child's perspective is in close focus, and the worlds of the senses and the feelings rich and enthralling. As adults, we lose some of this immediacy, and our survival depends on a different set of criteria, including the ability to scan the wider terrain of our lives and pick out what's important. To some extent, we disengage from the world. Our writing, however, can only gain from an ability to recreate the world, to look through different eyes, whether these be the eyes of a fly or a horse or a child or a flatfish or a kestrel; or simply an imagined character – a person with a very different lifestyle, agenda and values from your own; maybe from a different era or culture.

The eyes of the physical body, we know, benefit from switching near and far vision. Similarly the muscles of the eyes of the imagination are worked and strengthened by this conceptual shift.

We need both modes of vision – the mouse's and the eagle's. If you are by nature an eagle writer, it's possible that your writing tends towards the dry, or sparse: the abstract and disengaged. If a mouse, then you may overload with detail, sensory or otherwise, potentially swamping a reader with too many rich impressions.

Starting points

1

    a) For the next week, choose an animal whose perspective you will come back to at moments throughout the day. Research its habits; observe one if you can. Watch/learn how it moves, what it does, what it eats, what it fears, how it behaves in relation to its surroundings and situations. Really study your chosen animal.

Then write about it. *Be* that creature. Imagine yourself into a different world; write your perceptions in the first person and the present tense through the 'eyes' of that animal, whether it's a stray dog or a hedgehog, a swallow or a slow-worm, a rat, a pig or an otter. Engage your senses; animate your language, flood it with sensory perceptions. Saturate yourself in your environment; as far as we can tell, animals don't perceive the separation from their environment that humans do. Climb into that skin; feels its texture, its heat (or lack of it), its terrain; feel what it requires to pursue its survival needs or to avoid its enemies. Keep a journal for a week from its life (don't admit this to your friends and family, though). (I'm not asking you, by the way, to be anthropomorphic, attributing human characteristics and emotions to the animal; I'm asking that you imagine and engage with a totally different way of being in the world, with very different concerns and criteria.)

Play with perspective. Imagine the lives that are being played out at, or under, your feet, or beyond the far hills. Feel into the frost-wet belly and naked feet of a shrew on a winter lawn, the hundreds of insects it needs to catch each day to stay alive. Imagine the sensation of the uplift in the armpits/wingpits of a buzzard catching a thermal. Imagine swimming for long periods underwater, like a whale, or spending your life tunnelling in the dark, like a mole.

Or try this exercise from the point of view of a child.

b) Writers need to be able to imagine themselves into the lives of other people. How would it be to be an Albanian, Kosovan, Chechnyan or Tibetan refugee, for instance? How would it be to leave your home, work, family, to come from war or oppression or hostility in your own country, and to arrive in an unfamiliar country with unknown customs and language where you might also meet hostility? Without empathy there is no imagination, as well as vice versa.

Imagine hiding, because your life depends on no one seeing you. Imagine lying, consistently, about who you are so as to escape persecution... What is 'reality' then?

c) What would your life look like, what would your daily concerns be, and what details might be important, if you were:
i Housebound?
ii Homeless?

d) How might the life of a farmer, dentist, dustman ('waste operative'), trawlerman, aeronautical engineer or guerrilla differ from your own? What would a day in their life be like? (Be careful not to glamorise this.)

2

This is one of those great 'take your notebook and go to a café or restaurant or other public place' exercises:

a) Go to a café or other public place! Using the 'landscape' or 'buzzard' focus – the whole picture – sketch the place in which you are, finding ways to capture the atmosphere, its colour and its dynamic. What is the essence of the place? What is its purpose?

b) Start to sketch in some of the details of furnishings, objects, items: why might the proprietors have chosen these particular objects? What do they say?

c) Now focus on the relationships, perceived or imagined, between the people around you and the place, and between person and person. What characterises these things, each time?

d) Finally, focus on one person (discreetly!), one situation, or one object, and pay him, her or it detailed attention, making notes.

What happens to your writing, and your attention, each time?

'ONLY CONNECT'

Connessione (da Vinci) – A recognition of and appreciation for the interconnectedness of things and phenomena[1]

All things are in the universe, and the universe is in all things: we in it, and it in us: and in this way everything concurs in a perfect unity.
Giordano Bruno (C16th)

In the previous chapter I spoke of our living in a fluid universe, where the boundaries between things – indeed between things and 'no-things' – are perpetually in flux, and to some extent are necessarily arbitrary. There is a continuous exchange of molecules; everything is in a state of constant motion, even things we consider solid and stable – chair, house, multi-storey car park – these things are at a subtle and notional level dissolving and reforming all the time.

I said above that we are made of the same stuff as the rest of the universe. We are all created from starfire; and this is not just a nice gnostic metaphor – we are all the result of the first massive explosion; so we are actually, physically created of the same matter as the rest of the universe! We're all made, literally, of the same elements – the same elements as each other and as the stars: in chemical terms basically carbon, hydrogen, oxygen and nitrogen. This is a most amazing fact. *As above, so below*, said the ancients.

As a result of that first explosion everything we know, and a great deal more than we can possibly imagine, was created; and also space and time.

At a subatomic level we also know that the tiniest possible speck of molecular matter – in us as well as throughout the universe – behaves both like a particle and like a wave. At this level, it is impossible to differentiate state.

And then there are the cycles of things. The water you drink today might have been drunk by Boudicca or Vortigern, by a mediaeval serf or a Dark Ages warrior; the soil in which you grow your vegetables may contain a homeopathic dose of a Stone Age skinning tool or a Bronze Age cup, a chariot wheel, the hair of a mammoth, the tooth of a tiger, the claw of England's last wolf.

Does this happen too to time, as well as matter? Recent theories suggest that it does. So somewhere that same wolf is still prowling, just as King John is still signing the Magna Carta, Bonnie Prince Charlie is still rowing to Skye, Pythagoras is still calculating, the Easter Island statues are still in the making, the blue Prescelly stone of which Stonehenge is partially constructed is still being quarried, the Songlines, or 'Footprints of the Ancestors', of the Aboriginal peoples are still emerging from the Dreamtime; and the world that we know is just one continent.

Science, having fallen out with the arts and humanities around the time of the Enlightenment, is finally catching up with what mystics and various wisdom traditions and religions have said always: at a fundamental level everything in our universe is interconnected.

Physicist David Bohm has said: '...[the] inseparable quantum interconnectedness of the whole universe is the fundamental reality, and [the] relatively independently behaving parts are merely particular and contingent forms within the whole.'[2]

The 'butterfly effect', which illustrates the fact that small variations in initial conditions result in huge, dynamic transformations in concluding events, is one of the earlier principles of chaos theory as it began to be shaped in the twentieth century. This theory suggests that the minutest tweak on this underlying fabric of things here, right here, may be enough to wreak havoc, say, in Africa. 'Small variations in initial conditions result in huge, dynamic transformations in concluding events.'[3]

We know this effect to be true in climatology, as well as in such things as the stock market and global economics. Everything we do has an effect. And it is easy to be blind to the fact that – another 'for instance' – our demand for beefburgers in the 'developed' world sets in motion a chain of events thus: to satisfy the demand for more cattle, vast tracts of for instance – a true example – the Amazon rainforest are felled. Not only do indigenous peoples lose their homes and their whole culture, but there is now a problem with erosion and aridity due to the lack of trees. In addition the climate is destabilised, and droughts and flooding and hurricanes become more widespread, as we have seen over the last year or two.

Why am I, a non-scientist writer, banging on in a mystical quasi-scientific way about such things? We don't need scientific proof to know about cause and effect. The symbolism behind the butterfly theory is vast, important and profound. The Hindu tradition got there before physics: in this tradition the world is enmeshed in what is known as Indra's Net. At each intersection of the web is a glowing point of light, a jewel. Each of these jewels is a living being, human or otherwise. A tug anywhere on this net sends ripples throughout the whole. A rip affects everything.

Everything we do has a consequence, whether or not we see it. The least we can do is be aware of the dynamic. *Connessione*. 'Only connect' as Forster puts it in *Howard's End*. Relationship is all. What we write about – paint about, make music about, experience every second of the day – is *relationship*: the places where we touch Other, whether that 'other' is a person, a tree, a note of music, a colour, an idea, a space we fill with our physical presence, a thought. The way in which we touch, connect, sets other things in motion; so our touching, bumping up against, the world will always have a consequence.

It is impossible to create from, or in, a void, because 'void' does not exist, except as an intellectual construct.

So we write about our connections, our relationship with the world – the places where our inner world meets the outer. Or we write about where we *don't* connect, about our failures of relationship, our fragmentedness – a common theme in contemporary literature.

In drawing, there is the concept of 'negative space', where, in order to bypass your preconceptions which constrain you to think 'in boxes' and see what you expect to see, you are asked to draw the space *between* objects as a way of dissolving and reconstructing that object, as well as your thinking about objects. You don't focus on the object at all, purely on the relationships of spaces.

When I write, there is me and there is the world; and even when what I am writing is purely 'imaginary' it can only grow out of my experiences within, thinking about and feelings of and towards everything that appears to be not me – my life in relationship to this vast universe, and all its other inhabitants. So there is the visible world where everything appears to be separated and distinct, and there is this subtle world where we are held together in a fine mesh of connectedness, where everything affects everything else.

Quantum physics has demonstrated that it is no longer possible to separate the world 'out there' from those who observe it. In other words, 'the observer is [...] an integral part of the world he views and becomes a participator'.[4]

I step to one side and my shadow falls over the buddleia, and the peacock butterfly rises. The air is shaken by its wings; the ripples spread. The thrush quits the beech tree but the branch still sways. Dusk falls, the wind drops, and on the creek in the near dark the curlew's call reaches me from across the water, nudges my heart. The curlew calls, I imagine, whether or not I hear it; but I have, and there is now relationship between me and it.

From another continent, impossibly far away, my daughter's voice arrives in my ear via a piece of plastic. In a distant town the funeral of someone I don't know is a funeral of a part of me. At the same moment the birth of a baby I will never meet is a birth in me, whether or not I 'know' that fact.

And maybe this is what I want most to explore in my writing, and in my reading – the flavour, consequences and workings-out of our interrelationships, the subtle, potent, vast, forever-changing world of our enmeshment, of cause and effect – or of synchronicity, co-creation. Whichever, it is our relationship with it all. Our *connessione*.

The flapping of a single butterfly's wing today produces a tiny change in the state of the atmosphere. Over a period of time, what the atmosphere actually does diverges from what it would have done. So, in a month's time, a tornado that would have devastated the Indonesian coast doesn't happen. Or maybe one that wasn't going to happen, does.

Ian Stewart

[The Irish word] *Tuirigin* [means] nothing less than the birth of the true nature, for it is not until the soul has been fused with everything else that it assumes its true nature; the soul's many turnings bring about its wisdom. The Celtic *tuirigin* is about fusion – not the refining of the soul till it reaches nirvana, but a profound communion with everything that brings authenticity to the soul.

Caitlin Matthews

THINKING WILD

There is a wolf in me... I keep the wolf because the wilderness gave it to me and the wilderness will not let it go... I came from the wilderness.
Carl Sandburg

Of course it's the writer's job – or at least can or arguably should be – to engage with the social and political issues that arise daily in a largely urban culture. We need to write (also) about people and to be aware of our common humanity. To turn our faces away may be to shirk a responsibility. People need to speak out, and one of writing's many functions is that.

But too much contact with so-called civilisation – by which I mean urbanisation – is both brutalising and sanitising; not just to the poet or writer, but to the human being; and to the soul. 'The world today is sick to its thin blood for lack of elemental things, for fire before the hands, for water welling up from the earth, for air, for the earth itself underfoot...' said Henry Beston.[1]

The soul needs wild. It's a way of keeping sane. 'We simply need that wild country available to us, even if we never do more than drive to its edges and look in,' says Wallace Stegner. 'For it can be a means of reassuring ourselves of our sanity... a part of the geography of hope.'[2] It's also a way of finding our way back – or forward again. As the wild places of the world are decimated, something in us is laid waste too; something that may, if not addressed, prove to be irreparable. We have separated, and insulated, ourselves from the wild. '...[O]ther cultures', writes Barry Lopez, '...did not separate humanity and nature. They recognised the immanence of the divine in both. And they regarded landscape ... as integral to the development of personality and social order...'[3]

It's from the wild place in us that good writing – as well as good living, deep living – springs.

I'd like to talk a little here about the word 'wild'. I'm using it as Robert Bly does, meaning untamed, free, unconstrained, not savage or barbaric. The most inspired definition I know comes from poet, ecologist and woodsman Gary Snyder: 'The word *wild* is like a gray fox trotting off through the forest, ducking behind bushes, going in and out of sight. Up close, first glance, it is "wild" – then farther into the woods next glance it's "wyld" and it recedes via Old Norse *villr* and Old Teutonic *wilthijaz* into a faint pre-Teutonic *ghweltijos* which means, still, wild and maybe wooded *(wald)* and lurks back there with possible connections to *will,* to Latin *silva* (forest, sauvage), and to the Indo-European root *ghwer* base of Latin *ferus* (feral, fierce), which swings us around to Thoreau's "awful ferity" shared by virtuous people and lovers.'[4]

The wild is a way of keeping us alive and awake; we remember our roots, and draw the nourishment we need from the earth and the dark and the fertile places; from walking a little with the other nations, with our non-human siblings, learning their ways; from rain on our skin; from the green light of the canopy falling into our eyes; from the stones and the humus and the dung beneath our feet. We need this exchange with wild nature, just as we need sunlight, moonlight, starlight, water, wind. 'Something in us vibrates to the cry of wolves, to the play of bears; we are not some purely inward, acosmic stuff, but rather of the same flesh as birdsong and snow,' says psychotherapist Andy Fisher.[5]

'I pick things out of the wind and air,' Carl Sandburg said. Easy to forget how to do this, shut away in our sealed homes and offices, with artificial heat and light and noise; easy to become deracinated, our instinctual and intuitive selves, our sense of play and ease, split off, over-ridden and denied; our earthiness all shaken off. 'Whatever you have to say, leave / the roots on, ' says poet Charles Olson. 'And the dirt...' and that's a pretty good prescription for our lives, too. Let's not clean them up too much, block off all the places where soul might linger and dwell, in moist and fertile darkness...

It's a tradition so established as almost to be a cliché, that of the writer retiring to contemplate nature in solitude (I've spoken of this in earlier chapters). It's the most fruitful method there is of allowing, in Hemingway's words, 'the well to fill up'; and we cannot write from a depleted place, except about our depletion. Some of our best writers from the last hundred years, often of both prose and poetry, are those who are the modern equivalent of contemplative solitary mystics, at least part of the time. Barry Lopez, Annie Dillard, Gary Snyder and Anne Morrow Lindbergh are among the many who have all written books about their time alone in nature. Dylan Thomas had his little house down on the littorals in Wales; George Mackay Brown on Orkney. The philosopher and writer John O'Donohue preserves his solitude in a small cottage in the west of Ireland. My friend Kenneth Steven has his tiny writer's cabin in Scotland. I write in solitude in rural Devon. It's a way of letting your thoughts spool out unjerkily, uninterrupted; and, more, it's a direct conduit, writing outside or writing after being outside; a taproot into wild, primal and essential nourishment.

That master of wilderness time, Henry David Thoreau, wrote at length about his thoughts during the time he spent at Walden Pond, where he went to 'live deliberately, to front only the essential facts of life... to live deep...' 'In literature it is only the wild that attracts us,' he continues. 'Dullness is but another name for tameness.'

Gary Snyder talks about how we breed out the wild strains; how we have cultivated cattle and pigs, in the wild alert, quick intelligent animals, in our agricultural practices to become dull, 'sluggish meat-making machines'. (Ironically there is a price to be paid for this, of course: intensive agriculture practices, so far removed from the animal's natural habitat and way of being in the world, too often turn otherwise tranquil animals into aggressors, which is the savage face of wild. Clearly, there are parallels for humans, too.)

Practise the wild, then.

What does this mean? Firstly, of course, it means reacquainting ourselves with the 'old ways'. It means taking time out, outdoors. It means paying attention to the cycles of things: the day, the seasons, the moon – 'out there', but also within. It means finding places where – as much as possible, and this is a hard thing in Britain, especially in England – human presence is not too obtrusive; not just in terms of people themselves, but in terms of the marks of our passage, so much of the time so visible or audible.

It might also mean not being so quick to tidy things away, wash things up, neaten and clean and shine them, both literally and metaphorically. Allowing a little moss to grow.

Wild practice

1

Walk, cycle, ride, camp. Walk barefoot. Change your daily habits – if you can – so that your day begins with walking to work instead of closing yourself away in a vehicle.

2

Spend some time alone outside, with and without your notebook, every day if possible; even if for only five minutes. Get up very early and watch dawn break;

go outside at night. Go to the coast and watch the surf and the stars. Find a particular tree and watch it through the seasons. Examine the moss that grows on it, the cracks in its skin, the ivy, its changing faces, the beetles and birds that inhabit it. Feel its bark. Stand and sit under and by it. Write about it.

Find a bench in a local park, if you can't get to 'real' wilderness, and sit on it at different times throughout the year, again noting down the changes, as well as the things that stay the same.

3

Learn how to be silent. 'Where silence begins. I go forward and I people the night with stars, with speech...' (Octavio Paz)

4

Learn about nature. Identify the plants and the birds. Find where wild animals hang out. Watch their differing patterns of behaviour through the weathers and the seasons. Just watch.

5

Move between outer and inner. Gradually in your writings include yourself in the picture: where do you fit in? How do you respond? What does wild time mean for you? What are the connections, and what the disparities between inside and outside? Record it all.

6

Wild time may be to do with finding a balance between being and doing. Animals do this well. There is a routine in the way they live their lives, based on food supply, diurnal and nocturnal rhythms and season. You might want to reassess how you live your life: how artificial are your rhythms? What could change? For many people, the biggest change might be to allow yourself unstructured free time, outside, simply watching and listening, simply being...

I know that I love the day,
The sun on the mountain, the Pacific...
But I know I live half alive in the world,
Half my life belongs to the wild darkness.
Galway Kinnell

I would love to live
Like a river flows,
Carried by the surprise
Of its own unfolding
John O'Donohue

Only at dusk does the silence return to the forest
Quivering and vital as men go home
Returning to the firelight, a sense of knowing
Of having been there before.

Here is where we come to
When we stop...
James Crowden

To the eyes of the man of imagination, nature is imagination itself. As a
man is, so he sees.
William Blake

Nature is none other than God in things... whence all of God is in all
things... Think thus, of the sun in the crocus, in the narcissus, in the
heliotrope, in the rooster, in the lion.
Giordano Bruno (C16th)

THE SUDDEN GLINT - NOTES ON NOTEBOOKS
BY CHRIS NORTH

Collecting

Carrying a pocket-sized notebook seems a very obvious discipline – but I have worked with many participants in writing workshops who do not carry one and seem surprised that I place such importance on them. To me, and I think to most serious creative writers, maintenance of a notebook is an essential discipline. Notebooks are a positive creative tool as well as a simple repository of notes and information.

One enormous advantage of the notebook approach is the wealth of material you have permanently available to work on. This is most useful when immediate creative ideas are dry.

To gain the most from the notebook, entries should be frequent. They should, as much as possible, be undirected, unplanned and unstructured. Notebook entries should develop into a reflex.

Below are some suggested techniques for catching some order – some useable material from your journey through the chaos of each day. These are not meant as formal directions but as starting points to assist in maximising the notebook's use. Eventually every writer develops their own notebook shorthand and techniques.

All these entries should be unmediated, unrevised writing. Quantity is allowable. No matter how long your narrative is, it will still be an enormous condensing of the actual passing events of a day.

1

Firstly try *close observation*. Stopping and looking. You could say that writers are paid and valued for their ability to notice things that others miss. A writer detects patterns, spots real behaviour and picks up unconsidered trifles that others do not notice. At any gap in the mainstream of your day make a point of noticing and recording something. Anything. For example: note the way a flag moves on a breezy day; or how light changes through your room during an afternoon; examine and record the opening sequence of flowers on a teasel plant; or closely describe the way a small child ponderously inspects a bunch of keys. Concentration on the minutiae of passing moments can lead you to striking similes and metaphors.

2

A refinement of close observation is the *sense map*. This involves a slow examination of any encountered objects or exterior or interior space in terms of the senses, one by one: sight, smell, touch, sound and taste. You can employ synaesthesia, describing one sense in terms of another, or maybe explore a sixth sense relating to ambience, apparent presences, things glimpsed or sensed, etc. If you do this regularly you will be amazed at how much more you begin to notice, as you seemingly move closer to the essence of the place, object or moment.

3

Developing from these techniques are *character sketches* of people met or thought about. These can take the form of the 'character squeeze': i.e. just three or four noted words to catch the essence of someone encountered. For example: 'jiggling leg, chewed finger, mouth to mobile, curtain-ringed ears'; or your entries can extend to longer character sketches. Give yourself permission to write pages of excessive, inventoried description if you want. Honing is not necessary in a notebook.

4

Simply writing the *straight narrative* of a day's events, no matter how mundane they may have seemed, can uncover potent material, particularly if you note and worry out detail on the way. You will find that useable material occurs to you as you go through the process – indeed sometimes an insight will positively leap out as you write.

5

A variation on straight narrative is *stream of consciousness* writing. This essentially slows the narrative down to 'real time', so that events and thoughts are recorded as they are happening. However, you are not trying to record sequences of events in any kind of chronological order, but rather you are allowing the jumping sideways or back and forth motion that the unfocused mind exhibits. This kind of writing does not consciously 'select' and evaluate the material for recording; it simply 'allows' whatever appears.

6

Lists are potent devices, and opportunities for creating them are around all the time. I have listed the stripped down contents of individual letters published in a local paper, the various forms of London's many steeples and the sounds made by different sorts of revving motorbikes. All subsequently appeared in published work.

7

All writers have a licence to *eavesdrop*, and nowadays the ubiquitous mobile phone is providing ample opportunities for catching speech patterns, and occasionally interesting content.

8

Writing out your own *conversations* immediately after they have occurred can be surprisingly revealing – and I have found they frequently supply ignition points into fiction or poetry. In some conversations the interplay of two or three minds often create insights that would not arrive by normal thought processes. These insights need to be captured quickly. Found text is a similarly rich source of material. I remember Ken Smith, the late poet, recording in his notebook: 'Two hearts for 50p' seen in a greengrocers* – and 'Read the world' on the side of a van.

9

And *dreams*. I have a notepad on the bedside table to immediately record dreams. They are the product of the unconscious mind unshackled and at play. One way or the other they could be hinting at what you ought to be writing about.

10

Imaginings and memories. Also scraps of ideas, phrases, thoughts, and things such as news headlines, seen or heard.

Most of these notebook disciplines can be extended by using the 'free-write' techniques frequently employed in writing workshops. Every writer is different on the amount of time they can usefully free-write. I find ten minutes works for me – after that I start hesitating and the flow goes. But as all who attend workshops for the first time discover, a great deal can be written in ten minutes.

Creative play is essential. I enjoy doodling with words and believe that one should never feel embarrassed or self-conscious about scribbling what initially seems meaningless rubbish – sometimes such ramblings make the important breakthrough.

If the writer keeps a notebook permanently at hand for no other reason than catching the sudden idea on the wing, she or he will find it worthwhile. There is probably a book to write about the great short stories, poems and plays that escaped capture because some writer foolishly did not hook them immediately when they briefly showed themselves. Sometimes the sudden glint is just a line or phrase – but those few words can be a key. Once captured, the door it opens can be accessed any time.

Shaping

An important element in notebook discipline is, of course, using and processing the material gathered. I regularly empty out my notebooks into a master journal on a word processor. Any elements that are applicable to specific writing projects are pasted into the appropriate documents. The more speculative, free-write entries I place in a more involved system of work incubation.

Some years ago the late poet Peter Redgrove published a brief pamphlet on an incubation process that he had developed over a number of years. From his very structured and organised process, I have adapted a system that works for me.

In essence incubation is a way of allowing your unconscious to have as much involvement as possible in your creative process. Free-write work is systematically filed away for a reasonably prolonged period. Peter Redgrove allowed his pieces to incubate for some three months although I find a slightly shorter period is more productive for me.

If you file frequent free-write entries on a regular basis, a considerable bank of incubating work will develop. After a piece's period in apparent oblivion, it is revisited and worked on. When you do this for the first time you will startle yourself. A piece of more rounded work seems to step from that first free-write as if it had created itself. The work should be progressed further – perhaps by elimination of redundant matter and the introduction of approximate shaping – but as soon as you feel yourself hitting resistance then the work should be returned to incubation; as it should be anyway, once you have exhausted all the more obvious avenues for shaping this time.

By the time you visit your work for the third time the completed piece will be becoming visible. At this stage I usually release it from the incubation system and revision becomes more intensive and continues until the piece is finished.

* See the poem fragment by Ken Smith in 'The Poet's Career' chapter by Keith Jafrate

ETERNALLY OPPOSITE, ETERNALLY CONNECTED

'Poets,' says writer William Oxley, 'are not creatures of the intellect but creatures of the imagination.'

I'd modify that a little to read: 'Writers are firstly creatures of the imagination, and only secondarily creatures of the intellect.'

At the risk of introducing polarised thinking, it's relevant here to talk about the two hemispheres of the brain. Nobel prizewinner Professor Roger Sperry researched what have come to be known as 'left brained' and 'right brained' thinking styles. In effect, these are two different ways of processing information, and an ideal scenario is one in which both sides of the brain are nurtured and exercised, and where there is flexible communication across the hemispheres as well as the ability to integrate these different ways of processing information.

Left brained thinking is the one in which most of us function during most of our waking time. Our culture requires this focus of us, and has valued this state of 'doing thinking' over what we could call 'being feeling'. This state is one of high cortical arousal; logical, analytical, linear, language-based consciousness. It is in this brain activity that we plan and map and schematise or organise the way in which we move forward in our daily lives. In relation to creative writing we could call this function the editor, the town planner, the grown-up.

Right brain states are normally associated with the unconscious, or liminal states of consciousness. They involve a lower level of cortical activity, and theta brainwaves associated with that state of reverie (the hypnagogic state) experienced just before drifting into, or coming out of, sleep are connected with creative inspiration. These right brain states are non-verbal, image-based feeling states which are also associated with play, as well as with visual/perceptual modes of 'thinking'. It seems that the right hemisphere processes and retains verbal material better if it is carried in images, pattern, rhythm or feeling; hence the retention in the memory of song or poetry, sometimes even when other faculties have failed; and the reason perhaps for encoding important wisdom in poetry and story in the oral (bardic) tradition. This is the 'imaginer' part of the brain: right brain is the inventor, the artist, the magician, the child.

Both parts of the brain of course are in use simultaneously, and even maths requires both hemispheres (apparently in solving a mathematical problem the brain sends messages back and forth between both nine times) – and both, of course, need to be involved in creativity; but each has its own stage in the process, its own time.

Neuropsychology calls the right brained state 'primary process thinking' and the left 'secondary process thinking'. Each is characterised by its own level of cortical arousal, although some research suggests that these styles may not be so much related to particular regions of the brain as to differing levels of arousal on a continuum. 'Defocused attention', a kind of diffuse awareness that scans, reads and collects information across a broad field through a spontaneous, associative and connectional process, is characteristic of primary process and the earlier stages of creativity. 'Focused attention', on the other hand, is characteristic of secondary processes and is needed in the later stages of creativity, such as shaping, refining and editing.

For me, all this is another way of saying that both head and heart have to be involved in the making of a piece of writing; and the ability to see both detail and the whole picture.

As writers, our ability to communicate effectively – by which I mean inspiringly and excitingly, as well as via the arrangement of words/ideas on the page – depends partly on our ability to work from a balanced brain perspective, where intuition and analysis, play and seriousness, spontaneity and planning, lateral and linear, freewheeling and focused all come together.

Encourage the right brain with the exercises below, which in their ultimate expression rely also on the 'thinking' powers of the left brain.

Incidentally, using visual art – a picture, sculpture or image – as a prompt is a very effective way of asking the right brain to kick in; or writing stream-of-consciousness style while listening to instrumental music.

The exercises below ask for non-verbal responses. (When you're responding to any of the exercises in this book, don't feel you have to respond only in words. Try including drawing in some of your responses.)

Starting points

These are both best done with a partner, though it is possible to work alone.

1

Pictograms are, says Tony Buzan, the inventor of mind-mapping, 'a way of allowing the brain to talk to itself in its own language'. Certainly visual images are a good way in to writing for many people. Try this one:

Take a large sheet of paper, and use coloured pens if you prefer. On it draw, without thinking or premeditation, a number of pictograms or hieroglyphs –pictures/symbols/images/shapes/patterns/stick figures (10 or 12), leaving plenty of space between. They don't have to be neatly ordered in lines.

Swap (if relevant). Now write imaginative notes, words, phrases beneath each one. Again try not to 'think' as you do this – jot down the first thing that comes into your mind – allow it to be spontaneous, and don't worry about 'fitting' the words to the image.

If you're working with someone else, swap back. Work up the notes, adding and subtracting as you wish, to shape a piece of writing: a story or poem.

2

Pictogram 2: (This is an adaptation of an artists' exercise by Betty Edwards.[1])

Again, take a large sheet of paper, and turn it horizontally. Make three small boxes along the top, and again about halfway down. Under each one write the name of an emotion: grief, joy, rage, jealousy, passion, fear. Now, again without thinking, sketch a quick abstract representation of that feeling state.

Take one of the boxes. With reference to the *sketch*, not the word underneath, write a stream-of-consciousness piece without stopping or thinking.

A variation on this is to fill the boxes with quick abstract representations of people you know; and then do the same thing.

No longer divided
we walk together
with a single shadow
Helen Carter

THE POWER OF DREAM

We've all used the expression 'I'll sleep on it' – as if at some profound level we know that what our conscious minds can't solve or answer, our unconscious can and often does. Surprising resolutions and revelations occur when our conscious minds are switched off and our unconscious, most commonly expressed and accessed through dream, is given free rein.

If a participant in a workshop is unsure how to complete a poem, say, or needs to progress a plot, or – in a creative or personal context – has a situation that needs resolving, I often tell them to write the question on a scrap of paper and put it under their pillow before they go to sleep. People laugh, of course; think that I'm superstitious, or that the suggestion is facile or childish. Nonetheless, sometimes they try it, often against their rational opinion.

Never yet have I known it not work.

Crick and Watson, working on DNA in the '50s, finally cracked it in 1953, thanks to a dream in which one of the two scientists saw an image of two intertwined snakes, dancing. Who knows what Freud would have made of this; but in the context of the scientists' work it gave them the illumination which in turn led to the breakthrough they needed: the double helix form of two interwoven strands of which DNA is composed.

More prosaically, I had a series of dreams in which the enduring theme was water, usually the sea. Out of this came both the resolution of a personal situation (water is often taken to represent the feeling nature), and the central motif and context for a new novel.

The sea is also a symbol for the unconscious: the realm of feelings, memories, past experiences, internalised figures and events, instincts, unresolved issues, repressed material in general, stories and, amongst other things, dreams.

C G Jung is largely responsible for what we know of the realms of the conscious and unconscious minds. The latter is vast: picture egoic consciousness as a tiny rowboat on the limitless ocean of the unconscious. Dreams for the writer are treasure-chests; or, to use another metaphor, the nets we drop down to catch the fish – the imagery of poems, the ideas behind story.

Dreams are the most readily available gateway to the unconscious. We all dream, every night; even those of us who believe we never dream. (Dreams are, in fact, critical to mental health, serving the functions of recharging the brain and balancing psychological processes. In a well-known experiment, researchers found that a group of student volunteers who were allowed 'ordinary' sleep but were persistently woken during periods of REM [rapid eye movement] sleep – the stage in which dreams occur – functioned badly to the extent of hallucinating after a few nights of this.)

According to Jung, there are two main areas of the unconscious. First is the personal unconscious. Beyond this is what Jung called the collective unconscious, in which we all share. This is the realm of the archetypes.

Jung became aware of the existence of the collective unconscious through noticing, over and over, that the same primordial symbols appear both in ancient myths and religions, and in the dreams of modern people. To his astonishment, he found images appearing in people's dreams that relate to some very ancient symbol, perhaps from a completely different culture that could not possibly have been known to the conscious mind of the dreamer. Gradually he realised that our dreams draw on universal primordial sources that are not connected with our conscious knowledge and/or life experience.

A study of myth, folk tale and fairy tale, as well as theatre, film, general fiction and art will frequently reveal an infrastructure of remarkably similar figures and of course situations, regardless of era and culture. These figures in story have collective associations, which we collectively reinforce in the writing, speaking, hearing, seeing and reading (as appropriate) in our contemporary culture. Their outer appearance may take on the flavour and colour of the particular culture and era in which they arise, but the dynamic remains the same. In them we recognise parts of ourselves; in their stories we see reflected aspects of our own experiences.[1]

In our dreams, we may recognise representations of these archetypes, albeit less well defined. Our personal context and connections will be unique, of course, but the imagery is universal.

Dreams are a wonderful resource that is, in the main, disregarded. In terms of reflective writing, listening to them and working with them will offer immense insight into hidden aspects of our lives, and show us potential directions we might take. As tools for self-understanding and growth, they are of paramount importance. Once you are in the habit of paying attention to them, and are *au fait* with their language, the act of going to sleep can become as pleasurable as going night after night, for free, to a rich picture-house or theatre in which you are both spectator and player.

For the creative writer, too, they offer an unparalleled arena. Novelist Lindsay Clarke says that all his books have started with a dream image.

So how might a writer work with dream images?

The first thing is to *pay attention*. Recording your dreams immediately on waking is invaluable. As you practise this, you will find that you have better recall. The act of writing them down also seems to 'keep the channels open'; as if, once we start taking our dreams seriously, they oblige by becoming more frequent or more accessible; or we oblige ourselves by becoming more aware of our dreaming life.

If you are using your dreams as a way of progressing your own personal development, you will be exploring and questioning your dream stories and figures; assessing and interpreting. For the creative writer, though, interpretation is less important than insight into story dynamics, plot development and character construction. Assume that every dream is a story, and act accordingly. The 'teasing out' process required in conventional dreamwork is illuminating, but for creative writing purposes it may be more useful to apply the plot questions of 'how?' 'what if?' and 'what then?'. Take the characters in your dreams and inflate them: exaggerate and embroider. Tell their stories from the inside and the outside. Progress their stories to their individual ends. Work out what they want.

Look at their archetypal characteristics: can you recognise or develop the villain, the trickster, the helper, the jealous sister, the renegade? The saboteur in your dreams may offer exactly the character or plot motif you need to block your protagonist's progress towards his or her goal; in other words, to inject conflict and suspense.

You can build a character around one issuing from dream by noting down his or her appearance and improvising/inventing life situations.

You can also isolate his or her core identity or core theme. A friend has a figure in her dreams who continually misses trains and boats. Leaving aside all the personal psychological interpretations that are the property of that person alone, we could brainstorm this dream character. What's going on with this 'symptom'? Is she generally shambolic and disorganised, or is this symptomatic of some deeper disorder? What disruption might this tendency cause? How does she feel about her failure to arrive? Will she arrive in some other more creative way, or is she destined, like Sisyphus, to end up always where she started? Who's making the choices? Might she meet someone she otherwise wouldn't have met, or might she miss the one person or situation that could have radically changed her life? By exploring these directions we can build up a picture of the character as well as create a plot.

Dreams will often show us what is not fully developed or given space in our outer lives, as well as what is not working. This compensatory mechanism might also be useful to you as a writer: if all your stories tend to rework the same themes, if your plots lack dynamic tension, if your characters are all too nice – or too nasty – look to your dreams for possible alternatives.

Watch for the language of the unconscious – it tends to communicate in symbols and moods. Its processes are not rational nor necessarily linear, and are as likely to be communicated in riddles, mysteries and humour as in anything straightforward. Note down any images or symbols. What do they mean for you? Write or draw your associations to each, your feelings and memories.

Talk to your characters! Let them respond! Have your characters talk to each other, and to you, out loud or on paper; record what they say in pictures as well as words; borrow from Gestalt and allocate certain chairs to certain dream-people, then sit in each chair and 'speak for' that character (best to do this when alone, to avoid being sectioned, or petitioned for divorce). Ask the characters what they want; whom they love; whom they hate; what they're frightened of. Speak or write their response. (This does more than simply clarify; it sets in motion a dynamic that has its own momentum.)

Bear in mind that image I offered at the beginning of the tiny boat of the conscious mind and the vast uncharted ocean on which it sails. Dreams are a magnificent opportunity to start to map that territory; don't waste them!

Starting points

1

Continue the dream in writing: choose a time when you are not likely to be interrupted, and, in a relaxing environment with the phone off the hook, write the dream as far as it went, and then simply keep writing.

2

Reconstruct the dream through active imagination: make sure you're in a quiet place where you won't be interrupted, and lie on your bed (try burning relaxing essential oils), and enter the dream again. Without forcing, allow it to continue to unfold.

3

Pick a central image, character or situation and free associate by noting down without thinking and as fast as possible any ideas, images, associations, memories or feelings that arise in relation to that central motif.

4

Have the characters talk to you and each other.

5

Make a brief story map of the dream: this happened, then that, then that...(this is a more objective process than 1 and 2 above). Consider different possible endings.

6

Dialogue with the symbols: this sounds crazy, but if you start to question them ('What are you standing in for? What message do you carry? What do you want?') and so on, and then listen quietly, you will, over the next minutes, hours or days find that you will make connections. Simply notice what thoughts arise, and what things come to your attention, in either your inner or outer world. For instance, suppose you had a ladder in your dream. Maybe you ask it: 'You're propped against a wall. Are you for me to climb up, or someone else to come down? And what's the other side of the wall?' Then just pay attention; and be aware that these kinds of connections are subtle, unexpected and often illogical, and the answers may come in lateral ways, such as things you hear or see in your daily life; something someone says; or a thought that seems to come out of nowhere as you're washing up. A ladder may, of course, represent something current and fairly obvious in one's circumstances, such as job promotion, or the desire for promotion; or it may apply to something far more interior. What if it leads into a small, private walled garden? What might that suggest to you? What kind of soul-need might it be flagging up – time out, maybe? Or what kind of plot motif might it prompt?

7

Add 'what if' to the dream situation.

8
Explore the characters in your dream:

How do they talk?
What do they want?
What do they like?
Who do they resemble?
What are their archetypal characteristics?
What trouble might these characteristics cause, or what solutions may they offer?

THE CREATIVE PROCESS

Creativity is a mysterious process. Nonetheless, a lot of time and energy has been and is being expended on trying to define, encapsulate and understand how it works. Chances are it's different for everyone, but maybe there are elements in common in the progression of the steps to making something new out of, apparently, nothing. As with anything else, if we can understand the process, we may be able to replicate it – or at least be more patient with allowing the natural unfolding of the stages towards its ripening.

Earlier in the book I wrote about left brain/right brain modes of thinking, and their connection with the conscious and unconscious minds. The creative impulse, in my belief, arises in the unconscious. The conscious mind is primarily responsible for the shaping of the impulse. Metaphorically and temporally, between these two modes is a liminal or threshold area known as 'the zone', which I describe in 'Altered States'. As I experience and understand it, the act of creating something moves between these three states – sometimes in a simple unidirectional way, but more often, for me at least, wavering back and forth between them until the process is complete.

Researchers have been trying to formulate the various stages in the creative process for a while. Nineteenth century physicist Herman Helmholtz suggested three:

1 Saturation
2 Incubation
3 Illumination.

Later, mathematician Henri Poincaré added a fourth: 'Verification' (this 'checking out' parallels the 'control' process in science, and could be seen to prefigure our current 'reflective practice').

Jacob Getzels, a psychologist working in the 1960s, suggested that there was a preliminary stage which preceded Helmholtz' 'Saturation'. He suggested that this might be named 'Finding' or 'Formulating'. Another American psychologist renamed this first stage 'First Insight'.

So the contemporary model[1] looks like this:

1 First Insight
2 Saturation
3 Incubation
4 Illumination
5 Verification.

If only it were this simple! For me, however, the movement from the moment of inspiration to the final executed piece is more like finding my way over a narrow mountain pass between countries in the dark, on foot, alone and with no map or torch, and winding back and forth over the border at random... at least, a lot of the time.

My own experience, as well as that of others with whom I have talked or worked, suggests that the above model does not go far enough. I think that there are more like eight stages in the creative process, and that that process dips in and out of the conscious and the unconscious (there is, naturally, a flow and overlap to some extent between stages, and between states of consciousness). I think the model looks more like this:

1 Seed Idea (first insight)
2 Circling the idea
3 Saturation
4 Incubation
5 Gathering
6 Illumination
7 Ritual/Preparation
8 Embodiment.

A year or two ago I was thinking about all this just as a writing magazine commission came in for me – almost miraculously, as it happens, a piece on creativity – so I monitored the process as I wrote the article. This is how my process evolved, switching between focus and diffuse awareness.

Seed idea
(Conscious prompt; seed sown in unconscious)
Here's how it works for me: I receive a commission from a magazine for a piece of writing that is exciting, and also challenging for me; i.e. it doesn't necessarily

spring into my conscious mind fully-formed. Through discussion with the editor, and as a result of jotting down initial thoughts and images I focus on how I might develop the projected idea.

Afterwards I try and get a feel for the shape of the seed, start to feel inspired. Then I leave it alone.

Circling
(This process moves between conscious focus and a more diffuse state of awareness)
I feel enthused. Over a period of time (hours or days, depending on the complexity of the project), before starting the process at all, I occasionally 'circle' the idea in my imagination, without any agenda. Towards the end of this period I might jot down more images, especially if I find one that seems to be a 'core' image, or make a spidergram or mind-map (actually these terms are too glorious for my rough scrawled picture-notes).

Saturation
(Largely conscious but 'dipping in' to liminality)
I start to focus. For a few days I gather ideas; some of this is focused research; some is simply reading, looking at or listening to things that I find personally inspiring, which I know trigger creativity in me. In this case I also think about how I personally go about creating, and I talk to other creative people. I *consume* all this.

During this time I find that I need to do things that help me relax: walk, read, take baths, eat well. I always spend time with our animals, but during this stage of the process I find I seek them out. I used to think it was a kind of displacement activity, but I am beginning to recognise that it has a deeper purpose.

Incubation
(Liminal and/or unconscious)
I finish researching late the night before I want to write the piece and sleep. The next morning I write a few notes – quickly, without thinking – then I metaphorically look away. At the time of this particular article commission, it's May and I take the footpath outside my cottage. Wonderful: bluebells, campion, wild garlic and buttercups. Thrush song. I throw the ball for the dog and wallow in the scent of wet about-to-flower nettles mingled with gorse and bluebell

fragrances. It's rained and everything is clear and sharp. Swallows skim my head. I soak it all up. I don't 'think' about the piece I'm writing (though I do allow my thoughts to touch on it if they stray that way. Then – years of meditation practice pay off here – I bring my mind back to the present moment).

On the way back I'm alighting on snatches of poems: a piece of my own, as well as phrases from the 200-odd submissions I'm currently reading for an anthology. I'm still not thinking about the article. I get out of my own light, out of my head, into my body and feelings, and allow my brain to freewheel. Images tumble. I start to feel a kind of fizz.

Back in the house. Cup of coffee, wash the dishes.

Gathering
(Unconscious, then liminal, rising back up towards consciousness)
Hands in the water. Still not 'thinking', though I'm aware something is starting to emerge in my mind. I try not to influence or 'grab' at it as it takes a shape, though I watch it. I can feel creative energy building. Something in my imagination is gathering fragments – it reminds me of Clarissa Pinkola Estes talking about La Loba gathering bones to sing them back into life.[2] It's a very fertile moment, and in its way extremely focused – almost transcendent in the way that for a short while it totally possesses me. I feel utterly involved and alert, watching, listening.

In the 2003 Reith Lectures (Radio 4) Professor Ramachandran talked about his teacher Richard Gregory's Dalmatian dog puzzle picture, where, on first glance, all you see is a mass of splodges, until...

Illumination
(Sudden emergence of unconscious material through liminal space into conscious mind)
...suddenly all the disparate splodges come together and in a flash your brain makes DOG.

In just such a way my images cohere into a pattern of ideas, the opening quote presents itself from all my reading, and an awareness emerges of where I wish the piece to begin. Aha!

Ritual/preparation
(Consciousness deliberately maintaining liminality)

Grab coffee. Back upstairs. Shut door to study. Switch off phone. Clear desk. Stare out of window at the distant river a moment. Focus.

Embodiment
(Conscious)
Start to write.

I should say that the piece does not necessarily emerge whole, like Athena from the head of Zeus. Sometimes I come up against not knowing where to go next. I have learned to respect and trust, as they say, the process, and I know better than to force it. So when the flow stops, I leave it alone for a while and do something else until it presents a direction. The wisdom here, of course, is knowing yourself well enough as to differentiate between times when you're feeling lazy in the face of hard work and need to push on through, and when the idea simply isn't yet 'cooked' enough. But the writing process is more than merely the act of putting words on paper; in fact, that's only the palm tree on the island.

ALTERED STATES

For art to appear, we have to *disappear*... our eye or ear is "caught" by something: a tree, a rock, a cloud, a beautiful person, a baby's gurgling, spatters of sunlight reflected off some wet mud in the forest, the sound of a guitar wafting unexpectedly out of a window. Mind and sense are arrested for a moment, fully in the experience. Nothing else exists. When we "disappear" in this way, everything around us becomes a surprise, new and fresh... We see things just as we and they are, yet we are able to guide and direct them to become just the way we want them...

Stephan Nachmanovitch

Recognise this state? There's a point in the creative process where you are so completely immersed in what you are doing that there is no awareness of separateness; where you *are* what you are doing. It's akin to a moment of bliss: akin to those moments of near-transcendence – maybe in mystical or religious experience or meditation, maybe in moments of intense intimacy, maybe in the presence of an awesome elemental phenomenon, maybe – pregnancy's an obvious metaphor here – that moment when a woman who has been wanting to conceive hears that she has.

Or when an idea we have been 'circling' semi-seriously suddenly starts to sprout in our imagination.

This is not a state of unconsciousness, but nor is it a state we associate with our 'usual' state of wakefulness, which involves much brain activity and focused attention. Rather, it is a liminal state where for a while we have put our 'selves' and our thinking and judging processes out of the way and are not aware of separation between ourselves and our experience, between observer and observed.

It is a state of heightened awareness, of inspiration, of alert calm; a kind of relaxation which means, says Nachmanovitch, an 'alert poised equilibrium, attentive, ready to shift in any direction with the movement of the moment. In this state we are able to relax our normal ego defences so that we can "respond from a deeper source within".[1]

This is a twilight zone where the creator has access to both the conscious processes in the 'thinking' brain and the image and feeling-based states of the unconscious.

The key process in terms of creativity is that state of low cortical arousal/activity associated with right brain activity of which I have already spoken in 'Eternally Opposite, Eternally Connected'. Successful creativity, it seems, depends on our ability to enter or allow this zone of calm alertness. (It should be said that this is not a passive state of 'blobbing out' but rather an active, attentive but non-interfering – 'defocused' – state of freewheeling in full presence in the moment. This state of heightened awareness/elated calm will be familiar to anyone who practises meditation.)

Amy Lowell, writing over fifty years ago on the process of making poetry, suggested that the poet showed 'an extraordinary sensitive and active subconscious personality, fed by, and feeding, a non-resistant consciousness'.[2] More recent research bears out the fact that a sensitivity to as wide a field of one's environment as possible, plus sensitivity to subliminal impressions, coupled with a state of defocused attention, is associated with creativity.

It seems that, in addition to creative types, many people who excel in their own field experience this state: surgeons and chess players as much as dancers and musicians. (Athletes call it 'the zone', and describe being 'in the zone' as being in a timeless state of near-euphoria.)

The defocused attention, or diffuse awareness, so important to the primary process part of creativity, involves us in a broadening out. The metaphor I keep using – that of dropping nets into the unconscious to catch its 'fish' – is so apposite I shall use it again. The act of engaging part of our conscious brain with some activity that does not involve high stress and therefore much investment is an 'allowing' one. The unfocused parts of our consciousness are then free to fish... We can facilitate this process by creating, or allowing, the conditions in which it is most likely to occur:

> *Relaxed monotony* seems to be important. The idea that the best inspiration happens in such places as bed, on the bus, or in the bath (viz. Archimedes' 'Eureka!' moment) has become, amongst scientists anyway, almost a cliché.

> *Relaxing environment* A gentle environment that requires minimal focused concentration – that is, an environment that doesn't demand the processing of stimulus via brain states of high cortical arousal – but that may feed the senses or occupy the body is a fertile one. Einstein, living alone in the country, noticed how the monotony of a quiet life allowed his creative mind

to function. Numerous other creatives have found this, as we've already discussed.

Solitude While it can be immensely fruitful to brainstorm with other people, the digestion and incubation of ideas that may lead to immersion in the creative 'twilight zone' and then some kind of creative expression require solitude, if only for a short while, to give space to the 'maturing' quality without having to engage with the more active brain state which company usually requires.

Immersion in the moment, the experience, seems to be central to the process.

Other creative processes help: anything that stimulates feeling states. Reading poetry. Painting or looking at paintings; listening to or making music. (Einstein, when processing an idea, would leave his study to go next door and play the violin.)

Also:
Flooding the senses and/or exercising the body in ways such as walking, riding, gardening, running, swimming, dancing, massage with essential oils.

Occupations that involve repetition and/or monotony but leave the mind relatively free, such as walking (again), mowing the lawn, washing up or cooking.

States that involve movement but also containment such as constriction/ sensory monotony – e.g. driving, train or bus journeys.

Ritual and preparation Consciously making an atmosphere of quiet but intense containment, through the use of, say, candles, flowers, music and incense can help; even the act of clearing one's desk, sharpening a pencil, finding an attractive notebook can do it. It's an act of seduction and dedication. It is as if one is making a statement of intent by focusing one's awareness on the creation of atmosphere, and as one concentrates on the physical part of preparation in such a ritual another part of one's awareness is activated. If this ritual is observed each time one commits oneself to the creative process, accessing the necessary state becomes increasingly easy.

For some people, flowers and incense just won't do it. Stephen Spender talks of writers' personal rituals to aid the creative process: 'Schiller liked to have the smell of rotten apples, concealed beneath the lid of his desk, under his nose when he was composing poetry. Walter de la Mare has told me that he must smoke when writing. Auden drinks endless cups of tea. Coffee is my own addiction, besides smoking a great deal, which I hardly ever do except when I am writing… as I attain a greater concentration, this tends to make me forget the taste of cigarettes in my mouth, and then I have a desire to smoke two or even three cigarettes at a time' so that, he continues, physical sensations from outside might penetrate the walls of concentration.[3]

For myself, despite my *preference* for candles and incense, the creative frenzy is marked by a desire for poppadoms and dry Martini, a drink that I don't normally bother with… a weird lot, we writers.

Play

Dr Jung, at a critical point in his personal and professional life, gave himself over to play, making a model village in his backyard. It was in doing this that his freewheeling mind offered the ideas that took his work in the directions that have made such an enormous contribution to our understanding of psychology.

Another way of talking about this is to remind us not to take ourselves so seriously; to risk making a fool of ourselves from time to time, and simply remembering how to have a good time, without any attachment to an expected outcome...

WILD THINKING

As the wild duck is more swift and beautiful than the tame, so is the wild – the mallard – thought...
Henry David Thoreau

How can we make our words and ideas fresh, original, untamed? How can we find ways of saying things that will surprise, delight, inspire? Are there new things to write about? And, if not, how do we make the old things seem new?

In many years of working with adults I recognise that the process of unlearning is often a harder one than learning. Letting go seems to be difficult to the point of impossible for many people, especially in the western world.

It requires that we find a way to let our bodies and our hearts do the thinking rather than our minds – at least, in the initial phases. This is how the imagination does its work. We need to be able to flash our hand out quicker than lightning to catch that fleeting firefly in the dark and tip it in the jar: without thinking about how to do it, what it means and whether there are more. Like a good archer, we need to have our eye constantly trained to shoot our hand fast and true, first time.

This is the territory of 'first thought, right thought'; it means cultivating a direct and immediate connection between impulse and action, between image-thought and written-word.

The more educated people are the more difficult, often, they find it to let go into this more chaotic – because unpredictable – process. I think it's a product of a left-brain-trained society, where making sense, analysis and intellectual ordering are given status high above imagination (think how still, today, children are too often ridiculed for 'telling stories'), impulse and body-knowing.

I'm not saying that the less educated you are the better your writing and your grasp of the 'wild' – lateral, free, inventive – thought will be, clearly. What I'm suggesting is that the ordering, shaping mind, so useful in editing work for presentation, can be a strongly inhibiting factor in the creative process; it can actually, I discover, prevent the wild thoughts, often so grounded in feeling and imagery, from arriving in the brain at all.

The good news is that you can get into the habit of suspending the linear thinking processes, at least for a short time.

The essence of all this really is simple – as adults we need to remember how to play, as I suggested in 'Altered States'. It's hard for creativity to enter a straitjacketed life or mind. Allow a little chaos into your life. 'Chaos is the crucible of creativity,' said Miroslav Holub. Make space for idleness. Minor miracles need unstructured space in which to occur. Find ways to subvert your thinking patterns; do this consciously, by monitoring your thoughts and contradicting yourself, internally or out loud, for instance.

Drift. Disrupt yourself. Make new patterns and new maps.
Make your day a blank page.
Look beneath.
Look behind.
Look for what has been lost.
Ask questions. Ask essential, living, heart-opening and soulful questions.
Find one new thing every day. Tell someone about it. Write about it.
'Guess, follow absurdities and give the impossible a hearing.' (Kate Grenville)

Be a tabula rasa.

If you were to come this way in spring, say, or in rain; on a day
that might seem like any other day unless you were looking; for instance today;

If you were to take this trip differently, say backwards, or with your eyes closed,
using only touch, or sound;

If you were to sink your whole self into this day walking in this new way,
with the newness in your head of a blank recording screen with everything
erased except

NOW   THIS   HERE

how would you write it then?

The only way to write, or maybe the only way to be, is as if this was the first day and you seeing for the first time; with no points of reference, no expectations, and especially

no map home.

Here are some tips and starting points.

1
Disorientation and novelty seem to be keys to creativity; often it grows out of the juxtaposition of the familiar with the unknown. Next time you encounter a new situation, see if you can let it be exciting, an adventure, rather than something to fear ('fear is excitement without the breathing').

2
Routine stultifies creativity. Break your usual patterns. If you normally walk one way to work, walk another. Change the way you walk every hundred steps. Look up when you walk; look at the roofs and the sky. If you always have the same breakfast at the same time, change both.

3
Get up, or go to bed, at a different time from usual.

4
Try jotting random thoughts down at random times.

5
Wear new colours, or new styles of clothes. Notice how you feel in them. (I said this to one of my groups once; and a well-dressed woman in her fifties who always wore navy or beige turned up the next week in a screaming orange sweatshirt. I don't know what happened to her writing, but she took off for India for the first time not long after; and started painting, too. I guess I have to conclude that it worked...)

6

Listen to different music.

7

Go to art exhibitions – or different exhibitions from your normal tastes.

8

Learn a new art or skill.

9

Go somewhere you wouldn't normally go. If you're gregarious, go alone. If you're solitary, go with someone else.

10

If you normally do ready meals or takeaways, try cooking for a week. Or vice versa.

11

Set out to notice something particular each time you're out: the colour pink, the number seven, the letter Y, people with odd earrings, red bicycles – whatever.

12

Brush your teeth, or answer the phone, or especially *write* with your unaccustomed hand.

13

Try breaking your habitual patterns of speech with unexpected responses (this can be very liberating!). 'Talk crosswise,' says Jerome Rothenberg in his 'Crazy Dog Events' poem; 'say the opposite of what you mean.'

14

Adopt a new word or phrase each day (bring a word in out of the cold).

15

Give a coin to charity every time you use a cliché – and redesign the cliché, too.

16

Really listen to what people say. Eavesdrop. Write down snatches of conversation – especially out of context. Could you use one of these fragments as a starting point?

17

Acquire synaesthesia – seeing sounds in colour or tasting a word or hearing music in pictures... Practise!

18

Practise thinking in metaphors and similes as you go about your day and all that you encounter. 'What's this like?' 'What if this were a...?'

19

When you have written something, read it from the bottom up. Or tear the page in half lengthwise or crosswise and reassemble it in a different order.

20

Everything you do today, even – especially – the most menial tasks – do at half speed and full attention.

21

?

PART 2

THE PRACTICE OF POETRY

...I have said little about headaches, midnight oil, pints of beer or claret, love affairs, and so on, which are supposed to be stations on the journey of poets... There is no doubt that writing poetry, when a poem appears to succeed, results in an intense physical excitement, a sense of release and ecstasy. On the other hand, I dread writing poetry...the writing of a poem brings one face to face with one's own personality with all its familiar and clumsy limitations. In every other phase of one's existence, one can exercise the orthodoxy of a conventional routine... In poetry, one is wrestling with a god.

Stephen Spender

FRACTURED LIGHT
BY KENNETH STEVEN

For me the whole path is laid out in Robert Burns' magnificent poem 'Tae a Mouse'. The poet (also ploughman) has broken a mouse's nest in the field. A hundred thousand others might have passed on by, but Burns stops and bends to pick up the pieces he himself has broken. He sets the actions of humankind against eternity; he lifts that broken nest and holds it up to the light.

The poet is seeking what the Caithness novelist Neil Gunn called 'atoms of delight'. All of us are aware of what we might term *quotidiennité,* or 'everydayness'; in some ways we never quite allow ourselves to believe that the rest of our lives will be composed chiefly of the same mundane routine as always – that is too much for us to bear. We tend to see both past and future as idealised states of being – dangerously, yet understandably.

The poet's life is no different – it's composed of the same anxieties, the same struggles, the same moments of banality. But the little things become the big things. Carol Ann Duffy's woman on an upper floor doing the dishes is turned to gold by the geese that pass her window; Ted Hughes' hawk is transformed into an all-powerful dictator.

For me, memory holds one of the most important keys to this road into writing for the individual. Many feel the pen they would wield wouldn't be strong enough, or that it would simply repeat the things written by a thousand others before them. Not so, not if the person is truly allowing the imprint of their own life to fall on that piece of writing. There's no reason to be afraid of writing a poem about a sunset for fear it's treading ancient ground; if that sunset has distilled through one's consciousness and personal imagination, then what's created will be original and unique, not hackneyed.

And our memories hold the most precious repository of original things – rattle bags of jagged and angular things, shining things that refract the light as never before. The boy who used to stand barefoot outside the baker's shop on early Saturday mornings. The old opera singer who lived upstairs and who sang always when the flats went dark at midnight. The form of your mother hunched over the sink in early morning kneading new dough for bread. They are the stills, the black and white photographs that remain stowed away in the recesses of the head, that cannot be valued. They are priceless, and they are intact. Some of them hurt, but even in their pain they retain a beauty, a terrible beauty.

All of these things have the potential to be the beginnings of journeys. You alone know the secret of that attic room, the precise look of that figure, the exact sound of that tread. No one can capture those things adequately but you. We will not capture everything, we were not meant to. In Monet's attics were found hundreds of canvases attempting to capture one particular image, one specific moment of light. We see now the few that succeeded so magnificently, not the ones searching and striving and failing.

It's my belief that we need to attempt to make sense of this world as never before. Hugh MacDiarmid spoke of the age in which he wrote as one containing 'no more gods and precious few heroes'. The poet Ken Morrice said that 'these days we know more about the structure of atoms and how to get to the moon than about systems and how to be happy'. In many ways it would seem that we have more and more knowledge and less and less wisdom.

Shelley's words about poets being *the unacknowledged legislators of the world* may carry a ring of pomposity about them, but writers are important as people holding beacons for those about them, and for saying what may be unpalatable to a society that has gone too far down a particular road – into intolerance, materialism and darkness. It is for us to hold up the brokenness of our times to the light, and to see within its fragments the beauty that remains.

A Poem For Ivars

A picture of Latvia:
You as a boy lifting potatoes behind a horse,
Swallows ticking wings in a farmyard sky,
The generals of winter a day yet closer.

In the hungry faces, the simple hands
And this hard road through the furrows of Moscow,
I see a richer earth still living, wooden songs
That could pull your people's faith.

If a man should come now to your door
Selling motorways, a rustle of money in his eyes –
Do not buy his road, for it leads
To all our lost riches, our need of God.

Kenneth Steven[1]

WRESTLING WITH A GOD: MAKING POEMS

[P]oetry lets us imagine that certain arrangements of words, and nothing else – no camera, no lights, not much action – can tell us what it's like to be other people, and (in another sense) what it's like to be ourselves. In poems, we believe that language alone can reveal what Proust called "the intimate composition of those worlds which we call individuals and which, without the aid of art, we should never know".

Stephen Burt

A question I come back to with my regular creative writing groups is to do with why we read: what is literature for? The answers are always both various and numerous; amongst them to be entertained; to be transported; to learn; to be moved; uplifted; reassured; challenged; to be invited to question; to feel less alone; to have a glimpse, as E M Forster said, into other people's secret lives; to make sense of the universe and our part in it; to be changed...

This question is perhaps more immediately applied to novels; I suspect that people read poetry for slightly different reasons and maybe at different times in their lives. Nonetheless, the process of considering this in relation to poetry is a fruitful one. What do I want from a poem? Why do we read (or write) it?

All the above reasons apply. But there is an outstanding reason for me: what I really want is to be transformed, however slightly, by the poetry I read.

This means that I and the poem will be working in synergy. One is only changed if one is willing to put oneself into the process, into the crucible, with the poem. A bit of that poem, that book, will remain lodged with me; and in addition a good, by which I mean effective, poem will communicate something of the universal in the personal, and in so doing touches the transpersonal. And not all poems, by a long way, have that potential. Of the thousands I read annually, maybe a couple of dozen, maybe fewer, will have this kind of impact on me; or maybe it would be more honest to say any kind of impact. These few, for me, are poems which I can appreciate intellectually, but – and this is crucial – their primary and most significant impact registers in a place beyond the intellect, a place that's non-verbal.

So much poetry leans towards the confessional – the merely personal, or towards the abstract – the impersonal. Poet Wendell Berry talks of poetry where the speaker is present but the world absent, and the converse, where the world is present but the speaker absent.

How to contain and convey both? The challenge of achieving this synthesis, this holding of polarities, seems to me to be the pivotal creative tension which succeeds and which registers in the body – the solar plexus, the gut, the nape of the neck or hairs of the arm – before the intellect objectifies and admires. The litmus test.

So to come back to the question, knowing that there may not be an answer: what is poetry *for*?

Part of the answer, I suspect, is to do with hunger: a hunger, as Ben Okri says, that is to do with more life. Our lives have become narrow; their arteries constricted, he suggests.

A related answer must be to do with freedom; or rather freeing. I come to poetry sometimes for restoration. Good poetry may help in the reconnection of ourselves with something larger than merely ourselves, our small perspective.

Somewhere in these hieroglyphs, conglomeration of signs, must glimmer the seed of something larger than the word itself. Even when rooted in the ordinary, the small, as much of the best poetry is, it must contain the potential to be bigger, and to help us, however briefly, be bigger (like a healthy love affair). And a big poem might also be extraordinary, and maybe even immeasurable; it may also offer, in some way, the possibility of hope, or transcendence, or revisioning, or redemption – whatever these things might mean to the reader. The possibility that we could remake our lives.

That's not to say I want continual epiphany, any more than I want unmitigated gloom; but poetry needs to address both: the dark as well as the light, to set itself the task of recording the breadth and depth of being human.

I want a glimpse of the enduring beyond the merely human – whatever that might mean. A poem is successful as a poem both by being sufficient in itself, and because it gestures at something significant 'behind' itself – even, or maybe especially, if that something is silence. (How can we use words so that – Okri again – they themselves might become a kind of silence?)

For me, poetry will sometimes take me to a threshold and give me a glimpse of – something. Something *other*, something not entirely knowable. Mystery. If I'm lucky, it may even fly me over that threshold:

> A suspicion of light, sliding over leaves and then gone.
> A glimmer of something slipping away into the hedgerow.
> Your own hand rising to meet you, as if it were a wing.
>
> *(Roselle Angwin)*

For a poet, traditionally, has also been a shaman, a seer. 'Poets were specialists in liminality,' says Michael Dames in his book *Mythic Ireland*; 'they operated at the thresholds, between categories of space, time, or identity, in dangerous "frontier" conditions, among uncomfortable truths. These they shaped on behalf of the community.' He is speaking in the past tense, but perhaps this quality is especially important, if extremely rare, in our time – in a world of commercialisation that values the cerebral and the sound bite and what Robert Sheppard has called 'the poetry of the advertising agency'.

Having said that, even poets can't neglect *this* world; so poetry must also be, for me, in the loosest terms, political; it must question and challenge rather than simply uplift and soothe. It needs to take risks and to ask a reader to do the same. Becoming bigger only happens with a certain amount of struggle: 'the truth will set you free but first it will piss you off'.

In order to allow it to do that you have to be able to engage with it.

In the film 'Il Postino', an account of his European exile, the Chilean poet Pablo Neruda, when asked what poetry is, replies 'Metafore'. Metaphor is the core of poetry and in a way poetry is allegory: a way of telling something by means of something else; a fingerpost to another reality. We need to come away seeing with new eyes.

Of course there is also the sheer pleasure of the language and its aesthetics, and on a cerebral level I love linguistic skill and surprise. And I want to marvel at the shaping of the construction – without being distracted from what it might house. Some of the strongest poetry also employs the simplest language. The art of the poet is to employ uncluttered gleaming diction – simple but not facile.

It also appeals – or should appeal – to the ear: its rhythms and cadences, its patterns of consonants and vowels, its incantatory effects. Poetry is a way of making spells, of course; it's first cousin too to song and prayer and hymn, so it may also deliver a trance-like, spell-like state, taking us closer to the world of the imagination.

As we move forward through this new century it seems to me that it is time that poetry reclaim a synthesis of the heart and head; somewhat lost, for all the surprise and innovation brought by some aspects of postmodernism, in much contemporary work. And by 'heart' I don't mean sentimental or overt and unsubtle baring of personal angst. It's not easy to write poems that don't shy away from the feelings, but that do not slop over into mawkishness. And I want, dare I say it, soul. Seamus Heaney does it effortlessly and unselfconsciously:

> You are neither here nor there,
> A hurry through which known and strange things pass
> As big soft buffetings come at the car sideways
> And catch the heart off guard and blow it open.
>
> ('Postscript')

No explanation needed; no interpretation. We know what he's talking about even as we fail to articulate it in our common everyday language. Heaney embeds in this poem, too, strong images and a fluid musicality. (I recommend that you find and read the whole poem out loud; note the cadences, the risky and successful repetitions and near-repetitions, the reverberations of sounds. I suspect, though certainly he will work his poems, that the sense of rightness of those echoes and chimes inhabits him as naturally as breath.)

Imagery is the DNA of poetry; the primary building block. A good poet gives us the bones of the picture and lets us flesh it out. Here's John Burnside:

> alone in attic rooms
>   as spring begins:
> a rhythm in the light
>   a line of song
> the sudden taste of grass
>   high in the roof
> wind through the gaps in the beams
>   the rafters spiced
> with cumin
> and the aftertaste of nets.
>
> (from 'Settlements')

He puts us there in the salty gusty grassy attic, shifting light flickering on walls, a suggestion of journeys, a flavour of *temps perdu*, bittersweetness... What is the feeling tone of that excerpt? How does Burnside convey it? Not by telling us what to think or feel; but by letting light, song, grass, roof, wind, rafters, cumin and nets carry in their own reality the cargo of something else, something more human ('alone in attic rooms').

So let us have concrete detail. The life of objects is so much more effective than the use of abstract nouns: if you want us to feel joy, or lust, or loss, or grief then let us taste it, smell it, see it, inhabit it. Find something solid that will stand in for the abstraction.

Another of the ways in which a poem works is by setting up a resonance in the reader: 'Perhaps while looking for someone else,' says Jeannette Winterson, 'you might come across yourself unexpectedly, in a garden somewhere or on a mountain watching the rain.'

Good poems give something of themselves to you, whether or not you understand all the references or even all of the language, though the effort of working away at the poem will be repaid, and if the poem is sufficiently intriguing it may seduce you into researching. 'No one understands everything in a poem all at once,' says Ruth Padel. 'What matters is being open to some hook in it, a thought, image, feeling, turn of phrase or rhythm which feels important. When something in a poem starts mattering to you, the poem is doing what it was made to do, and you are beginning to make it yours. If it's a worthwhile poem, there will always be more to see in it.'[1]

Poetry that is linguistically too easy, too immediately understandable, exhausts itself in one go. This is one of those difficult balances: a poem, with patience, gives itself up gradually, but a reader needs to have enough of a glimpse through the doorway to be beguiled into wanting to push the door open, and allow that poem to go to work on him or her:

> ...So we are grasped by what we cannot grasp;
> it has its inner light, even from a distance –
>
> and changes us, even if we do not reach it,
> into something else, which, hardly sensing it, we already are.
> (Rainer Maria Rilke, 'A Walk', tr. Robert Bly)

In order to be so grasped, we should expect to have to work at some aspects of the poetry, including some of the vocabulary.

Too many poems are too easy, too trite, too banal, too spelt-out, leaving you nothing to work at, nothing to unpack or return to. Little originality, few surprises. A poem needs to resonate long after the first reading. These are the poems that remain with you, that revive themselves over and over in your feelings and imagination and memory. That doesn't mean to say they'll necessarily be easy poems.

One of the things that is important to me as a reader is a depth of psychological and emotional literacy in a poem. That of the intellect alone is not enough. Poetry is somewhere I go when I am looking to find the opposites reconciled: head *and* heart; material *and* metaphysical; language *and* content.

Other things I like: newness – of thought or of expression; preferably both. I love language and I love new and surprising diction, combinations and juxtapositions of phrases, contrasts and divergences, things left out, disruptions to the expected flow and rhythm, spaces and gaps, even fragmentation. In the workshops I run a common experience is that poems work better – or at least that the writers see new ways to go – after any or all of these interventions: cutting in half; starting somewhere else; avoiding neat endings; reading the poem from the bottom up; maybe turning it inside out by starting in the middle and reading a line at a time up and then down alternately; interleaving phrases from other poems of yours or of someone else's. It's the unexpected that so often lends potency. (And cutting, cutting, cutting again.)

But though I want to be surprised, something that feels contrived turns me off immediately. I don't want the poem to be exhibitionist and posey and lolling about and showing off. I want a poem with attitude but not necessarily inscrutable designer shades, labels and stick-on two-day stubble. I don't want to be distracted, either, by the poem's underwear showing; by which I mean that I don't want to have to grapple with a self-conscious structure or wildly in-your-face form; though I like poetry that takes risks and experiments with form, I don't want it to be at the cost of content. I don't want it to obtrude or be the whole point of the poem. I like to realise that something, for instance, is a modified sonnet only *after* the event, and be impressed all over again (for an example of what can be done with the sonnet form have a look, for instance, at the exploded sonnets of Colin Falck in *Post-Modern Love* [Stride]). That something is technically perfect or linguistically clever is not enough of a recommendation, either.

So I guess I also want subtlety. I might want to marvel at the architecture but I also want to go in and be impressed by the interior, to view the exhibition, to *dwell*. I want the infrastructure to be sound and innovative and challenging and permanent and impermanent all at once. I want views, I want to be invited to linger and discover new rooms and stairways and corners; and I want my poem, my dwelling, to be permeable, too, to let in the light as well as the darkness, to let in some of the wind and the smell of sea and birdsong and seasons. But I don't necessarily want games and shock tactics; I'm not sure I want my loo in the kitchen and my bed in the bath.

A poem, for me, needs to be a doorway into a country I've not yet seen, and yet which feels oddly familiar, rather like a love affair with a soulmate: *oh yes, there you are*. Or *yes, that's just how it is; only I couldn't have articulated it*. I want to be able to push open the door myself, but I don't want so many locks I need a hacksaw and oxyacetylene.

So it is important to work and rework our poems so that they are new, so that they surprise, without sacrificing the lifeblood of meaning, which gives them the power to convey value. Poems need shaping, containing. I'm loath to impose constraints of form, however, whether old or new, to the extent that the vehicle is more important than the driver or the destination; equally we need vehicles that are up to the demands of the 21st century and the contemporary terrain. To bend the metaphor, if I had to choose – and there are contemporary poets who won't agree with me – I'm more interested in whether I can cross the bridge than in its engineering, in as much as its function is lost if I can't get across. But I want the latter to be sound, unobtrusive, skilled; and is it too much to ask that it's also aesthetically pleasing, but not too tricksy?

So I'm back with synergy: vehicle *and* driver, journey *and* destination. As writers, if we want our readers to experience some newness of perception our efforts need to ensure that we work the form to carry the content as excitingly and synergistically as possible. Form and content need to work in tandem to sustain the creative tension.

Poetry is like a relationship: it may need to be worked at, yes. We may need to struggle with it, question it, meet it, be rebuffed and meet it again, win it over and be won by it. Like other things of value, it shouldn't have to give up its meaning immediately. A poem needs to promise more than it initially delivers; it needs to tantalise and seduce, it needs to give itself up a little at a time. I like its initial impact to be like a punch in the stomach that winds me; I want it to make the hairs on the back of my neck stand up. It should astonish me. It should sit and glimmer on the edges of my consciousness.

It needs to be many things at once for me. It needs to be inclusive not exclusive. It needs to be *of* life rather than above or beyond it. It needs to be a picture frame and the picture, a doorway and the landscape through the doorway, a set of Russian dolls, a hot air balloon, a diving suit, a microscope, a telescope, an interrogator, a bestower of blessings, both sacramental and wicked. It will be a lifeboat at times; it will always be a homeopathic dose. It needs to celebrate the life of the senses as well as the life of the heart and the spirit and soul. It needs to be somewhere I've never visited but always known, somewhere foreign and somewhere I can also imagine calling home. Norman MacCaig spoke of 'taking your mind a walk'. I'd like to suggest that what I require from a poem is that it takes the rest of me along, too.

I want it to reverberate beyond my intellect. I want to cohabit with it in some deeper, darker, altogether moister more fluid place than that of the analysing brain, a non-verbal place: the place in me that deals with love and birth and sex and loss and death, that watches trees grow, watches swallows return, watches people I love fall sick or suffer, struggles with relationship, understands about cycles and endings and beginnings. I want to wear it like a skin. I may not die from the lack of it in my life, but having met it I also know, like Adrienne Rich, that it's a means of saving your life.

Poetry is that
which arrives at the intellect
by way of the heart.
R S Thomas

What is called a poem is compounded perhaps of communication, invention, fecundation, discovery, production, creation. Through all the contention of intentions and motives a miracle has occurred. There is something new under the sun; being has emerged from nonbeing; a spring has bubbled out of a rock.
R D Laing

Poetry is… a form of magic, because it tries to change the way we perceive the world... Poetry... remystifies, allows the Edenic, unified view to be made briefly conscious... Poetry is the paradox of language turned against its own declared purpose, that of nailing down the human dream. Poets are therefore experts in the failure of language. Words fail us continually, as we search for them beyond the borders of speech, or drive them to the limit of their meaning and then beyond it.
Don Paterson

WHOLE FRAGMENTS

Baudelaire said that poets are the "universal translators", because they translate the language of the universe – stars, water, trees – into the language of humanity.
Lena Lowitz

There has been a subtle shift in the audience for poetry in the last half century. In England, at least, despite the fact that it seems that there are many more people writing poems now than at any time over the last forty years, ironically the audience for poetry seems to be shrinking, at least as regards the printed word. (Even more ironic, given that in popular culture both rap music and poetry slams have raised the profile of performance poetry.) Currently, poetry is given little space in bookshops, and almost none in even the broadsheet newspapers. Unless the poet is both popular and accessible, in the main the people who buy poetry books are poets themselves – and many of them don't.

Since the advent of modernism, which started the process of breaking apart the old formalism, and because poetry no longer occupies an important place in the school curriculum, many people are now anxious that they won't 'get it'; and this fear of not understanding acts as a barrier to trying. One of the reasons that those who don't read poetry don't, is because they fear that it will be difficult, obscure or irrelevant to their lives; and some poetry is, in truth. It is easy to get a sense that poetry is for the linguistically-sophisticated élite.

There again, a lot of what passes for poetry is trite, trivial and poorly-made. Poetry, like anything else of value, is a skill that needs learning.

My own conversation with myself, and with other practising poets as well as readers, on poetry, and its value and place in the cultural life of a society, continues. As long as this conversation continues it will, it seems to me, be nourishing and creative. (Similarly, no creative act – such as a poem – is ever entirely finished: as long as people bring their thoughts, responses and questions to it, it will continue to live, to breathe and to change. A poem will never be a fixed truth, though it will remain, as Seamus Heaney has said, a consistent 'teller of truth'.)

Here, as a kind of addendum to 'Wrestling with a God: Making Poems', are a few of my current thoughts, interleaved with others', about this whole crazy business of poetry, and why and how it matters; as well as reflections on how to approach it as both writer and reader.

So, firstly, I'm back with the question of what poetry is *for*. Since I explore this at length in 'Wrestling with a God', I'm only going to use as a yardstick here something Ruth Padel says in her *52 Ways Of Looking At A Poem*.[1]

Padel quotes Patsy Rodenburg, who works at the National Theatre in London, talking about teaching Shakespeare in New York: 'They were yearning for profound work, because you can go to great plays and not feel so lonely. I did *Richard 111, Julius Caesar*, plays full of envy, grief, murder, horror; plays about what they were facing in their city and the world outside... what's comforting is that it has happened before...'

So through our awareness that others have been there before, poetry can help us 'not feel so lonely'. Such patterning of words, she suggests, as well as the structuring of thought, echoes, validates and makes universal your own feelings; it may also heal. In the same piece Padel quotes Iris Murdoch: 'art should not console', but goes on to say that sometimes it is the only thing that *can* console; and it is true that people often turn to poetry, whether as reader or writer, in a crisis. Poetry allows us to swim into and under all aspects of human experience, and to deepen, re-imagine and re-experience our experience of our humanness, our commonality. 'When you read a great poem', says John O'Donohue, 'it reaches deep into regions of your life and memory and reverberates back to you forgotten or invisible regions of your experience. In a great poem you find again lost or silent territories of feeling or thought which were out of your reach. A poem can travel far into your depth to retrieve your neglected longing.'[2]

But it's not just about empathy, consolation and comfort, of course. Sometimes it's about waking up. 'One should only read books which bite and sting one,' stated Kafka. Good poetry raises questions. 'Poetry is a place where all the fundamental questions are asked about the human condition', said Charles Simic. It is, as in everything, the asking that's important; the willingness to sit and question, and then to listen. And to carry on sitting. 'Poetry doesn't give answers,' writes Neil Astley; 'but it engages readers intellectually and emotionally'[3] – so that hopefully they carry on asking the questions.

Another reason for the existence of poetry is to do with finding new ways to look at 'old' – i.e. universally recurring – situations; ways of re-visioning our world/worlds.

While it may be true that often the most profound subjects are most moving when spoken of simply, our sophisticated – or maybe overworked, dulled and desensitised – tastes, as well as the sheer quantity of media stimulus available to us all, all of the time, mean that perhaps we can no longer rely, in our writing of poetry, on a simplicity of form, a transparency of subject and an over-accessibility of language.

This doesn't mean to say, though, that we have necessarily to keep finding new and ever more obscure subject matter. 'The stuff of poetry is commonplace,' says David Constantine, 'the commonplace, what lies everywhere. At first a reader may not recognise this commonness, because it is the business of poetry to defamiliarise it. Becoming too familiar with the commonplace we may not be touched and moved by it. Poetry defamiliarises and revitalises what is in large measure common experience, recognisable by all.'[4]

It is a truism that there is nothing new to write; only new ways of writing. In modernism and post-modernism the creation of the new has been a priority. Constantine again: 'Yet many writers will have had the feeling... that they are, as they compose, after something which is [already] *there*; that the fiddling around with words, the arriving at a syntax, the act of uncovering, is the bringing out of something which pre-exists their particular project, is in fact *inventio*.' ('In the older poetics, a large section used to be given over to what was called *inventio*, which had a different meaning from our derived word "invention". *Inventio* meant not making up but actually finding, finding something that was there to be found...')

So the question is: whatever our subject matter or starting point, how can we now write in a way that is fresh, surprising and rich? How can we make poems that are alive enough as for a modern audience to want to engage and make a relationship with them? How can we find a way, via the 'pattern and music, song and flickering images, associative links that make poetry... to emulate, deal with and respond to the complexity and chaos of modern life without tidying it all into a final line or answer', to quote Rupert Loydell? (See also Rupert's piece 'The Unsettling of Language'.)

So maybe what we are striving for is to find a way to enable others to see with 'new eyes' – to revision the world, to come at a familiar experience from an unfamiliar direction. We as writers need, before we can achieve this in our own work, to bring new eyes and ears to the way we read and hear poetry. We need to be open to new ways, to be willing to be startled and astonished.

One of the challenges for contemporary poets is that, apart from other poets, the potential book-buying audience for poetry – as opposed to audiences for performance poetry – is still often comprised of people who were reared on poetry from the eighteenth, nineteenth and early twentieth centuries, where rhyme and metre were strongly prevalent. Ironically, this is also true of people who *aren't* poetry audiences: people young enough to have come into contact with postmodern thinking at college or university but who, having not read English at tertiary level, or through uninspiring teachers and/or a diminished poetry curriculum at secondary level, have no sense of the evolution of poetry, let alone its relevance to their lives; too often, their acquaintance with poetry has also been confined to classroom lessons on the *de rigueur* long-dead Greats.

Neil Astley, editor of the anthology *Staying Alive,* suggests that the audience for poetry was falling away already in the first part of the twentieth century. He attributes this to the then modern poets losing touch with their audience: 'Influenced by the experiments of Symbolism, the innovative Modernist poets of the early 20th century rejected traditional forms and realism as well as consensus between author and reader, producing highly complex work in response to an awareness, prompted by Freud, Jung and others, of the unconscious and the irrational.' Poetry has changed in a hundred years; audiences, however, are still catching up.

In a stimulating essay, Stephen Burt[5] explores the history of poetry in the late twentieth century. I want to paraphrase here, somewhat simplistically, his description of the state of poetry in the early twenty-first century.

Between about 1970 and 1985, there were two strong streams of poetry – and of course many and varied tributaries – coming out of the USA. (Clearly there was actually a multiplicity of poetries, each with its own creative, political and social agenda; but for the sake of simplicity I'm looking at two formative approaches.) These bodies of work have had a profound influence on contemporary European poetry.

The first was an accessible kind of poetry, often written in a personal and/or confessional language (e.g. Robert Lowell). Accessible poetry too was associated with the rise of feminism (e.g. Adrienne Rich). This kind of personal and/or political poetry explored and was grounded too in changing social mores: the new attitudes to love and sexuality, and also anti-war, black and gay politics. This poetry, building on but also disrupting the formalism and then modernism (e.g. T S Eliot and W C Williams) of the first half of the century, was championed and taught within the increasingly-common creative writing programmes in colleges.

Against this flow were the poets who preferred their poetry to be less overt, less 'naked', as Burt says: more oblique and challenging, not didactic. One of the most influential movements here was the 'Language' school of poetry (e.g. Charles Bernstein). Though this poetry included divergent voices and styles, what they had in common was a mistrust of 'easy epiphanies, the focus on personality and emotions, and the storytelling that (in their view) made so much sixties poetry (especially protest poetry) complicit with the social order it hoped to oppose. Some of these poets' academic champions liked that argument (others just liked very difficult poems).'

Burt goes on to describe how European theorists like Foucault and Derrida took the place traditionally filled by modern poets at the heart of many English departments, and this input started to influence poetic thinking, reinforcing the Language terrain. Innovative work appeared that upturned the way poetry had been made previously, and challenged its accepted function. (Throughout the history of poetry, of course, there have been innovations; and also poetry has often been anarchic and anti-establishment, occupying the territory of iconoclasm, challenging the norm. But Language poetry pushed this further, arguably, than has been seen before.)

This movement was about the fundamental uses and construction of language itself, and was (and continues to be) as terrifyingly cerebral and inaccessible to some as it is exciting to others.

Then the New Formalists in the'80s reclaimed lost territories of accessibility.

In response to all this, there was yet another upsurge: '(S)ome students sought something new – something more open to personal emotion, to story and feeling, than language poetry, but more complicated intellectually than most of the creative writing programs' poets allowed'. (This also raises a question about how poetry is taught, or disseminated. Ann Lauterbach[6]: 'As long as teachers think poems have to be translated, students will be fearful that they don't have access to the "right" language.' Poetry, she suggests, needs to be taught in such a way as to encourage students to become excited about the existence and use of language *per se*, in its own right. 'The logic of poetry is not the same as the logic of a story or newspaper article,' she continues. 'Poetry is often as much about the way language works – rhythms and sounds and syntax, musical rather than pictorial values – as it is "about" a given subject. The meanings which come to a poem are often just at the intersection between these elements.')

Somewhere with a foot in both the streams I describe above were, and still are, poets who blend the flavours of these differing approaches with their own particular and identifiable voices; and in their work the streams seem to successfully interflow. I would name, amongst others, John Ashbery here, Charles Wright, and Jorie Graham.

One of the innovations of the Language School's approach to poetry was reader empowerment. A Language poem – and by extension any poem that is less than transparent – through its non-prescriptive opacity, offers an invitation to the reader to co-create the poem. 'Some poems are more difficult than others,' says Lauterbach, 'but then, some experiences are too. It isn't the worst thing in the world to be confused, if the confusion is honest – that is, I don't set out to write poems that are difficult or confusing. I like to provoke; I want my poems to give people permission to think for themselves, on the one hand, and to be deeply responsive, on the other.'

Another important aspect that Language poetry addresses is that of questioning how we use language: its fluid nature, and the assumptions we bring as speakers, listeners, readers and writers. Language poets object to the easily-comprehensible more traditional narrative and personal lyric poetry on various grounds: two of the most obvious being that it offers nothing new; and also, as above, that, rather than challenging our ways of perceiving, it reinforces an entrenched, conventional and unsurprising poetic and political viewpoint whose relevance has passed.

For many people, however, Language poetry seems sometimes so inaccessible and conceptually abstract as to appear empty and virtually meaningless; these people are turned away from poetry at the threshold.

Phew. Where now? Is there, then, a way of drawing from both wells: that of the lyric/personal inward-turning poem, and that of the less figurative, and more outward-looking? Can we find ways to draw the reader in while still bringing innovation to our work?

In music, fusion is current. Borders are blurred; seemingly incompatible styles are combined to fruitful and synergistic effect, new possibilities are born.

Maybe the new poetry requires a both/and approach. Maybe syntax is disrupted, and then recombined. Maybe form is exploded and allowed to find new shape. Maybe it is possible to combine the surprising with the lyrical; the personal with the extra-personal; the surreal with the real; the imaginative with the experiential; the open with the oblique; the simple with the experimental. Maybe our palette is richer than it's ever been.

And that, I would suggest, is where we are now: looking for poetry that reflects our current perceptions of the whole human situation, with all its complexities, strangenesses, fragmentations and dilemmas; work that intrigues and moves a reader to engage and re-engage with a poem, and thereby with the world, as well as with him or herself; pieces that require readers to meet them halfway and do some of the work themselves; poems that survey the outer world and are also capable of travelling far enough into our interior worlds as to take up permanent residence, inhabit us.

Yet, like all the arts, poetry is alive sometimes *despite,* rather than because of, our interventions. It may lend itself to looking deeply, but it doesn't lend itself to analysis, other than of its outward technical form, without losing its mystery; it is peopled with shadowy figures and fragments of stories we only dimly perceive. As writers, often we do not know what we're going to say until we've said it; and we may be as astonished as anyone at the words that fall onto the page. Issuing as it does initially at least from the right brain, poetry will, if it's any good, continue to surprise us, and thwart our efforts to understand and order it. That's how it should be.

As for why it matters, if you read and/or write poetry yourself, you will already know. If you need convincing, then I would suggest that poetry exists partly as a kind of mapmaking tool: to attempt to chart what is not easily otherwise chartable; to make some kind of sense from what is not readily ordered; to make a language that speaks to more than the intellect; to find a way to say that which is not otherwise sayable; to speak for the voices which otherwise can't. Also to make a conduit, keep a doorway open, keep a room free for the uninvited, always present and often invisible guests.

Starting points

Commit yourself to taking time out for reading, *really* reading, slowly and with immersion, poetry new to you this week. If you don't already, subscribe to one or more poetry magazines, and go out and buy, or order from your library, some contemporary poets, including poetry in translation.[7]

...I have come to believe in the notion of whole fragments: pieces of experience, or language, which are understandable and complete in themselves, but which don't necessarily link up with or to a Big Truth or Story or Conclusion. I think our real lives are made up of just such discontinuous fragments – a cup of coffee, the sight of a cardinal [bird] in a tree, a kiss, a poem, a scrap of overheard conversation, an image from an ad on TV, an article about Rwanda....
Ann Lauterbach

Poets try to cut the line of a poem so that it lives and dances as itself. Poems are some of the most amazing presences in the world. I am always astounded that poems are willing to lie down and sleep inside the flat, closed pages of a book. If poems behaved according to their essence, they would be out dancing on the seashore or flying to the heavens or trying to rinse out the secrets of the mountains.
John O'Donohue

WHAT I LOOK FOR IN POETRY

Below is a summary of some of the criteria I have mentioned which I apply, more or less consciously, when I'm reading a poem. I'm told it's a somewhat daunting list, so perhaps I should say that these are just guidelines; a map which helps keep me on track in my own writing.

General

1

The *feeling tone*: I want heart as well as head in a poem. But I don't want sentimentality. I want it to have, and come from, soul.

I also want to feel it in my body, simultaneously with or even before my intellect's appreciation of the language and techniques.

I want to be drawn in by it, moved and changed by it, if only a little; I want to be engaged with it, to have my insight and experience deepened by it.

2

I want *authenticity*: I want to have a sense that the poet is writing from within the poem, rather than about something from the outside; I want to *feel* that poet's experience and imagination at work like yeast.

3

I want it to go *further and deeper* than just a poem about, say, landscape. I want to learn something from it, be changed by it.

4

I want it to convey something of the *universal within the personal*: I want both speaker and world present (Wendell Berry).

5

I'm 'looking for *enormity in the very small*' (Michael Cunningham, author of *The Hours*, on Virginia Woolf's writing).

Specific

1

I want *subtlety and depth.*

2

I want *rhythm and cadence and musicality.*

3

I want *colour, imagery, simile, metaphor, sensory detail.*

4

I want the *concrete world to convey the abstract.*

5

I want good use of *patterning:* to both eye and ear, on page, in phrasing. This includes use of space, as well as appropriate line and stanza breaks.

6

I want good use of *sounds:* alliteration, assonance and chiming words and patterns.

7

The sticky issue of *rhyme:* many people who feel alienated from today's poetry cite as one reason the fact that 'it doesn't rhyme'. The truth is that much poetry does in fact rhyme, but it may not use end-rhyme. Ruth Padel points out that classical Greek and Latin poetry (before the late classical and early mediaeval times) didn't rhyme – Homer didn't rhyme; and Shakespeare and Milton both wrote a great deal of poetry and drama, or poetry within drama, which didn't rhyme either; or at least, didn't use end-rhyme. Padel says: 'Asking a poet "Do you use rhyme?" is like asking a painter if he or she uses white paint: the paint you mix with every colour. You may not see white on the canvas, but it is there...' If the poet is successful, the sound-relationships within the poem are so closely interwoven with what is being said that each is integral to the other.

Certainly I prefer *near- and internal rhyme to full end-rhyme,* unless the form specifically requires the latter.

8

I want *imagination and originality and surprise; obliquity rather than linear narrative; leaps and jumps.* I want to be stretched.

9

Diction: *strong precise surprising words, and concision.* Poetry's partly about how few words you need rather than how many. A surprise to many people is that adjectives, by making poetry sound 'over-poetic', can too often weaken rather than strengthen a piece; the same goes for adverbs. I particularly notice good use of verbs. I *don't* want archaisms, clichés, tortuous inversions of language to fit the form.

10

I am not personally keen on traditional metrical forms, but I like to know that the poet knows about them.

11

I want a *fluid and dynamic movement* through and development within the poem.

12

Closure: I like *subtlety; a little tweak of surprise and pleasure rather than a fist of a punch line.*

And more

Read the poem aloud
Don't lose any opportunity to fine-tune the diction, refine the language
Consider re-ordering the lines
Most poets need to cut, cut, cut
When you think a poem's finished, take it a little further, a little deeper.

You ask if your verses are good... You send them to journals. You compare them with other poems, and you are troubled when certain editors reject your efforts. Now... I beg you to give all that up. You are looking outwards, and of all things that is what you must now not do. Nobody can advise and help you, nobody. There is only one single means. Go inside yourself. Discover the motive that bids you write; examine whether it sends its roots down to the deepest places of your heart, confess to yourself whether you would have to die if writing were denied you...

Rainer Maria Rilke

THE UNSETTLING OF LANGUAGE
BY RUPERT LOYDELL

Most of us, when we start writing, engage with our words as a way of self-expression: writing about what we feel, what we see around us, trying to make sense of the world. Later, most of us also ultimately experience some disillusionment with this way of writing – it simply doesn't go far enough – and have to find a way to resolve this problem for ourselves.

Andrew Duncan in his *The Failure of Conservatism in Modern British Poetry*[1] puts it this way:

> 'After working on one's poetry for several years, it is normal for the primitive autobiographical drive to come to an end. At this point you have the time to devise new ways of working: a new generator of the unpredictable is needed, and this is supplied by chance or indeterminate procedures, combined with rules chosen to generate new decisions...'

For me, the end of my 'autobiographical drive' came with a realisation – through dialogue with other poets, and the reading of new poetry and poetics – that the changing world around us meant I needed to find new ways of writing. It came with the realisation that we simply *can't* carry on writing the same sorts of things in the same sorts of ways as people have before us, because the way we 'see' things, what we 'feel' about things, has changed.

It's important, too, to recognise that just because something is 'genuine' or 'real' or even utterly heartfelt doesn't mean it makes a good poem. Poetry isn't just about biography or experience, it's also about language and – if you want – some notion of 'truth'. But truth isn't the same as experience or narrative, story or epiphany.

I've been reading some postmodern theology (Richard Holloway & Don Cupitt), and they point out that we humans are always slow to change, seem to be conservative by nature. We wanted the earth to stay at the centre of the universe, just as earlier we wanted the earth to be flat, and we're the same with language and psychology/philosophy. We now know that we don't think in narrative and neat order; instead we have ideas of rhizomes, fragments and cut-ups – chains of interlinked narratives – as a metaphor for the way we live. We know that to some extent we invent and reinvent the world through our language, and that language doesn't just 'equal' an object. Previously, photography and then film changed the arts; now science is having an effect.

So it's very difficult to make poetry in the same way as previous generations of writers because we understand the world in different ways from them. Well-worn images – like sunlight, or the blur of a bird's wing, for instance – can't carry what poetry needs any more, because we now understand these ideas differently. We know about chaos theory, we know about fractals, light/heat; the ozone layer; the time that sunlight takes to reach us, and the red/blue shifts involved.

We can seek solace in old-fashioned and traditional ways of writing – the familiar is always more comfortable – but I don't believe it can work anymore. We need new, complex ways of writing because we know this is a complex, changing world. We know, for instance, that we are media-led. We know that in England we are prone to romanticising the countryside, desiring a picturesque landscape with cows and green fields. Life isn't like that, though; it's about food chains, nature 'red in tooth and claw' and urban development; transience, change, secularisation. How can we mirror this more recent picture of our world in our poetry?

The exercises below are some of the ways I've found to try and represent, to write about, the complexity of the world we inhabit. They are only ways to write or make you think about writing, and like all processes they may or may not turn out useful to you. The poems that may or may not come out of these exercises still need shaping and editing, finishing and revising – but try and leave some of the awkward bumps in them rather than iron them flat. Syntactical jumps, mixed voices, new and sometimes strange ideas and images are often more interesting than the norm. Don't worry that poems written using such processes somehow take away 'your' voice – the poet's voice always shines through (and besides are you interested in the poem or yourself as poet?). And don't forget to allow your reader to construct the poem for themselves, or with you. The age of poems that dictate Truth or Fact has gone.

For myself I want poems that ask more questions than offer answers, poets who facilitate a way through unreason and uncertainty, disbelief and doubt. I'm not alone: poet/critic Charles Bernstein, in his book *My Way*[2], suggests that 'Poetry is turbulent thought, at least that's what I want from it. It leaves things unsettled, unresolved – leaves you knowing less than you did when you started.'

Here are some workshops to help you get things unsettled:

1

a) Find the last 12 poems you have written with twelve lines or more in it.

b) Use the first line of each poem to make a new 12 line poem, the second line of each to make another, and so on, until you have a set of a dozen twelve-line poems. Treat these as draft poems: revise, rework and edit them into something new. Try to keep some of the awkwardness and surprises in them though, don't try to smooth the poems out too much.

Have a look at Ted Berrigan's *Sonnets* where the author used this idea.

2

a) Stretch out a poem so it has a line gap between each of the lines and write lines that fill the gaps.

b) Make that a finished poem.

c) Also take the new lines you've written out again and work them into a finished poem, or stretch them out and write another one.

3

a) Take some novels or non-fiction books from your shelf and quickly skim through and write down 20 questions you find there, leaving a gap between each one.

b) Now open the books again, stick your finger in and write down a phrase as an answer to each question in turn.

c) Now revise, title and edit to finish your poem.

Here's a poem of mine that came out of this workshop method:

Conversation

Why insist on the word poetry?
It is the simplest thing in the world.

What have you invented?
It is made up of borrowings and collages.

Is this how chance must be defined?
There are accidents always and everywhere.

Form is unique, it does not repeat itself?
I hope to let words exist without thinking about them.

What kind of audible results will be produced?
The air is filled with music we cannot hear.

How is sound dispersed?
In nature, at every moment, there is amplification.

What is this movement into the air?
Circles of sound, laughter, and language.

Who speaks in your inner chambers?
I prefer the notion of conversation.

What 'other' are you talking about?
A stranger at the natural limit of our vision.

Where does devotion come from?
From trying to find the point of balance.

Do you suppose that tranquility exists?
That's what the nothing in between is.

What is the name of the noise of rain?
We no longer know the exact definition of sadness.

Rupert Loydell[3]

A poem is not a puzzle to be solved. A poem is an experience, an event, in and of language. It should be approached as such...
Ann Lauterbach

Do not forget that a poem, even though it is composed in the language of information, is not used in the language-game of information.
Wittgenstein

Art is even more than ideas. Art is the exploration of ideas... (A)rt is best at work when it's being prickly, querulous, and hostile to complacency of thought.
Janice Galloway

LAKES AND RIVERS
FORM AND FREE VERSE

The cadences of spoken English lend themselves most naturally to iambic pentameter, which is a line of five 'beats' of two syllables each, unstressed and then stressed respectively ('I'd like a pound of ripe tomatoes please,'). So even 'ordinary' prose has a rhythm, albeit patchy.

The movement from prose to poetry is a continuum. If prose is a relaxed muscle, then contracting that muscle a little will give us the prose poem, which blends the fluidity and unconstrained nature of prose with the tautness of poetry. Contract it still further and you have free verse; tighten it just a little more and you have metrical form. Each has its merits; each its *aficionados*.

Despite the fact that the concept of free verse has been with us since the late nineteenth century, there are many people who still feel that unless a poem scans in a predictable way and uses end-rhyme, it is not a true poem. In the same way as some people whose preferred music is folk or pre-twentieth-century classical might initially find jazz improvisation difficult to comprehend or relate to, some brought up on the notion that what makes poetry poetry is its strong metrical shape and end-rhyme feel at sea with free verse. 'But what makes it poetry?' is a common question. Others feel that anything with a consistent rhythm and rhyme pattern is invariably doggerel. What's going on?

Well, as I've explored already, poetry has undergone a number of shifts in the last century or so. The introduction of the concept of *vers libre*, pioneered by poets such as Baudelaire, Rimbaud and Mallarmé, and championed later by writers such as T S Eliot, was an important watershed. Vers libre, or free verse, was introduced in rebellion against the formal constraints of classical verse, which was seen as too narrow. (Free verse is not, as many people think, blank verse, by the way. Much of Shakespeare's work was written in blank verse: that is iambic pentameter without end-rhyme.)

Poetry is first and foremost a kind of music, and its lyrical qualities are defining features. This is one of the reasons why we don't have to understand a poem intellectually to be affected emotionally by it (the other major reason being to do with use of imagery, particularly archetypal images, which create pictures in the imagination, and thus an instinctual or emotional response [or both]). As in music, too, it happens that often the best improvisers – free verse writers – have a grounding in classical form, so that at least they can consciously choose to depart from it – and know what they're departing from.

Previously, of course, poetry's long history was oral; within the body of the poem, or ballad, or epic, was contained not only a tribe or society's history, but also its wisdom. Poetry was a kind of mnemonic: a strong metre and a memorable rhyme scheme ensured that the content was preserved.

With the Classical period, as the writing – as opposed to reciting – of poetry became more widespread, came a further sophistication of and emphasis on form and formalism: using ordered formal structures to carry over-arching ideas. I think of this period as Apollonian: grounded in the intellect. The Romantic period following was more Dionysian, with its freer, feeling-based more personal subject matter, often drawing on the natural world. Both of these traditions underpin our current views of poetry; both of them are valid; and there is still some creative tension between them.

Writing to a proscribed form, such as the sonnet or the villanelle, is undoubtedly difficult. It's hard to find a marriage between the container and the content, so that the former does not intrude. In the hands of an amateur, the classical forms can be dire – clumsy rhymes, awkward inversions and more archaisms than raisins in a fruit cake. In the lake of form, any depth of water, of meaning, simply evaporates. In the hands of someone like Seamus Heaney, by contrast, the frame or boundaries of the sonnet, for instance, exists to enhance the beauty of what is within. Form, used well, can be very liberating.

So if it's hard to write well within the constraints of classical metre and rhyme, that is not to say that free verse is any easier. In fact, in some ways, it's more challenging to write a good poem in free verse than a sonnet. A good free verse poem is not, contrary to populist belief, simply chopped-up prose. If you were to try to lay it out again as a prose passage, it would lose something vital.

Rather than add to the numerous books that address poetic form, here I want to look at the tools of free verse.

Clearly many of the devices used to make a poem hang together are common to both free and formal poetry. The main differences are to do with a reversal in emphasis. Where form is underpinned by a structure of consistent occurrences of rhythm and stress or syllable count, free verse is marked by an absence of these things.

Where formal verse generally uses end-rhyme, free verse generally doesn't. (Free verse does also use rhyme, but rather in the shape of echoes and chiming sounds. Internal rhymes are central to free verse. When end words that rhyme, or 'ghost' each other using near-rhyme, appear in free verse they won't be used in a consistent and regular scheme.)

Where stanzas are neatly shaped in formal verse, in free verse they may be ragged.

What this means in practice is that in free verse the other devices used in poetry have to work harder to tie the poem together.

Free verse does, in fact, have rhythm; it is just not a regular one. Patterning, both of sound and of layout, is connective tissue. Repetition can be very effective, too, as long as it's conscious rather than careless.

Alliteration and assonance are crucial ingredients, as are the usual components of imagery and sensory detail, and metaphor and simile.

Diction is important in that it needs to 'fit' or to be used quite consciously for effect if it doesn't fit. Vocabulary needs, as in all poetry, to be carefully chosen for effect: it can be surprising, precise, unusual, apposite and simple simultaneously.

Choices about line length and line and stanza breaks have to be made with care. Where a line ends will shed light on the emphases the writer intends by throwing weight on to the ending word, and also on to the starting word of the next line. It will also indicate or underline the emotional tone of the poem – short jerky lines with hard sounds will convey a very different feel to long languid lines with soft sounds. Most of us will use these mirrors unconsciously to suit the subject matter, but an awareness of the choices available may make the poem stronger.

The page, the white space around the poem, in my view is another aspect of the piece – both component and punctuation; how the poem looks visually is a clue to the weight of the poem and its flavour.

The use of punctuation and capital initials is a sticky area, and each poet has her own way of dealing with this. For myself, the poem itself determines how I punctuate, but most frequently I use as little punctuation as possible, allowing once again things like line breaks to do that work. I do usually punctuate within a line if the sense demands it, however. For me, punctuation and capitals work in tandem; if I were to write a poem with absolutely no punctuation I would probably also use no capitals. But generally I would use capital initials at the beginning of a poem, or after a full stop, and for proper nouns; but to my eye capitals at the beginning of every line simply do not look right in anything other than strictly-punctuated formal verse. But these are not 'rules', just opinions.

Flabbiness in free verse is as unacceptable as in form; but a bigger danger because you are not continuously counting syllables, stresses or feet and therefore the tendency to sprawl is greater. As always, 'less is more'. Poetry, like so many other things, can be a great way of remembering how little one needs, rather than how much!

Thinking about this notion of less being more, another issue is that of 'accessibility'. There are those who feel that poems should carry clear messages and meaning; there are those who prefer their poetry not to 'make sense' in the conventional way, but to challenge the way we use language. My own view is a 'both/and' rather than 'either/or'. Poet Ruth Fainlight says: 'Sometimes I do not understand the meaning of one of my own poems until years later. I want my poems to be clear – BUT – poetry is not primarily merely another method for conveying a message: the music of the words, their sound and rhythm – the language – is what makes a poem.'

I've said already that it is not necessary to 'understand' a poem intellectually to feel the force of it. We're not looking for information when we read a poem. All literature is arrangements of words, and yet the art, the task, of poetry is unique. We don't go to it for the same reason as we go to a newspaper, or a non-fiction book; probably not even for the reasons we read novels or watch plays. We don't go to it in the same way, either. Some things are better approached side-on, where they are allowed to give up their meaning slowly, so to speak.

Symbols are like this. And inasmuch as poems are symbols, as much as they stand in for something else, as all language does (an attempt to convey the ultimately unconveyable) – for lived experience, for imagined experience, for that towards which the poem gestures – they too are stronger, usually, for being oblique rather than direct. When I read – or write – a poem I expect, indeed want, to have to work at it a little. It's a two-way process – the poem approaches me and I approach it. Between us, at the cusp, there is a little seam of energy, a little fire-rip band, like a lit trail of petrol.

If the poem gives itself up at the first reading, and subsequent readings offer nothing more, for me that poem has failed. Yet it is for that same reason that so many people say they find poetry 'difficult', or 'inaccessible'.

Why should poetry be easy? A poem is not an essay. Its terrain is different, its syntax is different, it may challenge intellectually or emotionally. It works partly through what it leaves out. Our expectations of it are different. It's an acquired taste. And yet many people don't expect to have to learn its unique language or diction. Why is it not OK to have a do a bit of the work ourselves? Is it because we live in a 'sound bite' culture? Because we are used to being fed our knowledge? Because the media and our new technologies make everything so fast, so accessible that we are impatient, that we have minuscule attention spans, that we've become lazy?

It's easy to write a transparent poem – and to be fair there are times and circumstances when that is appropriate. It's less easy to write an oblique poem that is not contrived or pretentious, and that is seductive enough for a reader to want to work at it.

I don't find obliquity easy myself. But I do often use the device of apparently writing about one thing, which uncovers another in the gaps. How do we move towards something more impressionistic, less direct? I guess the easiest way is simply to think metaphorically. What are you really writing about? What vehicle would carry that best? One way, if you are wedded to meaning and sense, is to start by using one central metaphor:

Navigation

Riding the back of the Tamar
our keel cutting clean,
waves peeling away to the margins,
narrow channel, silver
among silvered mud,
hoisting the jib, rope snaking
past our feet, creak of breeze,
the deck tilting
between red and green lights,
Navy flotilla, open sea ahead.

Everywhere the world gives voice
unreservedly, over and over:
day crawling up the sky,
the lights of Saltash
multiplied and returned from water,
taste of light rain and saltspray,
that flock of squeaking titmice
shimmying in the pines
we left behind,
tea in this red plastic mug.

The sun, still rising.
What we need is faith,
a good wind,
a few kind words.

Roselle Angwin[1]

The language and syntax in this poem are straightforward. It is an 'easy' poem. But it can also be read on more than one level; for it is not, of course, really, or just, about sailing. I hope the last line would be the giveaway that would tempt you back into reading the poem again. The poem is about relationship, its difficulties ('navigation', the narrow channel between mud banks, the red and green lights, the Navy as a symbol for warring or peacekeeping forces [depending on your viewpoint], the uncharted sea ahead, the faith we need). It's also a poem about the low-key everyday details, the easily-overlooked reasons for gratitude, and too the perennial nature of relationship – the fact that the world still keeps turning, the sun still rises. So the poem has a bifocal awareness: the flatter straightforward detailing tone of the first stanza is brought into balance by the more celebratory tone of the second, and then the poem's real agenda is released at the end.

There's also another subtext, which comes, for me, from my Buddhist practice. Like the rope ('sheet', if you're nautical) snaking – in actuality it tears through your hands and you risk rope-burn, which is a good metaphor for me – I can lose myself in anxiety, once I have an idea in my head. Life pours, or burns, through my hands without my even being aware of it. Worries about the future or regrets about the past spin us out of the only time we actually have – the present. The poem, taken as a whole, is also about celebrating the 'now', this unique and passing moment, as a way of bringing me back, keeping me present with how things actually are. There's so much, every moment, to be grateful for, and it's so easy to slide into a mindset of noticing what's wrong and forgetting all the things that are right – with relationship, with life.

The poem started, for me, with the last line – a phrase that repeated itself in my head; but I didn't want to write a lecture on kindness. How might I carry what I wanted to say?

As it happens, a strong undertow in many of my poems is the sea, or water: I was brought up on the coast. Water too in some schools of thought and traditions symbolises the feeling nature. So to speak of relationship through these images was natural for me.

Starting points:

1

Have a look back at 'Navigation', above. Read it aloud. Within this poem are a number of poetic devices. You will see that the flow of the words and lines echoes the sailing theme. Each of those two main stanzas consists of one long sentence. This helps to keep a fluid movement. I particularly use assonance, and alliteration figures strongly too. Because of this there are a number of internal rhyming sounds: in that first stanza for instance, are a lot of 'c' or 'k' sounds, and the chimes of 'keel', 'clean', 'peeling', 'feet', 'creak', 'breeze', 'green', 'sea'. Then there are a number of 'a' sounds and 'i' sounds, too. There were decisions I made about line and stanza breaks, and verb choices. Some of these were unconscious; some were deliberate, building on patterns that were starting to emerge. Each of the stanzas has its own related but different tone and emotional quality.

2

Next time you are about to write a poem, reflect first:

What are you really wanting to write about?
   Brainstorm the comparisons/images that come into your head
   What would make the best sustained metaphor for the situation you want
   to address?

Note that it may not be the most obvious. My poem, above, could have been stronger had I used a more oblique kind of metaphor, and a more sophisticated approach. How might you write it?

It may be worth spending time thinking about all this before you begin writing a poem; or maybe, like me, you don't know what the metaphor will be or where the piece of writing is going before you've written it. In which case, do the first redraft with these thoughts specifically in mind, and consciously leave out the more obvious statements, restatements or comparisons that you make. Is the poem stronger for saying less?

THE PEARL FROM THE GRAVEL
STARTING TO SHAPE A POEM - BY KENNETH STEVEN

When a poem is born it will often be like a battlefield; it may pour out like an overturned jar of ink, fragments of ideas, notes, images and phrases tumbling and jumbled. This is how it should be – the subconscious isn't going to serve up something neat and polished as a school essay. That may take several drafts.

Often the unborn poem will kick at head and heart, eager to be listened to, and then it's time to hide away, to find cloistered space where the words may flow from the pen with as little interference as possible from the editor within. Allow the subconscious to deliver something precious. Work somewhere which, even for a time, is yours and yours alone. It's vital to claim this creative space as often as possible. You want to reach the part of you that normally lies dormant during the busyness of the day; you have to get as close to dream-time as possible. Both when writing and rewriting, give yourself time to descend into the chambers of the subconscious, to the place where the pen flows freely. And take your time 'returning': don't hurry back from silence.

Then leave the battlefield to cool – don't be in too much of a hurry to shape those ideas.

When you come back to that first outpouring, hours, days or even weeks later, listen to what it's trying to be. Read the passage aloud – not once but several times. I see every poem as a separate globe of sound, and that umbilical between sound and sense is of paramount importance.

You'll see the dross at once; strike out whatever is definitely chaff to clear the space for what is important. Be utterly honest with yourself about what works and what doesn't work; what is verging on cliché and what is less than original. No one has ever seen the world through your eyes before – let your imagination shape something startling and new; resolve to make something wonderful with words. It's better to end up with ten lines that truly sing than twenty that barely hum. Even if you end up with one magical phrase after pouring out a page of strivings, that's precious.

Allow yourself the freedom to play with language, to free it to sing in your writing. Always err on the carefree side – not all playfulness will work; some similes and images and aspects of diction will need to be moderated, softened.

But retain the spirit of playfulness: allow adjectives the chance to pretend they're verbs for the day, let a preposition go free. Every piece of writing should be pushing towards new things – the possibility of saying something in a new way. When you're fighting to capture a particular image, play games with sounds to create new words. Again, what you make up may not sound right in three months' time, but have the courage to release the energy of language inside you.

In my poem below, sound is at the very core.

The Birth of the Foal

My eyes still fought with sleep. Out over the fields
Mist lay in grey folds, from vague somewheres
Curlews rose up with thin trails of crying. Our lanterns
Rocked in soft globes of yellow, our feet
Slushed through the early morning thickness of the grass.

She lay on her side, exhausted by her long night;
The hot smell of flanks and head and breath
Ghosted from her spread length.
Sunlight cracked from the broken yolk of the skies,
Ruptured the hills, spangled our eyes and blinded us,
Flooded the pale glows of our lanterns.

There he lay in a pool of his own wetness:
Four long spindles scrabbling, the bigness of his head, a bag of a body –
All struggling to find one another, to join up, to glue
Into the single flow of a birthright. He fought
For the first air of his life, noised like a child.

His mother, still raw and torn from the scar of his birth,
Turned, and her eyes held him,
The great harsh softness of her tongue stilled his struggle.

We knelt in the wet grass, dumbed
By a miracle, by something bigger than the sun.

Kenneth Steven[1]

In the opening stanza everything is being dampened down to create a sense of linkage between the mystical pre-dawn landscape, the sleepy figures moving through the dew-damp fields and the silent sense of anticipation in each of their hearts. The single word 'slushed' attempts to draw all those strands together. 'Rocked' in a way anticipates birth, with its human associations with cradles and cradling. The long sounds in 'sleep', 'fields' and 'feet' all tend towards the hypnotic and gentle.

In the second part of the second stanza the hushed verbs used up until now are swept away by the startling ferocity of the whip crack of the sun's first rays. These violent and disturbing verbs are dark mirrors of the mare's long night; yet they are intended to represent a kind of staircase back to softness and silence. After the intensity of that first sharp spine of dawn light, things mellow – eyes grow used to the sun once more. My intention is that this should be conveyed in that subtle progression of verbs and through the sounds at their hearts: cracked, ruptured, spangled, blinded, flooded.

In the third stanza we've turned our attention to the hero, the newborn. But he's no hero; he's a disjointed bundle wondering what on earth he's to do with these extraordinary appendages stretched out over the early morning ground. The second line is the longest in the whole poem for good reason: the clumsiness of the words is intended to mirror the young foal's sense of confusion and awkwardness and helplessness. That torrent of broken phrases seeks to suggest that disjointedness. It's only in the fourth line of this stanza that a new order seems apparent; the language is easy and fluid, suggesting that the foal has tottered to his feet for the first time. (Of course real time and the poem's time are very different entities.)

I wanted this poem to be 'real', without sentimentality. In the fourth stanza – notice that the later stanzas are shorter now that the struggle is over – I seek to *show* the mare's maternal love rather than to tell it. At every turn I want to undercut, to understate. Hence the weight given to the one word 'held' in the second line, and the oxymoron of 'harsh softness' in the closing line of the stanza.

I struggled over that final stanza, unsure as to where the line breaks should come. Finally I decided that 'dumbed' should reverberate at the close of the first, allowing it to hammer home with all of its shades of meaning. Lyrically it is picked up by the sound of 'sun' in the last line, creating a closing couplet. It also hints at a third birth in the poem: the dawning of new understanding on the part of humans, we who think we have everything under our control. Even bigger than the sun which floods our lanterns and eclipses our puny power is the sheer miracle of birth, the giving and granting of a new life.

LATE SEPTEMBER

WRITERS AND THE UNWRITEABLE - BY MARIO PETRUCCI

Who could forget that surfeit of images? Exploding towers. Bodies falling from a hundred storeys up. Screened again and again, until they burned a despairing loop in our brains. The anger, suffering, grief. All the complex unravelling issues of blame and responsibility.

On being asked for a war poem, W B Yeats famously replied:

> I think it better that in times like these
> A poet's mouth be silent.

I have passed over Yeats' advice and written much about war; but usually concerning events already stratified into history. Ironically, that temporal distance can sometimes let you in, quite close. I can write about November 11th 1918. But September 11th 2001? I saw nothing 'poetic' in those horrific images. That's not to say that artists shouldn't scrutinise September 11th and its aftermath, either globally or personally. It's just that, close up to such a colossal event, most authentic poetic paths seem blocked.

One possible path, however, is to return to the personal, the everyday. A scale we can 'take in'. The humble dirt track rather than the media freeway. That's where I was heading, when I received a call from the BBC via the Poetry Society. I had started to look at September 11th through smoked glass to begin to gauge my own thoughts – thoughts which had grown darker but also, strangely, more resolved. I'd already jotted something down – privately. The BBC, though, wanted a poem. About September 11th. Quickly. Could I help?

I resolved *not* to do it. It felt parasitic. A kind of psycho-spiritual voyeurism. It was too easy to get it wrong. It was too soon. Then I remembered a small German poem, translated by David Constantine, recounting how on Easter Sunday on an island, a father joins his son in covering an apricot sapling against late snow. The poet is Bertolt Brecht; the title 'Spring, 1938'. The poem is so utterly bleak; yet so beautifully poised. It is testimony, in the face of impending war, to that resolve to carry on noticing and doing the things we can, however small. World events filter through to most of us through the slight and personal – those very things we may see in a fresh light when so much is threatened. And these things can help us. A fragile sapling, or a spider in its web, can bear enormous emotional and metaphorical weight. This, I felt, was the spirit in which to approach the writing of 'Late September'. A poem that wouldn't try to say too much. But I did want to say, and do, *something*.

The poem was recorded at Shepherd's Bush, and went out. I hoped to God I'd at least do no damage. But I was quite unprepared for the number of American citizens who contacted the BBC to say how the poem had supported them or helped them to escape, for a short while, the obsession and anxiety that was everywhere piled on by the media. The poem helped them to remember that life *carried on*. That was a turning point for me. If one of my poems had actually helped somebody, somewhere, to find temporary relief from such horror then Yeats was wrong. In times like these, the public *does* need its writers to speak for, and with, them (though, to be fair to Yeats, perhaps not too much – nor too readily). The response to 'Late September' added weight to my conviction that when we read Auden's phrase 'poetry makes nothing happen' we should place the emphasis on the verb 'makes', not the 'nothing'. Poetry is an 'unconstraining voice' which is there to remind and persuade, not to coerce. The relentless coverage of September 11th, its insistent focus, had facilitated the latter. It left many people with nowhere else to go.

If a primary approach to 'big subjects' is to be oblique, I must now also admit an opposite, or alternative, possibility. I have recently composed a book-length poem, *Heavy Water*. It is based on first-hand accounts of Chernobyl and, because of that, pulls no punches. Again, I approached *Heavy Water* with enormous trepidation; but also with a profound certainty – mistaken or otherwise – that artists need to bend to the work at hand and its internal imperatives. I believe (writing is after all an act of faith) that there is always some authentic nexus between artist and subject, some possible brush with the universal – and we can draw from deep places where all experience, however bleak, can be compassionately sensed. Indeed, Arundhati Roy tells us: 'Writers imagine that they cull stories from the world... it's actually the other way around. Stories cull writers from the world... They commission us.'

That's how I felt, composing *Heavy Water*. Commissioned. Those voices in my source texts demanded (in the main) to be heard. To be remembered. And let us not underestimate the act of 'remembering', the putting back together of separated parts. Even when understanding is in short supply, remembering remains a civilised and civilising act. Isn't it part of our job as writers – individually if not collectively – to reclaim lost voices; or at least to listen out for them, prepared for their sudden, sometimes terrible, commissions? Writers can (with sensitivity) tackle missing histories, even if those histories are not – on the surface – their own, even if it means sometimes getting it wrong. We owe this to people made see-through by political, social and intellectual neglect. Those who have been exposed to the invisible shouldn't become so.

Such 'commissions' may be rare; are psychologically, emotionally draining; they are never to be taken lightly. Yet *not* to ignore them is, I feel, an entering into the darkest folds of our creativity, a sounding of the few deep keynotes on our journey through the spheres. And so, as a writer, I find myself taking risks most sensible people steer clear of. I overhear myself as I challenge and contradict, as well as stand by, my own advice concerning the taking of such risks. It's the kind of thing that makes writers so incorrigible, so indispensable. For there is no 'answer' to the big questions: we must discover each part-answer to each part-question, as it arises. I take comfort in the fact that, in the end, a poem is only a poem. No more – though no less – than that. No doubt we shall see many more 'September 11th' poems, probably with that very title (far fewer, perhaps, on Chernobyl or Bhopal). Blessing? Or curse? I know only that writers walk that dangerous winding path between the plains of silence and the markets of speech. There are times to stay and learn in the plains; times to swallow our doubts and enter the mêlée. We can only hope our timing is right.

Last Wish
(Chernobyl, 1986)

You bury me in concrete. Bury me
in lead. Rather I was buried
with a bullet in the head.

You wrap me in plastic. Wash me
in foam. Weld the box airless
and ram the box home.

You seal me in powder. Cut the hair
last. Then take the trimmings
and seal them in glass.

For each tomb that's hidden a green
soldier turns. None decomposes.
Nothing for worms.

A shoe. A pencil. Break one thing
I left. Give some small part of me
ordinary death.

Mario Petrucci[1]

Late September, 2001
(after Bertolt Brecht, 'Spring 1938')

There'd been dew. Maybe a light rain.
And a blot drew my eye to that plot of light
through the kitchen window. Closer. I saw

pincer legs measure out each wire. That
pause of the abdomen before it dipped
to spot-weld each link. I took a chair outside

to stand on. Craned. I wanted to live.
It let me brush a fingertip across the velvet
brown of its back, against the nap, and again

till it froze mid-air, eight legs outstretched,
still as a child roused from a trance of play.
There – the same black volts I'd raise my

slipper to, hunt across rug or duvet to end
in a smudge. Wouldn't have it in my hand.
In my hair. Yet it – she – went to all that length

to snare mosquito and bluebottle – those
who'd ruin a soup, or blood. Hours. For once
I took time. Saw the target complete, her radii

strung high between window and washing line.
I thought of the twist of cells that can work
such wonder. I thought of poets whose words

don't reach. Spider just – does. Can read
angles. But not this freak thunder, its blown-up
tongues of birds. Everywhere. Birds swooping

for spiders. And I feared something might
skim, unknowing, through that hard-earned web.
A swift perhaps, far too late. I saw spider

hung in her patch of unsafe sky.

Mario Petrucci

It is equal to living in a tragic land
To live in a tragic time.
Wallace Steven

THE POET'S CAREER: A SHORT GALLOP AT FULL SPEED, OR THE FLIGHT OF A BIRD
BY KEITH JAFRATE

We write to make contact, to be heard, to be seen. So, sooner or later, anyone who write wants to be published. Then we think of a career, how to make money, how to be recognised, how to be a success. But, like it or not, with money and support the reasons for poetry will change. Or, to put it another way, to define a poet's utility in terms not of what he or she writes, but by what he or she can do for others, whether as therapist or golden goose, changes poetry. Somehow, the poet and the poem begin to diverge, to separate. In my own life, and in the lives of poets I admire, poetry has been a vocation, a calling, not a profession; and I think it should be written from a sense of passion and compulsion, rather than in hope of reward.

To put it another way again, we should try to write through a fascination with the poem itself, not what it might facilitate. Which does not mean that poetry can never be didactic, political or *utile*. I can think of dozens of poets I won't name here who would claim they are fascinated and compelled by poetry, but who really write to get the next reading, the next publication, the next scrap of attention from anyone who'll listen. To me, it's best, while we mature as poets, that we try to resist the distractions of opportunity. As for how we eat, how we make a living, I think we should trust the world to provide something somehow for us, just as we trust it to send us language.

But I'm not suggesting a kind of blissed-out passivity. We need to consciously emphasise the bardic and shamanic aspect to the making of poetry, the discovery of organic and original forms responsive to spoken language and to music, and I guess I think we should be politically radical and culturally eclectic as a way of opposing, or infecting, the contemporary mainstream. I suppose I'm trying to work into a form of radical English lyricism that goes back to Blake but doesn't forget the likes of Bunting and MacDiarmid, and doesn't ignore wonderful Americans like Robert Duncan and Gary Snyder.

I say we should write through a fascination with the poem, not what it might facilitate, but I'm not being strictly accurate, in that the tradition I'm trying to write from sees the poem as an act in itself, a call, a crossing, a magic. It does not so much facilitate as *create*, it is a transforming music that changes the reader or listener while it happens.

I would say the purpose of the poem in this sense is to reveal, to make known and conscious aspects of reality that are normally concealed or inaccessible, in the manner of an hallucinogenic drug or a rite of passage. Behind this process, for me at least, is a commitment to tenderness, a forceful compassion, that the purpose of the poem is to make us bigger, more sensitive, more awake. This is not an ideology, more a belief that the magic of poetry can make us better attuned to the universe, and that this tuning process will erode what might be cruel or exploitative or indifferent in us.

I'm writing this straight after reading Ken Smith's 'Then the heart' from his big book *Shed*, the spell of which woke me up to what I was trying to say:

> all summer long, writing *Heart*
> *like the fennel root. Heart*
> *like a great horseradish. Heart*
> *like a loaf of hot bread new minted*
> *from the oven, keep beating,*
> *brave messenger, bearing news of yourself.*

It seems to me Ken doesn't confuse his heart with himself here, though they are one and inseparable. In the poem, his heart becomes the central emblem for the force that makes poems, their root, and Ken speaks to it as if he were not the owner and creator of his poems but the beneficiary of them. The poems are the message *and* the self that Ken wants to continue, and here is no choice about it.

So, for Ken, and for me too, you can't turn a poem into a form of currency, a lever to get a job or to conform to a publisher's tastes: it just has to be whatever we can manage to make it. And just as we should be wary of the materialism implicit in contemporary literary culture, we should also remember that the poem doesn't need to offer news or information of the factual or statistical kind. Poems should be revelations of imaginative worlds, both big and small, that the news either cannot or will not tell us about, and they have no obligation to be sensible or logical, or even to make sense in the ways we make sense to one another socially.

There are plenty of English poets writing political or moral or socially conscious poems, but it seems to me the form of their work often undercuts and disables their good intentions. In the world of the performance poet, for example, forms are mostly simple to the point of banality, and represent no great challenge either to their immediate audience, or to a wider readership or listening public. And I think it's true that some of our most 'successful' contemporary poets, of any description, work through an aesthetic that views the poem as a kind of object rather than as a kind of act. In this tradition, it is the degree of self-containment and detachment achieved by the poem that seems to determine its success, whereas for me the attempt is to break through the poem to some other kind of relationship, to change the space around the poem while it happens.

It's the difference, really, between admiration and participation, between making a vase and making a fire. I think, in the end, I'd say that the fire is more valuable.

How to light that fire? I would say work at times of elemental transition, work at dawn and sunset, work towards solstices and celebrations, but also work outside any habitual time or situation we may have made for ourselves. Ignore rules, especially any I may have suggested.[1]

...although they must feel answerable to the world they inhabit, poets, if they are to do their proper work, must also feel free.
Seamus Heaney

HAIKU, TANKA AND HAIBUN

As much of the emphasis in this book is on mindfulness of the present moment, it would not be complete without some words on the practice of writing haiku and related forms.

Haiku, tanka and haibun all have a connection with some of the fundamental Oriental Buddhist teachings on stillness, transience and the importance of an awareness of the present moment.

They all, in some way or another, emerge out of the numerous creative tensions to which we, as human beings, are subject; for instance the juxtaposition of:

Inner and outer worlds
The personal and the universal
The world of nature and the world of human affairs
Awareness of self and other
Open, authentic and genuine contact with life and its attendant vulnerability
Transience and permanence
The cycles of life and death.

I like these definitions by Noragh Jones:[1]

'HAIKU – a breath length poem characterized by concrete images, a heightened sense awareness, and connectedness with a deeper consciousness than our surface mode of being.'

'HAIBUN – a poetic prose narrative interspersed with haiku and permeated with haiku characteristics – heightened awareness, concrete imagery and resonance. Basho's haibun in *Narrow Road to the Deep North*, his journals of travels or pilgrimages, are resonant with a sense of place, past and present, with nature's moods, and with affection for humanity.'

THIS BRIGHT MOMENT
THE PRACTICE OF HAIKU

Haiku is both a poetic form in its own right, and also an expression of a philosophy, a way of being; a living 'way' and practice. Connected as it is with Zen Buddhism, it exemplifies the Eastern approach to life.

Like Zen, haiku is very much about the present moment, written about in the present tense. It's the poetry of everyday life – what is happening in this moment in this place. Paying this quality of attention to the moment allows us to see the extraordinary in the ordinary. For a reader, a well-written haiku may offer new insight – an 'aha!' moment. It will take one both deeper into the moment and the experience, and also beyond it, to the bigger world. It may even kick you into a moment of transcendence. For this reason, haiku tend to work more effectively if they also contain something of the natural world beyond the manmade, human and egoic.

The word haiku derives from *hokku*, meaning 'hook'. If we reduce it to its simplest intention, we could say that a haiku offers us the briefest sketch, an outline, on which we are invited to hang, metaphorically, our own feelings and life experience.

In many ways this approach is diametrically opposed to our English Romantic tradition, where poets such as Keats, Wordsworth and Shelley paint detailed word-pictures overflowing with feeling. For the English Romantics, think English country garden. For haiku poets, picture a single branch of plum blossom in the simplest of clear glass vases.

Haiku stands in relation to, say, the epic poem as a 50-word mini-saga stands in relation to a novel. If you are someone whose work tends towards the over-wordy, haiku is a wonderful discipline. Over and over you practise paring back; you focus on what you're really trying to convey. You learn, eventually, how *little* one needs, not how much.

Alan Watts called haiku 'the wordless poem', and there's something in this: a good haiku takes us about as close to silence as words may.

Traditionally written in Japanese *onji*, for which the nearest translation is 'syllable', the prescribed form was 17 syllables arranged in 3 lines of 5,7,5 syllables respectively. (In Japan, a haiku is more usually written in only one line.)

Generally, in English, a form of 12 – 14 syllables – or even fewer – often conveys the poem better.

But what is more important than the syllable count or even the number of lines is the spirit of haiku: its essential nature, a record of the 'now'. Gone into the making of a good haiku will be four things:

Sensory observation of a particular moment
A suggestion of relationship between apparently separate ideas or subjects
A drawing together of human and non-human
The poet's own felt response.

However, although that moment may have inspired a feeling response in the poet (which in turn inspired the poem), he or she conveys but does not impose that response on the reader. The poet draws the sketch by noting the details and circumstances of that moment and allows his reader to experience their own emotions as directly as possible. Robert Bly talks of the need to allow the Shadow to rise up and invade a haiku – this will give it 'bite'.

Haiku looks easy, yet a good haiku is exceedingly difficult to write and requires years of practise; indeed it can be, and often is, a meditation practice in itself, allowing you to look deeply into the nature of *what is*. The art is that of capturing the essence of a moment, distilling it into a few potent but not portentous words and laying them on the page in such a way as to make what is a highly-skilled technique look simple and spontaneous.

'Essential ingredients for haiku', says Gerald England, 'are simplicity of language, directness of communication, rhythm and the relative absence of the narrator'. In addition, a haiku should, suggests Gail Sher, work on three levels: firstly the surface, literal level, which should please; secondly, a deeper layer of meaning beneath; and thirdly the possibility of a moment of enlightenment.

Here are some basic suggestions:

Use the present tense
Haiku don't use simile, or rhyme
Be specific, not general: *this* moment, *this* tree, *this* room; singular rather than plural

Avoid abstractions and conceptualisation; root your writing in concrete sensory detail – the image is the poem

Avoid 'little' words as much as possible

Keep adjectives and adverbs to a minimum

Avoid cliché of course, and sentimentality

Avoid flowery 'poeticisms'

Sketch and suggest rather than explaining or forcing your emotions on a reader. The haiku should not be 'unfeeling' but should subtly suggest feeling response and hopefully trigger the possibility of a reader's immersion in the experience of the poem

Use punctuation sparingly, if at all. Let pauses and line breaks and space do that work

Juxtaposition of elements in the poem – creative tension between the lines and images –allows a reader to make a leap. (Haiku teacher Dr Ichiki says: 'The pause or gap involved in haiku may perhaps be likened to (+) and (-) in electricity, separated by a gap. The "spark" jumps the gap between two apparently different or unrelated ideas, and makes a connection.') This is particularly effective if there is a tension – shock, even – between the second and third lines

Nonetheless the haiku should be smoothly-flowing and authentic in feel

Good haiku point towards what may be unchanging and eternal by sketching what is transient and changing

Haiku tend not to be titled.

While writing – and reading – haiku, stay in the *experience* of the moment until 'saturated' by it. Don't rush to write, and 'allow' the images to speak rather than forcing them. Stay with the 'how', the process, until the 'what' is ready.

Ken Jones, in his piece 'Joy and grief – One Brush' expands on all this. He also offers you some haiku to consider. Haiku, more perhaps than any other form, repays deep attention and study. You need to read and read and then read some more, until you can recognise what it is that makes certain three-line poems haiku, while others remain simply three-line poems.

For now, a flavour:

the sea grows dark
the voices of the wild duck
turn white

even in Kyoto
when I hear the cuckoo
I pine for Kyoto

the temple bell stops –
but the sound keeps coming
out of the flowers

Basho (C17th)

sudden piercing chill
in our room my dead wife's
comb, underfoot

Buson (C18th)

And two contemporary examples:

out in the cold sunshine
planting early potatoes
uncertain who I am

Ken Jones

this white sand
those seabound footprints
not coming back

Roselle Angwin

It's worth spending some time with these haiku (any haiku). Often they only yield up their heart after intense contemplation, even though you might think you've absorbed their message immediately.

Starting point

1

Begin by saturating yourself over several days or weeks in haiku (see the notes accompanying Ken Jones' piece).

2

Practise starting to 'see' in haiku moments – lifting threads from the wider fabric to examine.

3

If you don't already, start to carry a small notebook everywhere with you. Just note details of the passing moment, wherever you are. Keep your notes grounded in the world of the senses.

4

Start by making simple three-line poems recording these passing moments. Don't struggle with this, and keep practising it over a period of days or weeks. Think of them as 'working drawings'.

5

As you note these moments, be aware of your emotional response to what you are observing and recording.

6

Go back through your three-liners. Firstly, have a look at those third lines. Do they surprise? How could you change or re-write them so that they might? What might you include – or exclude – to lift the poem from being no more than 'mere' nature-observation? (Harold Henderson suggests that a basic definition of a haiku is 'a record of a moment of emotion in which human nature is somehow linked to all nature'. How might you create this effect without spelling it out or labouring the point?) Try leaping sideways yourself, and finding an altogether different last line. Often changing the order of the lines makes a difference. Look for that leap of surprise between the 2nd and 3rd lines.

7

Start to pare back. Let the little words go. Don't think in sentences or even complete clauses. Check for present tense. As in all poetry, use strong verbs – but without making it seem contrived. Look for active verb forms: 'flees' is likely to be more potent than 'fleeing'. Check for concrete images – is it pictorial?

8

Rewrite it so that it contains a maximum of seventeen syllables.

9

Read it aloud!

As Auden and Valéry before him said of the poem, no haiku is ever finished, it is only abandoned. So the reader keeps getting on where the poet got off.

Raymond Roseliep

JOY AND GRIEF — ONE BRUSH
HAIKU - KEN JONES

Those in line
watching the wind
sweep the earth

Thus Saito Sanki, on the hunger years of post-war Japan – or anytime, any place in the terrible twentieth century. You can see that not only is a haiku such a little thing – hardly the length of a breath – but it is a half-said thing. At its most effective this tiny coiled spring can release a subtle, fleeting, liberating freedom from the ache of wanting-it-otherwise.

Much quiet delight and gentle healing awaits the explorer of the haiku world. Haiku have traditionally been the most popular and accessible of literary forms (millions write them in Japan). But you do need to have the *haiku knack*.

Some guidelines

Don't search after haiku. Instead, cultivate alertness so you are inspired by authentic experience when it arises. The clarity of such a 'haiku moment' should be infused with some warmth of feeling, a shared humanity, as with Shiki:

Pitiful … fearful
those poor scarecrows look like men
in autumn light

Just relax and keep it simple, without any straining after effect. Avoid cliché, cleverness and wordiness. Thus, Basho:

Water jar cracks –
I lie awake
this icy night

SHOW – don't TELL. Try to express your experiences through the images that you use, rather than actually saying that you are 'sad' or 'lonely'. This gives space for readers to experience such feelings in their own way, as in this by the eighteenth century master, Buson:

> The ends of the warriors' bows
> as they go, brushing
> >the dew

Similarly, avoid explanations, abstractions and philosophising. Prefer allusion and understatement. Tread lightly.

Many of the best haiku present unexpected and *contrasting* images. These can arouse profound and subtle emotions and can convey layers of subtle meaning. The Western convention is to write haiku in three lines, but four- and two-liners are acceptable where that makes the best 'fit'. Often the first line sets the scene, within which the second line makes an observation. The third line then presents an image contrasting with the second line, throwing our normal expectations out of gear, as it were, and opening up a wider perspective which may be both allusive and elusive. There is a mysterious spark of a wider truth here, which is left to the reader's awareness (an 'open metaphor'). The first example below is from Cicely Hill and the second by Ogino Yoko. The inkstone one, by Mitsui Suzuki, is more complex, recalling William Blake's 'love and grief are woven fine, a clothing for the soul divine'.

> Pausing to watch
> breeze over the hayfields
> forgotten names

> Hot bath water
> cold on the breastless side
> spring thunder

> Inkstone cold
> joy and grief
> one brush

Finally, are there words which you could omit that would make the haiku work better? And what happens if you change the lines around?

Haiku and not Haiku?

The authority of the above advice rests solely on its helpfulness in enabling us to develop the full potential of the haiku form. But within this mainstream haiku tradition there are, of course, many variations and controversies. For me, the Way of Haiku is part of my Zen Buddhist practice:

For company	Pushing my reflection
an empty chair	this wheelbarrow
	full of rain

Most Westerners write in free form. That is to say, they do not stick to three lines of five, seven and five syllables each, though every haiku needs to have some music to it. However, there is general agreement about keeping the haiku short ('one breath'), and 17 syllables is commonly regarded as the maximum. Again, Westerners are generally little concerned with 'season words', which play an important part in conventional Japanese haiku.

There are also less orthodox haiku, like these by Jim Norton and Nagata Koi respectively:

With melting hearts	How lonely it is
two skeletons	cultivating the stone leeks
vow to meet again	in this world of dreams

And there is a haiku variant called senryu. These deal humorously with human foibles and follies. Here is a traditional Japanese senryu and, on the right, for comparison, a haiku by Issa:

She suckles her baby	Those two tired dolls
'On the shelf	in the corner there – ah yes,
you'll find some sardines'	they are man and wife

'Spam' (or 'spoof') haiku is the name sometimes given to those entertaining little three-liners which constitute the bulk of what popularly pass for 'haiku'. In fact they have only a superficial resemblance to the poems discussed here. At the other extreme are the 'pseudo haiku' commonly found in mainstream poetry magazines. These are in fact conventional three line poems that may appear flowery, exaggerated and self-absorbed when compared with the authentic product.

Now try your hand...

Here is a mixed bag of published haiku, displaying a wide range of strengths and weaknesses. How does each relate to the criteria offered earlier? Which do you like best? And which least? And why?

1 Family picnic
   the new wife's rump
   bigger than mine

2 Clothesline
   the widow's black lace panties
   covered in frost

3 Holiday romance
   the smell of suntan lotion
   on the pillow case

4 Poky hotel
   no room for my shadow
   to unpack

5 Discussing divorce
   he strokes
   the lace tablecloth

6 Last day –
   a cold spark from two flints
   and then the paper catches

7 How cold –
   leek tips
   washed white

8 In one shrill cry
   the pheasant has swallowed
   the broad field

By, respectively, Roberta Beary, George Swede, Andrew Shimield, David Cobb, Alexis Rotella, Caroline Gourlay, Matsui Basho, and Yamei.[1]

TANKA

The tanka form is older than haiku, but less well-known in Britain. Tanka originated as formal though often playful poems about love: love of place, nature, and predominantly the love between a man and a woman, and/or the loss of that love. Similar in essence to haiku, they allow more scope for subject matter, direction and development.

Tanka, in brief, differ from haiku in the following characteristics:

> Their traditional form is 5 lines of 5,7,5,7,7 syllables respectively, as one stanza of 5 lines or two of three and two lines respectively (as with haiku, the spirit is generally considered more important than an exact syllable count nowadays). Sometimes they are written by two poets: one poet to write the first three lines, another the concluding two (these are known as renga)

> Tanka can include metaphor to aid meaning and power; they may in themselves be metaphorical

> In typical tanka a natural phenomenon may be given a metaphorical value in the second part, where an emotional twist changes the whole poem.

As in haiku, the spirit is more important than the exact syllable count, though five lines is still the accepted form; but linked sequences and changes in layout are possible. There's scope for humour and satire.

Starting point: tanka-by-numbers

Five lines:

> 1 location/weather/season/time of day (situating the poem)
> 2 development/detail
> 3 personal presence: self or other
> 4 & 5 tangential/surprising new direction; or an addendum/juxtaposition
> that may throw new light on the previous lines.

Yew*

the falling of light
and the place where it pools
between us

if you were to come back now
I would eat your red berries

(Roselle Angwin)

*NB: titles are frowned upon, but this one depends upon the title for its meaning.

Much of the charm of haibun derives from the way it occupies several thresholds: prose, poetry, prose poetry, journal and diary writing, autobiography, travel and nature writing, non-fiction and even fiction...
Pamelyn Casto

Still largely unknown in the UK (though better known in America) is the haibun, an exciting form with huge scope for experimentation, innovation and play, which deserves to be much better known. Haibun is the prose equivalent of haiku: intense, literary, a particular form of prose poem. It usually incorporates haiku: sometimes as an envoi, sometimes to begin; sometimes embedded in the text. (Traditionally it also includes *haiga*, brief pen or brush sketches.)

Honed, intense, vivid and deceptively simple, it normally encompasses a philosophical point or mood. It '...strives to be interesting, informative and inventive...It is not private writing...literary haibun strives to share a story, an experience, an insight, a journey of whatever kind as it attempts to touch its readers emotionally, sensually, intellectually and spiritually'.[1]

Basho's *Narrow Road to the Deep North* is the best-known example of a classical haibun; this is an extended piece, but a haibun might also be just one vivid paragraph. Its greatness 'lies in its doing so much with so little...'[2]

This form lends itself well to marking a journey, literal (external) as well as personal and interior. Like the haiku, the prose passage(s) is rooted in concrete imagery, but unlike haiku has enormous flexibility in content. The strength, simplicity and vivid brevity of its diction and linguistic style is important, however. Like haiku, understatement should also carry profundity.

In his Introduction to *Pilgrim Foxes*[3], George Marsh defines something important about these prose poems: '...[I]n the haibun we have two parallel realities, related, but with different rhythms. Every so often there is a Narnia wardrobe or loose manhole cover and one falls from the quotidian domestic business into a place where the reference points are eternal and death highlights the profiles of all things. These two places run in parallel and there is no contradiction between them... If you live... drawing continually on the sense that everyday reality is the arising of life from the silence, the ground of being, and the continual recreation and annihilation of that life and return to silence, then the form that represents a parallel world of poetry under a parallel world of prose is the perfect instrument for your expression.'

The main challenge for a haibun writer is to give equal weight to both the prose passages and the haiku, so that neither is subservient to the other. They need to work together and be equally integrated, without simply mirroring each other. Each should throw light on the other, without the prose being merely explanatory notes for the haiku, or the haiku standing in isolation. Marsh again: 'The haiku in haibun are more than a typographical intensification device, like a sinister chord under a line of film dialogue. They are the manifestation of a particular view of reality with terms like delusion, vast emptiness, no-self, the ceasing of notions, interdependence, and mindfulness.'[4]

The main points to bear in mind when composing haibun are:

> The language is heightened and tight, closer to poetry
> Present tense
> Use of concrete imagery as a foundation, but more abstract 'commentary' can be used
> Includes reflective, personal and/or philosophical 'asides'
> Focused and vivid
> Simply stated, rather than over-intellectual or flowery
> Moving but not sentimental
> A touch of humour maybe, or lightness
> Grounded in the moment
> Any accompanying haiku should not simply reiterate but provide something fresh and surprising.

As with any poem, the title needs careful thought, so that it is not so transparent that it detracts from the power of the text. (Such a title is like the difference between a gift seductively wrapped in a way that will also hide its contents, and one that is unwrapped.)

One of the most exciting, and fruitful, creative projects with which I have been involved was a collaborative email sequence with Rupert Loydell, following on from a course he co-tutored with Sheila E Murphy, an innovative and experimental American poet who introduced me to this form (which I have continued to use as a regular creative and meditative discipline).

Rupert and I agreed that our prose poems would be loosely based on the haibun form, and that we would set ourselves an exact count of 100 words per prose piece, closing with a haiku-like envoi, and that we would complete our sequence of 100 linked prose poems in 100 days which, give or take a day or two away, we did. The results were published, virtually unedited, as *A Hawk Into Everywhere*[5]; and the book remains something that neither of us would have been able to create alone.

(49) Arrival and Departure

Figgy 'obbin and stargazy pie; lardy cake and saffron. My great-grandfather skippering the last tea-clipper out of Falmouth, the *Water Witch*. How you led me down these lanes (the Carrick Roads) – blue-eyed as speedwell, forget-me-not – and in this spring the salt wind catches me out and here you are again. Always these choices: jump, or turn away; and inside here this heart beating – the one that lies, and tells the truth; the one that rages and forgives, the one that wants to burst out of my chest and launch itself like a hawk into everywhere

Madhouses and holy wells: memory turns and runs

Rupert Loydell & Roselle Angwin

Trekking Poles

A dream, a lightning flash, or cloud
So should we view this world
(The Buddha)

Mountain tent
cold and sleepless
I unpick the years of my life

To a tattoo of hailstones I unzip this, my twenty-seven thousandth mortal day. In the dawn light a damp, gleaming still life of odds and ends lies heaped in the bell end of the tent. A solitary stonechat sings a little song. Yet all this began in sunshine…

Climbing the mountain for the umpteenth time
striding shadows
of my trekking poles

But then holed up by unseasonable weather. At freezing point the little stove struggles to boil water for my coffee. I wrap my hand round the cold gas cylinder, and it hisses louder.

Crawling arthritically out of the tent, I remember to turn sharp left above the hundred foot drop that is just outside. I have abandoned the neighbouring damp cave of saints, poets and warriors. It serves now only as an oratory, a flickering bright refuge in a howling wilderness, where I chant the morning and evening office. The cast iron Buddha has his hand raised in benediction, until he too will rust away. Sometimes there is a little company to be had here…

In candlelight
a scuttling beetle
her shiny back

Likewise at dawn and dusk I climb up above the cave onto the flat slate top of Stallion's Crag. From here Owain Glyndwr evaded his English pursuers and leapt from history into myth.

A hero's war horse
hoof prints set in stone
my walking meditation

Twenty-one brisk circumambulations around the edge. Down through craggy pinnacles, in mist and thin rain, stretches the great trackless valley where no one comes. Joy swallows me up.

Today I must leave, struggling against the wind across the ridge and down the spur to the road-head an hour and a half away. Back through the magic door. On which side lies the dream?

Everything moves on –
the drifting shadows
of clouds

Ken Jones

WHERE BOUNDARIES BLUR
THE PROSE POEM

...the most that we can say about prose poetry is that it exhibits certain characteristics...
Peter Johnson

As I said in the chapter on form versus free verse, I think of the prose-poetry spectrum as being a continuum, through from prose to prose poems to free verse to metrical form. In anatomical terms, I likened it to a muscle: if prose is that muscle relaxed, metrical poetry represents that muscle contracted.

The prose poem sits between these two, but still has its own aesthetic.

It should be said at this point that in many ways the prose poem can only be arbitrarily defined – it is a form that is still evolving, and there are no absolute 'rules', and what I've written here is my own opinion informed by conversations and readings of prose poems, and of the theory behind them as written by Those Who Know What They're Talking About. I'm aware that, however, by attempting to define it, I'm in danger of suffocating it. Nonetheless, here goes...

The prose poem has been described by Charles Simic as a literary hybrid, including as it does many faces of prose, from anecdote to allegory to fairy story to journal to reflection to dream imagery to *écriture* and *pensée*, all bound together using some of the devices of poetry.

That's one description. This is how Peter Johnson, editor of an international prose poem journal[1], puts it: 'Just as black humor straddles the fine line between comedy and tragedy, so the prose poem plants one foot in prose, the other in poetry, both heels resting precariously on banana peels.'

What all this means in practice is that the prose poem will share some of the attributes of general poetic expression: imagery; heightened intensity of content, thought, and feeling; compactness; patterning and repetition; as well as showing sound and syntactical elements common to poetry. 'The prose poem', says Michael Benedikt, one of America's best-known exponents, 'encourages a tremendous flexibility of dictional, imagistic, and tonal approach'.[2] It will also include metaphor. 'An ability to create metaphor – to let metaphor out of the overly rational cage in which our more numbingly conservative poets sometimes practically imprison it, so that metaphor can perform for us and entertain us – is a prerequisite for any writer of prose poems', says Benedikt[3].

In some ways it is easier to talk about what the prose poem isn't, or doesn't do. What it won't include are traditional rhyme schemes and typical poetry layout with line breaks; generally it will appear on the page in a continuous sequence of sentences, though this is not a hard and fast rule. The diction will be poetic, but less conventionally so than in poetry. It will tend more towards the vernacular: conversational and colloquial. It may include echoing sounds and a rhythm that is tighter than ordinary prose, but any 'rhyme' and 'rhythm' will not be formal or overdone.

Although there is no reason why it shouldn't include 'embedded' lines of poetry (and in fact my long prose poem *The Present Where*, co-authored with Rupert Loydell, does), it generally doesn't; unlike in a haibun it is not a prerequisite.

There is an inwardness about the prose poem that allows a personal content, and that also often conveys the kind of imaginative material that gives it a dream-like flavour. Often there is a strong visual element.

Although it may have a narrative content, it is not simply a linear short story, even though it may have aspects similar in kind to the mini-saga, which became popular in Britain in the late '90s. It sometimes has an aphoristic feel to it, though it is not a moral parable or fable. It may be a vignette involving both inner and outer detail, and its informal structure often gives it a compelling immediacy.

When I think of the prose poem I see it visually. It's layered. For the sake of ease, I want to suggest that – and this is a generalisation – we could describe conventional prose and traditional poetry as proceeding along a horizontal, unfolding in time. For me, the prose poem is more a multilevelled chunk, in 'section', rather as an archaeologist might cut through successive layers of soils to reveal differences in the strata. George Marsh, whom I quoted in the haibun chapter, talked about two worlds co-existing in the haibun in a Narnia-like way; I think a prose poem is like that, recording different facets, or levels, of human experience.

A good prose poem will have an element of spontaneity about it; something of the sense of 'stream of consciousness'; and to that extent it will appear less 'worked' than a poem proper (though that is not to say that it hasn't been). 'It ... seem[s] to me that there is a shorter distance from the unconscious to the prose poem, than from the unconscious to most poems in verse,' says Michael Benedikt.[4]

Nonetheless, the writing will have a kind of tautness about it. This springs partly from its simultaneous occupation of two (at least) thresholds: the intimate, imaginative and associative 'interiority' of poetry, and the more narrative territory of conventional prose.

Partly as a result of its relative newness, the prose poem is a fluid form that encourages originality and improvisation. It will also have a texture of what could be called organic looseness about it, especially in terms of 'meaning' and 'sense', that marks it out from both more formal verse and from prose, whether fiction or non-fiction. (This is paradoxical in view of what I said above about tautness; but what I mean here is that it is not constrained by either the conventions of formal metre and diction, or by the need to have a 'direction', 'thrust' or 'destination'.) Prose poems may be of any length, though most often they are short, self-contained 'stand-alone' pieces.

Its original proponents were the French avant-garde from the mid C19th and the early C20th; it is intimately connected with both the Symbolists and the later Surrealists (like Surrealism, the prose poem draws directly on the unconscious), and Baudelaire, cornerstone of the French Symbolist movement, is generally seen as its originator. He wrote of his ideas of poetic prose – a form which needed to be both fluid and muscled, without rhyme or rhythm, yet still musical; a form which was suited to the lyrical flights of the soul as well as to dream states and reverie; and one which also took account of the impulses of the conscience. In the rewriting of some of his verses as prose poems, he was aware that he was working with a new and as yet unformulated mode of expression; and today, 150 years on, this still holds true, in the sense that there are few formal 'rules'.

However, before Baudelaire, in the early part of the C19th, Aloysius Bertrand was already experimenting with the prose poem. His surreal little visionary pieces read as remarkably modern passages in their use of imagery and format, although the subject matter is archaic and Romantic.

Undoubtedly Bertrand formed the foundation on which Baudelaire, and then others, built. His work also inspired the composer Ravel, who based a composition on a prose poem sequence of Bertrand's. Unlike Baudelaire, however, who engaged with contemporary cultural and political concerns in his writings, Bertrand did not develop the form to address both the interior world, and also exterior contemporary life. The prose poem in Baudelaire's hands became something both psychologically and socially 'aware' and aesthetically relevant, and allowed an as it were 'conversational' following of the twists and turns of the imagination in a way that more formal verse, by its nature, could not.

Baudelaire influenced other French writers such as Mallarmé, Rimbaud, Valéry and Eluard. A number of other well-known European writers from Baudelaire's time onwards have also found this an exciting form with which to work.

The prose poem offers, within its own parameters, tremendous freedom and fluidity, yet it is only now really beginning to find and hold ground in the English-speaking world, despite having figured in the writings of numerous poets from the Modernist and Postmodernist eras. The last twenty-five years, however, have seen an upsurge of interest in this form.

In France, the prose poem is still better known than in the UK, and a number of contemporary French writers use the form. In America it is well established, despite the dismissal of its existence as a genre by some critics, and there are many proponents.

It offers itself both to exploration and to experimentation, and there are whole books written in this form, the majority of them collections of individual prose poems; but it offers scope for experimental novel-like work, too.

It's my sense that the prose poem as a genre has a potential that is as yet still unknown. 'If the prose poem has a long-term (i.e., centuries-long) future,' says Benedikt[5] 'as an alternative to verse (and as an expression of the unconscious, the imagination, or whatever), it will I think have to develop in ways that are increasingly more far reaching... And proceed by extending itself – like dreams – into the various other areas of our lives which are vital to us all. I see that as the essential challenge to, for example, the American Prose Poem... into the 21st [century].'

Andy Brown, in his essay in this book 'Shifting Arenas', has a prose poem; see also his book, *Hunting the Kinnayas*.[6] There are a number of prose poem writers now in the UK, one of whom is Rupert Loydell, with whom I have collaborated on various poetry and prose poetry projects.[7]

As an example of this form (though not intended in any way as a definitive representation) is the following extract from a short sequence of my own ('Gardens').

Like tomorrow

Sometimes in the night I think I hear your footsteps, see you stretch a hand to lead me into your country, your mind which is incandescent with lights like Christmas candles, or still like a deep pool inhabited by golden carp, thoughts which fan the water as delicately as fins, barely rippling; or flick in a shower of neon across to the other shore, leaving me gasping for breath.

Sometimes you arrive like a flamenco dancer; sometimes a small wind swimming through leaves, and as I turn you've already left, and only the trees swaying to show your passage.

Sometimes you are an incantation on the lips of someone else
a vowel not quite uttered
a syllable just caught
a faraway tune.

Sometimes you are a hawk hanging on the wind.

I like it best when I turn from the kitchen where sunlight is stroking the tiles and walk out into the summer morning, grass still wet and the garden shaking off night, and you're there in the extravagance of hibiscus, or under the lime tree; or waiting on the doorstep in the basket of bursting figs, bloom still untouched, like tomorrow.

Roselle Angwin[8]

Speaking here as a poet... and also as an occasional literary critic, it seems to me that the nature of the Prose Poem itself particularly encourages qualities having to do with [...] evolution and transcendence and – yes – even outright experiment. In particular, transcendence of its own norms and seeming limits and boundaries, when it threatens to acquire them. And not only encourage such transcendence, but perhaps demand it!
Michael Benedikt

In a special issue on the prose poem in the journal *Verse*, Charles Simic states, "Writing a prose poem is a bit like trying to catch a fly in a dark room. The fly probably isn't even there, the fly is inside your head, still, you keep tripping over and bumping into things in hot pursuit. The prose poem is a burst of language following a collision with a large piece of furniture."
Peter Johnson

PART 3

STORYMAKING

It is easy to forget how mysterious and mighty stories are. They do their work in silence, invisibly. They work with all the internal materials of the mind and the self. They become part of you while changing you. Beware the stories you read or tell: subtly, at night, beneath the waters of consciousness, they are altering your world.

Ben Okri

HEART OF STORY

Stories are, in their fashion, a kind of thread that connects us to immortality. They spin into visibility a web of which, through story, we may experience ourselves a part, but which is too often invisible. They also remind us of our shared humanity, at the same time as taking us, somehow, outside of it. 'I believe in all human societies there is a desire to love and be loved, to experience the full fierceness of human emotion, and to make a measure of the sacred part of one's life… the most dependable way to preserve these possibilities is to be reminded of them in stories… It is through story that we embrace the great breadth of memory, that we can distinguish what is true, and that we may glimpse, at least occasionally, how to live without despair in the midst of the horror that dogs and unhinges us,' says writer Barry Lopez.[1]

In 2004, I created and led a week-long course called Storymaking. This evolved out of a course I had tutored for seven years ('Creative Novel Writing'), and was also a way, for me, of returning to my source of 13 years' before: workshops founded in the psychology of myth. The main difference from the previous years' novel courses was that I emphasised our personal relationship to story – the fact that without even knowing that we do it, as humans we live out archetypal themes, often shaped by the stories we have heard or read (or watched) through our lives (this forms the main content of my first book, *Riding The Dragon*). It was an exciting week for all of us, and our work felt very alive. What follows in the next few chapters is that course in brief. (A comprehensive course on the principles of writing a novel is given in my book *Creative Novel Writing.*[2])

Before you begin
Storytelling has always sat at the heart of every culture. It's central to being human. Though of course these days it is more often conveyed in print than it is orally, as a writer you are continuing this ancient tradition.

In order to start to focus on and shape the story you want to write, it may be fruitful to consider these questions. It will be helpful to you to record your responses.

Starting points

1

Do you have at least a faint glimmer, a slender thread, of a story you want to write? Is there a half-heard story in your imagination that needs to be written?

2

Consider the idea that we inhabit story as much as it inhabits us. What might this mean for you?

3

What stories, from your early life, have affected you and stayed with you? Why?

4

Then I would like to suggest that you think of a book that has remained strongly with you from your reading (and it may not be through a clear memory of the plot, but rather through an atmosphere, mood, the subject, theme or a character). You might wish to jot down ideas: why has it stayed with you? What was its theme? What was it that appealed to you? What light might it shed on your own life and its themes?

5

Lastly, give some thought to what kind of book you would like to write. You also might want to think about the form: stories do not have to be written as a linear narrative. There are books that don't 'fit' the stereotypical movement from beginning to middle to end... if none comes to mind, look out for examples of these next time you're in a bookshop (see also the essay on plots).

For every writer, I suppose... all writing is an act against forgetting, an act against death. As well as I can, I write against forgetting. The ground of it all, in one shape or another, is love.

David Constantine

I am very taken with Marcel Proust's philosophy of revisiting the past and making something of it, so it isn't wasted or forgotten.

Vicky Raden

OUT OF THE LABYRINTH

[T]he best we can have of those substantial truths that guide our lives is metaphorical – a story... the truth reveals itself most fully not in dogma but in the paradox, irony and contradictions that distinguish compelling narratives – beyond this there are only failures of imagination: reductionism in science; fundamentalism in religion; fascism in politics.
Barry Lopez

Once I attempted to earn my living as a storyteller, travelling around schools. However, after I'd forgotten or nearly forgotten, too many times, either the most significant details of the plot, or the ending, I realised that live storytelling, sadly, is simply not my forte (I should have known; you ought to hear me trying to tell a joke).

Sitting down to write this, I realise that I no longer consider myself a storyteller – despite the fact that in addition to my various non-fiction books I've written several short stories (all published), two and a half novels and hundreds of poems. I've had a lifelong interest in myths – my first book was based on them – which should give me a good foundation. What's more, I've had a life – fairly exciting and occasionally mildly dangerous in parts. My psyche is crammed full with stories.

I also spend a very large part of my life encouraging and supporting other people in the telling of their stories: often their life stories, the events, people and choices that have shaped and defined them, impassioned and enraged them, filled them with joy or grief, taken them to the edge of survival or up to the threshold of paradise. I've sat and wept with scores of people; I've sat and laughed. I'm never left untouched or unmoved by what I hear, and my life is so much the bigger, so much the more profound for the stories I've met.

We all have shoals of stories milling about inside us, just waiting for the right fly to bring them to the surface. Everyone, then, is a storyteller. And I am also reclaiming the term for myself.

There's something profoundly life-affirming about storytelling, both as teller and as listener. The sharing of stories, as with poems, is an act of intimacy. Storytelling is a currency, a vital exchange. As Adrienne Rich remarked of poetry, I think maybe stories, too, can save your life; look at Scheherazade!

With stories we remake history, revision our lives. Telling story is also a way of sifting through the clutter of our lives, finding the 'pearls of great price'; as we tell we mark the significant moments and events, we make sense of the difficult ones, we gain a different perspective, we learn to discard the stories that don't count, that don't serve us, that hold us back – even if only by selective telling.

We choose who we are, then, by the stories we tell: we tell too who we were, who we might now be, who we weren't and who we'd like to be. And who we're frightened of being. We shape and we reshape our lives.

In the act of storytelling we go through the great dressing-up box that is our past, putting on all the people we've been; and our future, or maybe a parallel present: who we haven't been, or might be.

We inhabit stories as they inhabit us. Storytelling is the heart of culture, all culture. It comes from the origins of human life; we know that it's been around since at least the last Ice Age. It's a way of preserving the wisdom of our species, of feeding the soul, of keeping our inner fires alight, a way of healing, of weaving spells.

In Old Welsh the word for storyteller is the same as that for seer.

Jung found common ground in stories from all over the world, on which he based his thesis of archetypes: the same themes and motifs occur in every culture, and as far as we can tell throughout history. The great mythologian Joseph Campbell built on this work in his *Hero With A Thousand Faces,* in which he tells the story of Everyman. There are the 'big' stories, the overarching stories of humankind – the perennial issues that concern us and that catch our imagination, that shape the way we move through our lives; and there are the 'little' individual stories, which are rather like the ripples created by the big ones. Their universal importance might differ, but they are all interconnected. Your story is both my story and your own.

Stories are in part about longing and belonging. The right story is an Ariadne's thread: leading us out of the endless labyrinth of our confused and confusing lives towards some sense of meaning; leading us deeper, too, into our own psyches, both individual and collective; connecting us to our joint and separate pasts. Storytelling can help us in finding our way back.

Somewhere our belonging particles
Believe in us. If we could only find them.

(*W S Graham*)

Stories restore you from the inside out; and, rather like the feeling of falling in love, they can invest everything with a depth and glow. 'The feeling of an inexplicable renewal of enthusiasm after storytelling is familiar to many people,' says Barry Lopez[1]. 'It does not seem to matter greatly what the subject is,' he continues, 'as long as the context is intimate and the story is told for its own sake, not forced merely to serve as the vehicle for an idea.' It also doesn't really matter whether the story is light or sober, uplifting or sad; what matters is that it is authentic (not the same thing as 'true', by the way); that it comes from and speaks to the heart. Making the story one's own, and setting it in some kind of personal or community context, whether by use of language and idiom, or by frames of reference (setting, names and physical detail, for instance), takes it deeper for a listener. Master storytellers know this. We bring feeling to story, if it's any good; and we manage this better if we have pictures in our imaginations from the telling, and if that story seems to spring out of soil we recognise.

Appropriately for an intimate art, ultimately stories are about relationships: with ourselves and our place, with other people, with other species, with history, with the land. In the patterning they offer us they have the power to reorder a state of psychological, emotional or spiritual disarray.

The natural world offers a model of easy fluid harmony: everything has its own proportions, everything its own territory, function, pattern; everything both stays within that mould and constantly flows out of it, relating to and interacting with everything else. Everything appears to be in perfect homeostasis, balance; and yet nowhere does it look planned, straitjacketed or neat and tidy. What an achievement! – And a good story achieves this too; in itself, in its loops and twists and turns on its way to its perfectly sense-making destination, and in what it helps shape inside us.

The principle of entropy suggests that the universe, with us included, moves towards a state of disintegration or decay. However, we also know that everything, on our planet at least, tends towards renewal: the seasons return, the tide comes back in, death is followed by birth, dormancy by growth. This is true of course in the human body, which is, it is said, renewed in every cell every seven years; and true of the interior life too. However, there is a tension between these two principles: that of entropy and that of renewal. If our psychological makeup, our emotional and moral elements are, as the Navajo believe (Lopez again), subject to a persistent principle of disarray, we might wish to set against that a conscious reordering.

One way of doing this is through restoring our relationship with the land; another way may be story.

Better still to bring both together.

Among some native peoples, the land is considered to portray a model of sacred order. Lopez draws parallels between the natural world and the personal interior world. If an individual can order his interior landscape, says Lopez, in accordance with the exterior, he will be able to achieve a state of balanced mental health.

The writer's task, I've said already, is to notice, to pay attention to, everything in your environment; the world's stories. What are the components of your immediate environment? What is the fabric of your picture? Is it peopled with humans, or buildings, or wildlife? With silence or voices or traffic? How do these things influence your inner life, and your writing?

For me, as a lifelong countrydweller, these are what make up my immediate world: that blackbird landing in the beech tree, the blood-red splashes on the holly tree, the line of badger droppings at the margin of the wood, the deer tracks in the mud, the sound of the pebbles rolling against granite bedrock under my feet on the bridle path, the sudden sharp tang of fox in the air that the dog lifts her nose to, the scattering and whirring of the pheasant who's given up trying to hide amongst the dead thistles, the cerise and orange spindle berries, the delicate twists of wild clematis, the stench of death in the undergrowth, the stormy light silvering the water in the creek below me, ragged cloud and lit shafts of rain over the Cornish moors in the distance, the smell of fungus and the sludge of hazel and chestnut leaves beneath my feet, the gunshot in the fields behind the house, the little snake of the two-carriage train crossing the bridge over the river – these are the stories of here, the moment before I came in to climb back up the stairs to my study to continue; and now a sudden squall of wind and rain at the window. Somewhere else, solar flares are causing electrical storms and chaos, affecting power supplies, radar tracking stations, even the Hubble telescope. Here there's a new moon rising, and the sky seems glassily green; the few torn clouds on the horizon look uneasily dark and swollen.

The countryside is not all flowers and birdsong, of course. It too has its underbelly: predator and prey; the lamb with its eyes pecked out; the hunt stopping up earths, digging out foxes, having them ripped apart by hounds; the realities of intensive farming, pesticides, nitrate run-off; crop failures; acid rain; diseased trees; the shooting of the wild geese, pheasants, rabbits, pigeons; myxomatosis in the rabbit population, which has them crouching by the road incapable of movement in broad daylight, struggling to breathe, eyes swollen and pus-filled. For the farmers, there is the struggle against weather, cheap imports, poor prices for stock and crops, isolation and a government which doesn't understand rural issues; and so on. It is my job to notice these things too.

I have, in my thirty-minute break from the computer, saturated myself in all these elements; in the story of their relationships. Whether I consciously choose it or not, this environment influences how I write, and becomes so often my starting point. It is both a strength and a weakness in the content of my poetry. This is my element; this is where I feel comfortable; it is what I know. I spend a lot of time on my own or with animals.

My view is biased towards the rural. I said earlier that too much contact with urban realities can be brutalising. But I am human: no contact at all leaves us insular and insulated, strangely devoid of empathy. I need to consciously connect this landscape with landscapes that include people and noise and commerce; with landscapes of poverty and war and deprivation; with heat, or hurricane, or flood; with offices, hospitals, slaughterhouses, prisons, dark alleyways. I need to remind myself. I may not live with these other elements on a daily basis but they are part of the larger web of relationship. They don't go away, whether or not I see them.

It's worth being aware of where you write from, and how your imagination can broaden that – *must* broaden that.

Nonetheless, *here* is what I know and what I love re-learning, day by day. This is how I deepen my own connections with life. The relationships between all these exterior elements, Lopez says, are what makes the landscape – any landscape – comprehensible. 'One learns a landscape finally not by knowing the name or identity of everything... but by perceiving the relationships in it – like that [bird] and the twig.'

The other landscape, the inner one, Lopez likens to 'a kind of projection within a person of an exterior landscape'. The inner landscape consists not only of all the interior physical processes which go on unaided by us, but also of the total of our thoughts; our history and past experiences; our imaginations; our feelings; the people we've loved, the places we've lived; the work we do; our dreams and longings; our spiritual perceptions; our values. There are relationships within and between all these processes; and these relationships are affected by where we go, what we see, the people we meet, where we live and what we can imagine.

Lopez suggests that the purpose and power of storytelling is in its achieving of harmony between the two landscapes; using 'all the elements of story – syntax, mood, figures of speech – in a harmonious way to reproduce the harmony of the land in the individual's interior'.

When we are disconnected from the outer world, the circuit is broken. When we are disconnected from our own interior life, the circuit is broken. Story is a way of throwing the switch so that the energy that powers us can flow again.

'Story', says Clarissa Pinkola Estes[2], 'is meant to set the inner life back into motion again.'

Storytelling starts right here, with this moment, with you in it, you, human being like me, gathering of atoms and molecules, standing here at the nexus of outer and inner worlds. Close your eyes; see all those stories perched inside you, wings folded, waiting for dawn.

Starting point

So here's a way in to storytelling: get into the habit of noticing, really noticing, paying particular attention to relationship and connection. Yes, it's good old writing practice again.

1

Take a notebook everywhere and just note down, in as exact and vivid a way as you can, *everything*. The sound of the traffic. The feel of air passing into your nostrils. The smell of books, coffee, wet dog, car exhaust, a woman's perfume or man's aftershave, a bakery, stale beer, garlic. The clattering of those bins. The note of a collared dove above the sound of lawnmowers. The minute rush – slipstream – of air as you pass another person. Whether your eyes meet or not; what your intuition – and your imagination – tells you about the individuals you pass. The way the light falls on the puddles. The taste of rain. The different distinct voices of everyone on the Tube or the bus. Especially keep your eyes and ears on the alert for the funny, wacky, quirky, unexplained/inexplicable, surreal, extraordinary. Note it all down.

2

Then practise seeing and recording the connections (and juxtapositions) between things. Some of these will be visible – the interconnected events: the bus splashing that cat, that woman's legs; the man exiting from the pub who steps into the road and that puddle to avoid bumping into the woman whose legs have just been splashed.

Some will not be visible. Think about the air you're breathing: how it's shared; how it's been inhaled and exhaled by so many other beings before you. The water you drink that passes through your body, gets purified and passed on, that evaporates into the ether, that collects as cloud, that falls as rain, that makes the puddles through which cars travel which splash your legs, which drains through into gutters to swell the rivers or nourish the soil or journeys out to sea where it evaporates to make cloud... or maybe gets drunk...

3

Now put yourself in the picture. You, recording. You, responding. Your notebook getting wet as the bus throws up puddle-water. You rushing or trudging or slipping or strolling between moments. Your reactions to and involvement in these things you're noting. Move between inner and outer.

4

Make these four aspects of writing part of your daily practice:

> How it is
> The connections between things: context and contact, relationships
> Where you come in as human, observer, recorder and self
> Keep a flow between these things, and between inner and outer.

5

Create imaginary relationships between people and people or between people and place. Develop that minor detail about puddle, cat, woman, man. Ask 'what if?' Sit in a public place and watch: watch what happens and eavesdrop on what is said; imagine what might happen or have happened 'out of the frame'; what isn't said.

Practise 'growing' story through developing fragments. Journalism uses these six focal points to create a news story: who, what, where, when, why and how; they are of use too to the fiction writer.

6
Remember the bringing together of observation, imagination and research...

A story is a candle lit against the dark.

ONCE UPON A TIME

...out of the whole symbol-building achievement of the past, what survives today (hardly altered in efficiency or in function) is the tale of wonder. The tale survives, furthermore, not simply as a quaint relic of days childlike in belief. Its world of magic is symptomatic of fevers deeply burning in the psyche: permanent presences, desires, fears, ideals, potentialities that have glowed in the nerves, hummed in the blood, baffled the senses since the beginning.
Joseph Campbell

I spoke earlier about storytelling being an act of intimacy; something vital also to the life of the soul. Stories are a kind of collective web, to which we add (this of course begs the question of the kinds of stories we need; a question raised in Jeremy Thres' piece, and one on which I'll touch again later).

The 'outer world' demands our daily lives make on our consciousness mean that it is easy to lose touch with inward forces and processes. As we've explored, story is life-furthering; a way of restoring balance, bringing us back. Joseph Campbell wrote that stories 'tell us in picture language of the powers of the psyche to be recognised and integrated into our daily lives, powers that have been common to the human spirit forever, and which represent the wisdom of our species by which we have weathered the millennia...'

Through the dialogue of dream, myth and story, Jung suggested, we can come back into touch with the greater horizon of our deeper wiser self. He saw this dialogue as a continuous interaction between the unconscious and the conscious mind.

As I've said, Jung found that the same symbols and motifs recur throughout culture and history. He concluded that there were universal symbols embedded in the human psyche, each of which plays a part in the way we live our lives. He called these the archetypes: 'the inherited unconscious ideas and images that are components of the collective unconscious'.[1]

In fairy story and folk tale we see these archetypes played out in the form of characters such as the king, queen, prince, princess, hero, villain or anti-hero, stepmother, wise woman, hermit, helper figure (often magical, sometimes in disguise) trickster, dwarf, giant, or animals or objects: dragon, frog, goose, swan, golden ball etc.

Each of these characters has a counterpart, or is symbolic of a process, in the human psyche. Fairy tales and myths are teaching tales: they preserve the wisdom of a culture. Myth particularly will, in one way or another, show us some kind of primal wound in the human being, and depict the way to heal that wound.

These archetypal stories are so deeply embedded in our psyches that they still have an impact on what and how we write, what we think and even what we value. Much film and literature today is still influenced by some of these story foundations and the kinds of plots they centre on.

Many writers have speculated as to the number of basic plots in existence. Aristotle said two: tragedy and comedy. Others suggest there are many more. Seven seems to be a consensus favourite:

> The Quest (e.g. the Grail cycle, Lord of the Rings)
> The Eternal Triangle (e.g. Arthur/Lancelot/Guinevere)
> Battle of Good and Evil (many fairy stories, Lord of the Rings)
> Nemesis (consequences of past actions – Shakespeare liked this)
> The Tragedy of Romantic Love (Romeo and Juliet; Tristan and Iseult)
> Virtue Rewarded (Cinderella)
> The Hero with the Fatal Flaw (e.g. Achilles; Shakespeare liked this one too).

Joseph Campbell, building on Jung's work, found in his study of myths and stories from all over the world and throughout history that the great unifying story was that of the Hero's Journey. He named this the monomyth. (I believe this could equally be called the Quest.)

If you investigate books, films, plays in the light of the seven plot themes above you will see that many popular works fit one – or more – of the models (there are many overlaps). However it seems to me that the Quest motif underpins most of the others: so often in story each of the characters is on a journey to find his or her heart's desire, and, consciously or otherwise, him- or herself. Sometimes that person achieves the desired outcome; sometimes he or she remains stuck somewhere on the journey, thwarted by others, by him- or herself, by circumstances.

Loosely, the hero's journey (in *Riding The Dragon* I've named this The Heroic Quest) can be seen to be the journey from immaturity to maturity, from ignorance to wisdom, from undifferentiation to individuation, from ego to what Jung called 'Self' (in his terminology this is a bigger transcendent function, incorporating the idea of soul or spirit, which allows us to think of the greater good rather than our petty personality-bound self-seekingness, so that the hero learns to move from seeking to fulfil only his own needs to an awareness of his place in the wider world as a compassionate being), from partialness and fragmentation to wholeness.

Abbreviating and generalising enormously, many of the stories with which we resonate will take the major components of these themes in one form or another. (Assume 'he' represents both he and she throughout.)

This is the shape of a 'Quest' story.

The Call to Adventure So we see at the opening our hero – male or female – in a challenging situation. Whatever the original reason, the Call will be manifest as a kind of restlessness; an awareness, articulated or not, that somehow life as he knows it has become too small. There are many ways in which someone will initially do everything possible to avert or avoid this sense that something has to change, from lopping off bits of oneself to try and fit the old life to taking refuge in drink or drugs or food or work or affairs. Eventually, though, the knowledge can't be avoided; a change needs to be made.

Answering the Call involves him in leaving behind in some way everything he has known and stepping out into unfamiliar terrain, with all the terrors, excitement and possibilities that offers. Yes, it can be tough; and yes often he will wish to turn back and block his ears. If he looks out, though, there will be, amongst the adventures, ordeals and antagonists, support, gifts, and helpers along the way.

Crossing the Threshold At some point there will come a big test; the hero then has a choice (though not much of one): to continue, or not. (The latter wouldn't make much of a story; nor offer change and transformation in the protagonist's life, which is the point of both story and – arguably – a life.) This test takes the protagonist over a threshold beyond which there is no return. In archetypal psychology, the stepping across this threshold – the full acceptance of The Call, in other words – represents a willingness to look more deeply into one's life; to face the unknown and unconscious aspects of one's personality, as well as the sides of oneself one would rather forget. It's a journey towards the soul.

Time of Tests In this place there are more tests: both to put the hero on trial to test his or her mettle, as they say; and also to temper personal shortcomings. We refer to these kinds of experience when we say things like 'ordeal by fire'.

The Supreme Ordeal & the Sacred Marriage In many novels, there are a couple of crises that push the story on and create a situation for the protagonist where a major crisis will be inevitable. This forms the climax of the book. In the monomyth model, two things happen almost concurrently. The first is that the protagonist is tested to his limits, until he breaks down or breaks through – often both, as it happens. It's a kind of symbolic death – to the old life and the old self. Assuming the protagonist wins through (lets go), he is then honoured with the 'sacred marriage', which is often depicted as taking place in the outer world but which symbolises an internal state of wholeness and harmony.

Time of Blessings For a while – often a long while – this is enough. Who doesn't want to stay and play in paradise? And after such a journey he deserves his joy and his rest. But sooner or later the hero needs to make the journey back out of his or her personal paradise (the land of satisfied ego needs and, now, a place where he has connected with his true nature, the Self).

Crossing The Threshold – back into the upper world bearing his whole self to give back to the collective, along with what he's learnt. Once more, in crossing the threshold, there may be a last test; but after that we're on the home straight.

Return as King/Queen The hero returns as a whole and worthy member of his or her society, empowered, authentic and authoritative; symbolised in myth as the King returning with his Queen to give back their wisdom to the collective.

All this to the modern ear can sound very quaint, and even 'unrealistic': we are so used to 'sophisticated' stories that we may see as the norm tales of dysfunction, violence, desolation, despair and cynicism. Try examining the main storyline or a subplot in a few of the novels you have recently read – or films you have seen

– in the light of the above cycle; and explore what of the protagonists' lives this model might reflect. You may be surprised.

Starting points

1

Explore the monomyth, or Quest, motif in the light of:

a) your own life; or
b) the book you are or are going to be writing if you know enough about it; or
c) a book you've read recently.

2

Note down the primary threads and qualities of any stories you can remember being told by your parents in your family of origin, or by your teachers. What underlying beliefs and truths did these carry? What picture of the world did they convey?

CREATING THE UNIVERSE
CREATION STORIES, SACRED NARRATIVES &
THE ORIGINS OF THE UNIVERSE

No matter how far the cutting edge of physics, or cosmology, takes us, our fascination with the origins of everything, and, if we can resist cynicism (sometimes masquerading as sophistication), our sense of wonderment in face of mystery remains as alive as ever. Books with titles like *A Brief History Of Time, A History of the World in 101/2 Chapters* and *A Short History of Nearly Everything* become bestsellers, each taking its own unique factual, fictionalised or combined route towards explaining everything. We want to *know*; or if we can't know, at least to speculate and imagine...

Stories are in part about how we came to be here; in part about what we're doing here and how we're doing it. We've always, it seems, wanted to know how we got here. Common to every culture, creation stories are the bedrock of a people.

In our Western culture, the Bible story of Genesis has supplanted other stories of origins. Here is a brief and fairly arbitrary selection of abbreviated creation stories and sacred narratives from Western and other cultures. (I have sometimes collated different versions.)

Clearly, there is a connection between the kind of creation story a culture retains, and the way in which that culture lives, the beliefs and values that are prevalent. Look at the differences, for instance, between the Aztec and the Hindu...

Genesis

In the beginning, the earth was without form, with darkness over the abyss and a huge wind on the waters. God said 'Let there be light', and there was light, and he separated light from darkness and day from night. Evening came, and morning came, the first day.

Then God separated the waters, making heaven and earth. Evening came, and morning came, the second day.

Then God gathered the waters below heaven into one place, so that dry land appeared; he called the dry land 'earth' and the waters 'seas'. Then God called on the earth to produce fresh growth, seed, trees and fruit. Evening came, and morning came, the third day.

Then God made the sun and the moon and all the stars. Evening came, and morning came, the fourth day.

Then God called on the waters to teem with countless living creatures, and the skies too to be filled with birds across the vault of the heavens. These he commanded to multiply. Evening came, and morning came, the fifth day.

Then God made cattle, reptiles and wild animals.

Then God made man in his own image, forming him from the dust of the ground, and breathing into his nostrils the breath of life. Then God created the Garden of Eden for man, away to the east, and gave him care for and dominance over all that lived. Then God saw that he was lonely; and from man's rib he created woman. Evening came, and morning came, the sixth day.

Thus heaven and earth were completed, and God rested. Evening came, and morning came, the seventh day; which God made holy.

Ainu (Japan)

In the beginning, there was nothing but swamp, where nothing could thrive, or even survive. But in the six starry skies above, and the six foggy skies below, lived gods and demons, and animals.

In the highest sky lived the Creator God, Kamui, who made this world in the form of a vast disc of ocean, balanced on the spine of a massive fish. The fish regulated the tides by swallowing the ocean and then spitting it out again; when the fish moved, it made earthquakes and tidal waves.

Kamui decided one day to make something of this watery sphere, and sent a bird, a water wagtail, to earth. This bird eventually, through the enormous work of treading and beating the mud and sand with its feet and wings, managed to create some small areas of dry land. The world was made so beautiful that the animals from the starry heavens begged to be able to go and dwell there, which they were permitted to do.

Then Kamui made other creatures to populate this world, amongst them the first humans, whom he made from clay, with spines of willow and chickweed hair. Then Kamui sent the divine man Aioina down from the skies to teach the first people, the Ainu, survival skills, such as how to hunt and cook.

When Aioina returned to the heavens, he stank so much of humans that he was sent back to cast off his clothes on earth; as he did so, new species were born from his discarded garments.

In some versions of this story, the Divine Creator was called away back to important heavenly business, and asked Otter to fetch another deity down to complete the task of finishing everything. Otter, though, became so absorbed in play that he forgot... which is why humans are not quite perfect...

Australian Aborigine – the Dreamtime

In the beginning, there was no life, and no death. There was only darkness. Under the featureless plain of this embryonic world, sleeping, were the stars, sun and moon, and the eternal Ancestors.

One day, in the Dreamtime, the Ancestors broke through eternity and came to the earth, and wandered. Sometimes they took animal form, sometimes plant form, sometimes both. Sometimes they were almost-humans.

Two of these beings, having arisen out of nothing but dust, were the Ungambikula. The Ancestors created hair for them from eucalyptus bark – one head straight, one curly. They breathed into their mouths, noses and navels, and the two beings came into life as the first true humans.

As the Ungambikula wandered the world, often, beside the beginnings of water holes and salt lakes, they came upon shapeless forms of half-finished human beings made of animals and plants. These people were like clay balls, unmoulded as yet, limbless and featureless. So the Ungambikula sang these beings into people, giving them heads and faces, bodies, arms, legs, hands and feet, until humans were made. Then these ancestors, these totemic beings who sang out the name of everything they met, who sang the world into existence, left; back to their long sleep, or into rocks, trees and waterholes, leaving living sacred trails wherever they had walked.

These trails are the 'Dreaming Tracks' or 'Songlines'; 'Footprints of the Ancestors' or 'The Way of the Law'. The continent is crisscrossed with these dreaming tracks.

Chinese

In the beginning, heaven and earth were still one. Chaos reigned. The universe was like a big black egg; and inside it was Pan Gu. After 18 thousand years, Pan Gu woke from his long sleep. Feeling claustrophobic, he smashed the egg with his axe and cracked it, whereupon the light, clear part of it floated up and formed the heavens, and the cold, heavy matter stayed below to form earth. Pan Gu, afraid that the two realms might again mix and create chaos once more, stood in the middle, holding the sky and the earth apart, his head touching the sky, his feet firm on the earth.

When Pan Gu died, his breath made the wind and clouds, his voice the roaring thunder. One eye became the sun, one the moon. His body and limbs made five huge mountains, and from his blood poured the tumbling waters. His muscles made the land, and his veins made tracks and roads. From his hair and beard sprang all the stars; flowers from his skin, nourished by sweat, and trees from the fine hairs on his body. His tears watered the earth. The marrow of his bones made precious stones, his eyes created lightning.

Some say that, finally, from the insect life on his body, or maybe from his pores, came the ancestors of humans...

Other versions differ in this way: many centuries later, a goddess named Nü Wa found herself alone, roaming Pan Gu's world. Catching sight of herself in a pool, she realised that there was nothing like herself anywhere. So she took up mud, and made forms of human beings, like herself, who each sprang to life as their feet touched soil. Nü Wa made more of them, and flung them to the edges of the world.

However, although she was no longer lonely, each time one died she needed to make another. So she created her mud humans as two sexes, so that they could love each other and save her the task of making new ones herself.

Eventually, without Pan Gu's holding them apart, the heavens and the earth started to crack and crumble, letting in fire and flood. Nü Wa laboured to patch and heal the fragmentation, which eventually she achieved, by plugging the holes in the sky with molten river-stones, and installing a giant turtle to support the sky with its four legs. Having saved the two realms from chaos once more, Nü Wa, exhausted, lay down and died, giving her body for the further beauty and abundance of the earth.

Aztec

In the beginning was the Great Catastrophe.

Coatlique, She of the Snake Skirt, was the Great Mother, fallen from the heavens as the universe broke apart. Created in the image of the Unknown, she was decorated with skulls as well as snakes, and though her great body was unscarred, her hands were cut and torn.

A goddess could only give birth once, and then only to divine offspring. After having been impregnated by an obsidian knife, Coatlique gave birth to the (female) moon and (male) stars. But she once again became pregnant, this time with the fiery god of war.

Her original divine offspring, in anger and jealousy, planned to kill her, but the god of war, enlisting the aid of a fire serpent, murdered these other offspring, dismembering them and then scattering the remains throughout the cosmos, where they stay, fragmented.

Boshongo (Bantu, Africa)

In the beginning was the great god Bumba; and besides him, only darkness and water.

One day Bumba, out of the immense pain of a stomachache, spewed up the sun. In its immense heat it allowed land to arise, as some of the waters evaporated.

But Bumba's pain had not receded; and so he continued to vomit until first the moon emerged, then the stars, then the first animals, and then finally the first humans.

And still he vomited.

Everything that is now in existence once passed through the great god Bumba's mouth.

Hindu

In the beginning, this universe existed only as the indistinct and unknowable non-shape of darkness, sunk in sleep. From this sleep arose the Divine One, who, though unknowable and indiscernible himself, dispelled the darkness and brought the elements and all that came with them into form.

Through his own will, the Divine Self-Existent One who is perceivable only by the inner eye but who creates and contains all beings, shone forth; and with a single thought created the waters, into which he planted his seed. From the seed in the womb of the waters grew a golden egg, bright as the sun; and after a year had passed, from this egg he came forth as Brahma, and he formed heaven and earth from the two halves of the egg.

Between heaven and earth he created the middle sphere, the oceans and the eight directions. Then he created the mind, the ego, and the soul, as well as the five organs of sense.

From the joining of all these things with each other and with himself, he created all beings.

And two from students on my 'Storymaking' course, summer 2004:

1

In the beginning there was already something there. It was a space.

The space was everywhere and into the space there came breath.

In the breath was water, warmth and dust and in the midst of this, words stirred and whispered. At first they were words about shapes. The words became louder until the shapes took on form.

The faint line of moon became full as the words became louder.

The roundness of the sun became hotter and brighter.

And day came.

And as the words became a chant the forms took on colour.

The words multiplied and created song.

And as the song grew louder and sweeter, the body of the first bird appeared.

Birds flew freely in the light and warmth of the breath. They flew in and around the sun and the moon. The flapping of their wings stirred up the dust, and stars were created in the space and made way for night.

In their dreams the birds longed for a place to land and they awoke to the first dawn of the world and they sang louder and their chorus stirred the souls of the people who were aroused and given form out of the earth.

When the night came again the sea arose from the pull of the moon.

The people understood the words of the song and they sprang out of their own mouths and with language the words joined them.

Then the people went together in pairs and knew much joy.

Jo Bellchambers, Becky Gethin, John Richardson-Dawes

2

Before the dawn of time, everything was merged; there was only a naïve unknowing harmony, a co-existence of light and dark.

Sun and moon exist but are unaware of their existence and their separateness. They move together, maintaining a twilight.

The moon begins to be jealous of the power of the sun and the light. The moon works together with the sea and the darkness to create a storm to flood out and drown the sun. The moon and the oceans whip up a storm which threatens to overwhelm everything.

The sun looks on with horror, and calls upon the wind to put a form to her colour and light, and together they force a way through the water and from the divide a rainbow bursts forward and paints the colour of the earth.

In this explosion and recognition of beauty, the storm and the conflict ceases and a new respect and equilibrium is confirmed.

From this time on the sun and the moon agree a new pattern, a sharing of day and night.

Clare Tamplin, Juliet Crittenden, Pippa Dobson

Creation story according to physics
This is my brief summary of Bill Bryson's[1] brief summary of the origins of the universe, according to current scientific thinking.

In the beginning, maybe around 14 billion years ago, was nothing and nowhere; and no time, either.

Imagine, then, in this no-place, shrinking a proton – which is already an infinitesimally small part of an atom – down to about a billionth of its normal size. Load this unimaginably small dimensionless non-thing – which by the way is *not* hanging, just waiting, in darkest space, as there is no space, and no darkness either – with about an ounce of matter. In a single blinding explosive pulse, says Bryson, the universe will start to inflate, expanding outwards, creating space for itself as it goes. In the first second gravity is born; in about a minute the universe has a diameter of about a million billion miles; and by about three minutes in, 98 percent of all the matter that has ever been, or will ever be, created, will have emerged.

So there you are. A selection of 'histories'. What do they have in common? Which inspired you? Why?

Starting point

Invent your own creation story. It doesn't need to be long; it does need to be imaginative.

THEMES

The theme of a story could be defined as the impulse behind the plot. Usually this can be summed up with an abstract noun or short phrase; for instance, jealousy, revenge, ambition, betrayal, love, the loss of love, growing up, the need to possess, etc.

Theme is the underlying motivation and unifying principle, and also provides the dynamic of the story, as well as the likely conflict. It could be described as the 'why' of the book.

There is an intimate correspondence between the theme of a book and the character's, or characters', central problem(s). It's useful to remember this. The overcoming of a character's central problem – the way s/he resolves – or doesn't – a particular theme or issue in his/her life, is often the lynchpin of a novel, providing the thrust of the action and the tension.

Themes and their bearing on stories & plots

So *theme* is the impulse behind the plot.

Story, according to E M Forster, is the narrative of events arranged in their chronological sequence. This is composed of the characters' movement through time and their lives. Story could be said to be the bones of what happens: this, then this, then this; in other words, the 'what'. He uses as an example of story: 'The King died, and then the Queen died.'

The *plot* is the psychological 'flesh and muscle' caused by the interaction of characters with others and with the world. It is the web – and the map – of relationships. It's the narrative of events, now dramatised by the linking of cause and effect. If, as Forster says, story is to do with the characters' life in time, plot is to do with the 'life of values and meaning'. Forster's example of plot: 'The King died and then the Queen died *of grief*.'

So plot is to do with the human aspects: it's about connections, relationships, consequences; the psychology of it all. Like theme, plot is fluid and dynamic in a way that story isn't: the latter is more 'fixed'. It's the 'how' and the 'why', and it hooks us by way of our curiosity.

Summary: plot-building through theme

1 The creative tension inherent in your novel is intimately connected with your theme

2 Connect the theme with the motivations, desires and needs of the main character(s)

3 Thwart these things through conflict, circumstance and character interaction: this generates tension and suspense, provides the crises that constitute turning points and climax, and moves the story on

4 Check periodically: does what I'm writing still relate to this theme? What is happening to my character as s/he moves through the story?

5 Novelist Mandy Sutter, writing in *Mslexia* magazine, offers a helpful suggestion. She says that a novel has two important characteristics in terms of plot dynamics:

> First is the high personal stakes of the main character – their investment in whatever their main desire is
>
> Second is what she calls the 'dramatic question', e.g. (her example): 'Will Quoyle *(The Shipping News)* find love and happiness in a remote corner of Newfoundland, having not found it in New York?'

Checklist: it will help you in your writing to know:

1 The central character's problem (the critical turning points and climax will show him/her stuck between a rock and a hard place. What is this about?)

2 His/her motivation. (What drives him? What does she want?) How does it relate to the problem?

3 The gist of the major conflicts and turning points. How are they related to each other, to the theme, and to the central issue?

4 What kind of story you want to write

5 Whose story is it? (In other words, do you have the right central character?)

6 The basic theme, in a few words

7 The plot, in two or three sentences

8 Working title. Does this give a key to content and style?

Starting points

1

Look back at your responses to question 2 in 'Once Upon A Time'. Think about the familial and cultural stories that underpin how you see the world. What are your family myths and stories – in the broadest sense?

2

Note down all the themes you can think of which have operated in your own life.

3

Re-list the themes in 2 above according to:

> Recurring themes
> Similar themes
> The ones that have caused you the most trouble
> Opposites (good dramatic potential in opposites): by which I mean themes that tend to come in pairs, like dependency and independence, which tend to be resolved – or not – around conflicts
> The ones you find most interesting, objectively as well as subjectively.

4

Now pick out one theme in your list that translated into a specific problem. Note down the problem. Write a very brief plot outline for a story built around that problem (it will probably be easier if you 'give' the story to an invented character and then write it in the third person).

5

Consider what themes interest you enough as to spend about 70,000 words exploring them...

PLOTS

Plot or character?

(As I cover this at length in another book, this is a brief resumé.)

Ronald Tobias in his book on plotting[1] suggests that it's helpful for you to know whether you are primarily interested in people, or in story. Most novels will, of course, in some way consist of both plot and character, but one will normally take precedence. So there are books – usually genre-type novels – which are action- or plot-driven, and there are books – and most contemporary literary fiction exemplifies this – where what is important is the development and progression of the characters, in which case the plot acts as a way for the characters to grow and change. (Characters change in such a book in the way that humans do: we are not left unmarked by events; especially if they are significant enough as to form the climax of a piece of fiction. In a plot-driven book, however, this is not necessarily the case: the characters exist largely as tools to develop the action.)

This doesn't of course mean that you can sacrifice the one for the other. There will be the two strands interweaving through the book, but one is likely to be subservient. So, says Tobias, it can be summarised thus:

Pattern of plot, where the plot is the dynamic force that will guide you through the action; and

Pattern of character, where the actors in the plot provide a dynamic force of behaviour that will guide you through your characters' intent and motivation.

Whichever your main interest, you will also need to pay attention to the development of the other. If you are concerned particularly with character development and the psychology of interpersonal relationships, a danger is that you neglect the narrative, so that it either rambles or degenerates into a string of unconnected events. (It helps to be aware of Aristotle's fundamental maxim: a story unfolds through the portrayal of *crisis,* followed by *complication,* followed by *outcome/solution.*) If you are more interested in the constructing of a plot, there is a danger that your characters will remain undeveloped and 'flat', more ciphers or stereotypes than 'real' people.

What is important to remember is that no matter which is your primary interest, what you must do is involve your reader sufficiently in the story and in the characters who people it for him or her to care about what happens to them; and then you need to put your main character(s) between a rock and a hard place...

Storylines

If we look at a storyline in it simplest shape, as a line on a graph, it rises firstly from the opening situation, which, conventionally speaking, shows the main character at a critical moment: about to leave home, at a point of change, in a tense situation, in the middle of an event which will change his or her future, and so on. The line will continue to rise – via some peaks, troughs and plateaux – through one or two more major crises to the climax, which constitutes the 'point of no return' towards which the previous plot developments have inexorably led. After this, the plot line falls off sharply to the end of the book.

It's worth considering in advance what the main crises, or turning points, might be. What does your main character want? And what is going to get in the way of that? Bear in mind that your protagonist will need obstacles and an antagonist – or else there is no story. (The archetypes mentioned in a previous chapter, incidentally, usually come in pairs, in story as in life: for each hero there will be a villain; for each wicked stepmother there will be a wise woman. One force moves us forward; the other holds us back.) Bear in mind, too, that the antagonist may not necessarily be, or only be, external. Our own weaknesses and negative character traits hold us back just as much as external circumstances or other people; the less aware of them we are, the more likely we are to manifest them in the outer world, through the psychological mechanism known as 'projection'. (More on this in the chapter on character.)

So that's the 'received' approach. But there are many ways of telling stories that 'don't involve realism or conventional narrative,' says writer and publisher Neil Astley.[2] 'It isn't the storyline that makes me keep turning the page, it's my engagement with the characters, with the language... and with a whole different world I inhabit imaginatively and emotionally for as long as the book continues.' So the challenge is to create a credible and engaging world for your reader; one which he or she leaves with regret at the end of the book; and which lingers in his or her memory.

Many publishers, in Britain at least, are not only open to, but actively seek out, new approaches to writing fiction. A commissioning editor at Chatto & Windus, interviewed in *Mslexia*, Summer 2004, says that what she is *not* looking for is the 'linear a to b plot that isn't doing anything exciting'. A narrative 'has to be striking, unless the writing is exceptional'.

Consider how many ways there might be to approach your story, besides the obvious and well worn. There are increasing numbers of books that don't 'fit' the stereotypical movement from beginning to middle to end... if none comes to mind, look out for examples of these next time you're in a bookshop. Approaches can include beginning with the end of the story – a flash-forward, and then working towards it; and ones that include flashback. These too are reasonably conventional; so what of others? Here are some:

> Sebastian Faulks: *Fool's Alphabet* – chapters are titled by place names beginning with each letter of the alphabet, so locating them in space, but the time-sequence jumps around
> Martin Amis: *Time's Arrow* – written 'backwards'
> Carol Shields: *Happenstance* – this book's jacket is identical front and back, though upside down in relation to each other, and you can begin at either end. The two stories – husband's and wife's – meet in the middle
> Julio Cortázar: *Hopscotch* – to be read as suggested by the title, in different sequences; read as a complete book or skip the 'expendable' chapters for a different story
> B S Johnson: *The Unfortunates* – '27 discrete sections offered up for sale in a cardboard box – drop on table and read at random'
> "   "   *Alberto Angelo*: 'small holes cut into pages to give readers advance notice of plot developments'
> "   "   *Housemother Normal*: 'geriatric comedy set in an old people's home, in which individual letters are chucked randomly about the page'.

Other possibilities include novels written as a collection of postcards; in the form of letters, text messages or emails; as a 'collage'; or in one long unbroken narrative, dramatic monologue or soliloquy (e.g. *Separation*, by Dan Franck).

Starting points

Part 1

1

Think of a book

Note down central character's problem

Note down theme

Note antagonists

Sum up plot in 1 or 2 sentences.

2

Creating a storyline

> a) Invent/note down a one-line possible outline scenario; e.g.:
>   – woman meets man in secret place; or
>   – overheard snippet of conversation: 'You mean you never knew?' or
>   – finding half a letter.
> b) Choose one line and note down: i) the most likely explanation; ii) the most inventive
> c) Invent a story around this scenario. Avoid predictable explanations and go for the more surprising and gripping.

Part 2

(This is a stereotypical pattern of storytelling development)

1

> Summarise the *plot* of <u>your</u> book in one short paragraph
> Now can you do that in one sentence?

2

Central character

> Name
> Physical details/circumstances in brief at opening: family/job/location etc
> What is this character's goal, aim, driving need or desire? (The central 'dramatic question')
> Why is this important?
> How is it linked to the theme of the story?

3

Central conflict

Who or what constitutes the antagonist/main conflict/central problem?
How would this affect the protagonist/or stop him or her achieving their goal?

4

Obstacles and problems

What is the first difficulty? When/how does it appear?
How is it overcome – or not?
What further complications/problems does it lead to?

5

Final crisis/dramatic climax

What is the major crisis?
What will it change?
How will the protagonist be changed as a result?

6

End

What is the outcome?

CHARACTERS

Novels are generally about *people*, and about the broad spectrum of human activity: the situations, relationships and circumstances in which we do, or might, find ourselves. Ultimately, they're about people in situations that will leave them marked and transformed. As readers, we need both characters and situations to be sufficiently credible for us to care about them.

Conveying believable characters takes skill, hard work, imagination and empathy. Characters won't come alive to the reader unless they have first come alive to the writer; so you need to be involved, emotionally involved, with them, even if they're not necessarily likeable people. *You* need to care about what happens to them.

E M Forster[1] suggests that one of the reasons we read novels is to have a glimpse into people's secret lives. A person has two sides, he suggests: the 'outer expression' consists of what we can see or know of their world through their actions, words and what we perceive or are told of their history, and what we might guess of their existential, emotional or spiritual life through these things.

Then there is the 'inner life': the private, yearning, dreaming, romantic, passionate, joyful and fearful private world that may not emerge into daylight so easily.

The novel's chief function is to lay this inner life bare, says Forster. 'We cannot understand each other, except in a rough and ready way; we cannot reveal ourselves, even when we want to; what we call intimacy is only a makeshift; perfect knowledge is an illusion. But in the novel we can know people perfectly.' This is why, he suggests, that characters in a novel can seem more 'definite' than real people, even our friends; 'and... we can find here a compensation for their dimness in life...'

Forster's words above were delivered at Cambridge in 1927. Since then, the world has changed: we've lived through the 'sixties; we are collectively aware of the importance of 'expressing our feelings'; counselling and psychotherapy are commonplace; and the post-war generation and their offspring tend towards a generally less inhibited way of being. Our cultural mores have shifted. Nonetheless, there is still a truth in Forster's words. Something in the human psyche is slower to change than external events and outward behaviour. In 'real life' we can never know another human being right through to the core. As a writer, it is your job to know your character as perfectly as possible, and to convey that to a reader.

Our major characters, at least, need to be whole people. What this means is that they need to be multifaceted and changeable like human beings. They need to be capable of surprising us (as writers and readers). They need to exhibit simultaneously consistency *and* unpredictability, just as we all do.

Forster famously divided the characters in a novel into 'flat' and 'rounded'. Although it may be a useful formula, I don't think this polarisation lends itself to the postmodern novel. Even in more traditional storytelling, it's more like a continuum: there are the one or two, maybe three, main characters in the book, in the foreground. In the middle distance are the major characters whose lives have an impact on the main character(s). In a supporting role are those who don't really have a bearing on the outcome, but contribute to the overall texture, the 'background' of the story; to create depth of field, dimension and substance; to lend credibility.

When thinking about character dynamics, it's useful to remember the idea of 'helper' characters, and 'adversarial' figures: in folk tales[2], these appear in such guises as the donor, talking animal, despatcher on a journey, crone, wise woman, princess' father, dwarf and other such archetypes. Sometimes their role is obvious and overt; sometimes it's a disguise (all is not what it seems). The point of this figure in the folk or fairy tale is to test and teach the main character; by helping or by hindering (which may also ultimately help).

Often in mythology these come in pairs: the hero's antagonist will be the villain; the beautiful princess will be partnered by a Loathly Lady, the ignorant young lad venturing out into the world by a wise old hermit. Folk and fairy tales will exaggerate and polarise traits for 'visibility', so that both hero and anti-hero are larger than life: exclusively good or exclusively bad, in a way that humans beings are not.

In practical terms, for the novelist, these offer two useful tools. One is the creation of other characters whose role in the book is to act 'for' or 'against' the main protagonist. The other is to see these figures as representing *internal characteristics* – positive or negative – that may further or hinder the protagonist in his or her life and the story.

We can look at these figures as psychological blueprints. Archetypally speaking, these fairy tale figures embody internal aspects of the psyche; so one facet of the novelist's job is to develop the psychological aspects of the main character so that his or her inner traits become visible: for example, how does she thwart her own achievement of her goal? What is it in him that insists on throwing spanners in the works? What provokes his anger/wisdom/love, and how does it show? How does her courage manifest? What needs to be sacrificed or faced up to? (And so on.)

Robert Bly talks about folk tale figures such as the dwarf who can be seen as representing the protagonist's underdeveloped mean side, something small and cramped in him, the part of him that keeps the biggest portion for himself. If we assume that we meet ourselves mirrored in the 'outer world', the 'dwarf' might be portrayed in the folk tale as someone who challenges the protagonist constantly with petty obstacles. This reflection of the protagonist's 'small' side in folk tale is often mediated by a 'big' figure, the positive face of the 'giant' – whatever is generous in him, his large, open side – to bring balance; or the wise advisor to give him an overview. The meeting and overcoming of such obstacles and antagonists in folk or fairy tales suggests that the hero does the necessary work – inner work – to develop these qualities in him (or her)self, in order to achieve and be worthy of whatever his goal is, his 'heart's desire'.

We all contain all these archetypes; some are well developed, some less so; others we don't even know exist in ourselves, even when we're quite adept at identifying them in others. Folk tales offer us maps of the psyche. We could suggest that fiction offers us tools in developing not only our fictitious characters but also the underdeveloped sides of ourselves which, once brought to our attention, can then be integrated and incorporated into our consciousness. They will then also be available to us when meeting the challenges we all encounter. Bringing this kind of mindfulness to our reading and writing will give both much more richness and depth.

So sometimes it can be helpful, when constructing your plot, to think about the various roles of the characters within it in relation to these archetypes.

Every protagonist needs her opponent, inner and/or outer. The tension created by pairing opposites, we've said already, will push the story forward. Celia Brayfield in *Bestseller*[3] says a central character needs two well-differentiated and probably opposing characteristics that are the focus and pivot of his/her central problem. Their cardinal quality drives them forward; the opposing holds them back. For instance, a person might have an appetite for life and a curiosity about the world, but still be held back by fear. Or courage and carelessness. Or a lot of talent but low self-esteem. Or someone might be a romantic who longs for intimacy, but is so shy she doesn't ever go out to meet anyone. Brayfield uses as examples Hamlet, who is vengeful but indecisive; and Shirley Valentine, who is adventurous but feels she doesn't deserve her dreams. Which of these ultimately triumphs becomes part of the creative and psychological terrain of the novel.

A common beginner's mistake is to 'tell' a reader about the novel's characters rather than have them demonstrate their 'who'-ness through their actions. Show your characters by what they do, how they do it, and through their relationships. Marina Oliver[4] suggests you show them by:

> What they say and how they say it
> What they do
> How they do things
> Why they do things
> Their past actions
> Their beliefs, habits, tastes, preferences, interests, hobbies.

You can also shed light on them through others, of course:

> How other people see them
> How other people talk to and about them
> How other people behave towards them.

When you are writing, try and picture these people in action; engage your senses. If, for instance, you are creating an encounter, and do not find it easy to visualise, picture yourself in a similar kind of situation from your own life, and call upon your memories of your surroundings, your feelings, the participants' body language and the remembered action and words. A reader will have a better chance of staying with you if they can 'see' the scene unfolding in front of them, as if on a stage.

Starting points

1

Thumbnail portraits – no more than half a page each, describing the quirks as well as physical and emotional aspects of:

 a) Someone you love (what makes them who they are?)
 b) Someone you don't like.

2

Take b) above, and write a brief – no more than a page – diary entry in *the first person* for this person.

3

Reflect on this. What did you learn?

4

Make notes in response to all the below:

Think of someone you don't like/trust – it might or might not be the same person as 1b) above. What are this person's main characteristics? If this person were a character in a book, what trouble might these characteristics cause?

Now list the characteristics of someone you like/love/respect/trust (ditto). Positive attributes can cause as much trouble as negatives: for instance an overly kind person might be taken advantage of over and over, which could have at least five kinds of repercussion: she might have loose boundaries and never be able to say no; she might lose others' respect or trust; she might be so at the mercy of others she neglects herself or her family; she might suffer a loss of self-esteem herself in being a martyr; she might have a secret store of resentment or self-pity.

Briefly: list the characteristics you as a person value; and then the ones you hate (to work with these will give your writing the depth that comes from an emotional charge).

Now list the characteristics in yourself you dislike. (Some people find it helps to give each characteristic a name; e.g. Critical Christine, Smartarse Simon, Grump, The Whiner, Dog-with-a-bone, etc.)

Do any of these have a particular charge for you? Ones that you *really* hate in yourself? If you were to look back over the work done so far in 1, 2 and 3 above, do you see any connections?

Choose one characteristic. What trouble could a person with these traits cause in a story as an antagonist?

List the character traits of your main character, positive and negative, and consider what bearing they might have on the plot.

5

   a) What does your main character want?
   b) Who or what is thwarting him/her?
   c) If what, how? If who, what is the antagonist's agenda?
   d) What would your main character not under any circumstances give up?
   e) What would be i) an obvious way of jeopardising this, and ii) a more subtle way?
   f) What do you want your main character to have realised by the end of the book?

6

Write a short scene – no more than a page – which shows your character in action; maybe under pressure or in a situation of conflict. Don' t think too hard; just let your pen flow. You might want to try writing it in the first person.

THE ALCHEMY OF OBJECTS
BY JANE SPIRO

I have an idea for a story but at this stage it has not yet incubated so that I can feel its anger and its bite. The story is still at the level of:

I want to write about the experience of work/life as cheap in a business-obsessed culture.

I want to write about the experience of emi/immigration into a foreign culture that you trust will be safer than the one you left behind (but is not).

I have the characters – Sol and Minka Elderkind, who have run the family company for three generations, and their 10-year-old son. I have the settings: an evacuation from northern Poland just before the war, to the cold northern England coast. I have the tension: a tragic secret that makes the marriage of Sol and Minka merely for show, and for survival. I have the dramatic thrust: the fate of the company when transplanted to England, and how this affects and symbolises the fates of all the family members.

But I know there is one ingredient missing: a magical object, one which I meet when evolving a story, which has an alchemic quality to it when I throw it into the mixing pot of my characters.

In my first novel, I started with the magic object, and the whole novel evolved backwards from this. It was a wall I was led to on one of my trips to Poland, set alone in the middle of a field of snow, and which on closer encounter turned out to be a patchwork of broken tombstones. This wall, its isolation, its non-wall qualities dividing nothing, holding up nothing, the suddenly intimate encounter with personal names, the desecration of the stones, their jumbled resurrection: all of these were the moment of transformation. This wall became my first novel.

So I am clear that, with my second novel, I have issues but not yet real, passionately experienced story. So what can I do, to leap from the one to the other?

It is, for me, this single alchemic object which precipitates the leap, and which transforms random pieces into plot. This object seems to me to have the following qualities:

When you meet it, it embeds itself into your story, or even becomes the
story

The more you explore it, the more symbolic and representative of your
central themes it appears to be

As you allow the object to play amongst your characters, it begins to echo
your characters and even become your characters

The object is like the repeated refrain of a poem: each time you return to it,
it has acquired a different nuance or meaning

It is an object you are able to love in some way.

In Flannery O'Connor's *Everything that rises must converge*, a white woman from
a southern state of America is reluctantly travelling on the same bus as black
people. To her dismay, a black woman climbs onto the bus wearing the same
large blue hat as hers.

In Raymond Carver's *Errand*, a valet is asked to deliver a bottle of Moët to
Room 211 after midnight. He does so, but in the morning is told the guest has
died and he must summon the mortician. As he leaves, he notices the cork from
the Moët bottle, which has rolled onto the floor. The guest is Anton Chekhov.

In Tracey Chevalier's *The Girl with a Pearl Earring*, it is the pearl earring that
turns the picture into a painting that represents the girl herself, who both belongs
but does not to the image she is portraying.

In *The Great Gatsby*, it is Gatsby's silk shirts that finally win Daisy and make
her cry.

Now I am searching for the alchemic object that will ignite my story. I know
the object, when I find it, will have all the qualities listed above. I am looking for
an object that will, like the pearl earring, turn the picture into a painting.

It happened one day, walking along the Tamar looking over to Plymouth where I
used to work. The scene from this side of the Tamar was idyllic and the release at
being on this side and not the other was great. I thought how the sea transformed
what lay in, near and under it, and yet how neutral the sea was. And then the
object sparked in my mind.

Amber.

Perhaps it came, because at that moment I was echoing the story of my
own characters, watching the wash of the sea from the safety of one shore, but
remembering both the beauty and the rejection that emanated from the other.

Perhaps it was because, at that moment, I was wearing the amber necklace my parents had bought me. They returned to Poland after 50 years, but despised the idea of returning to the familiar (and probably no longer standing) places. They preferred to visit the places they had never been allowed to go to before: the old cities of Warsaw and Cracow, and the salt mines where they bought this amber necklace.

Why had they left? Where did they go to when they left? By what complex route did these amber beads reach me and follow me here?

Amber became the thing which my characters loved in the story; and also the thing which they became: tough and bright, with all life trapped within them; shuttled from shore to shore; secret, hidden under the sea and disguised by layers of grey.

Minka was strong, and the nails in the wrench creaked like mice as she bent them back, and they strained together against the threads until a crack of light spread around the lip of the box, and they prised it open and stared, awestruck, into the place.

Inside, was a cave of luminous amber, dulled now in its strange nesting place, a huge creation workshop of shapes and colours mined 6 metres deep below the electric beaches, polished so the healing resin flaked away to reveal, here in the grey northern England hallway, a wildlife trapped in liquid dances, arabesque flies and minute mite constellations, a breathless undersea museum, his Baltic, his captured globs of sun.

Rubin knelt beside the box. Here was his planet, the sealed golden heart of the Elderkind dynasty. As long as the Elderkinds had this, they need never be afraid.

It was the thing that gave the anger and the bite. A generation later, Rubin's son Joel is forced to sell the family name to a company that makes cheap plastic imitations.

"Don't make a fuss you mean? Go quietly you mean? Blitz, do you know where this company would be if my family had just gone along quietly? Do you, Blitz? Do you know where you and your little scheme would be now if my family had gone along quietly without making a fuss?"

"I know what you're saying, Joel, –"

"Oh no you don't, you cosy little yuppie. My family have nursed this business for five generations, a world war and two continents: your staff team have been around five minutes, and all they know about are cheap imitations and quick fixes. I bet your 'staff' think five generations is some rock band. This business is just a load of pretty coloured Smarties to you lot. Do you know the difference between *this*, machine-made trash: and *this* – look at it, one is a dead, stupid glass eye: the other is an eye that sees, a living eye! Get it?! It's the eye of the sea – look at it! What you're doing isn't just stupid, it's inefficient, it's ignorant, it's –"

"I'm sorry you feel this way, Joel, I knew it would be hard for you but –"

"It's murder, it's murder," and Joel was sobbing now, because the wound had done its journey from the skin into the blood and coursed itself round his veins and it had reached his heart and stabbed him there, sent his heart and all the memories mixed in it into spasm.

Joel has become the amber: the amber has become Joel and all his history.

The more I learnt about amber, the more it spoke:

It is buried 6–20 metres under the sea
Only Baltic amber possesses medicinal qualities in the resin. It is rubbed onto skin to help with rheumatism and arthritis
In Arabic, the word for amber is also the word for electricity
When it is mined, it is covered with a slate-grey resin that makes it looks just like any other pebble on the beach
Its first colour after polishing is milky white like the sea's foam
Whole sea creatures are trapped in amber so it acts as a snapshot of the sea's mite population while the amber was forming.

Amber was the thing that brought together my two themes: emi/immigration, and the cheapness of work/life in a business-obsessed world. Amber represented the neutrality of nature: its continuity and durability; the beauty of those things that lie hidden. Amber represented electricity and ignition, the spark of my story that brought my characters to life.

Story alchemy

Starting points

1
Choose your object. What is *your* amber?
Move amongst the objects in your life, until one of them ignites.

> Something you wear all the time: a wedding ring, a watch
> Something you always travel with: a hat, a bag, a wallet
> Something you have kept since childhood: a teddy, a love letter.

2
Work backwards in time, unravelling the story of how that object came to be with you now: where from? Who gave it to you? Under what circumstances?

How was the object made or created? (In a sweatshop, from under the sea, carved from Carreras marble?)

3
Explore the symbolic significance of your object. Let yourself 'travel' through all its meanings, and research these if necessary, in a dictionary or on the Internet.

Let the ingredients take you where they wish to go, and trust the alchemy.

STRANGER THAN FICTION

Making a story from real life

One of the problems with writing from life is that if we've had a full or exciting life, it's so packed with good stories that we assume each is sufficient in itself, without drafting or editing, or adding to, subtracting from and restructuring. But part of the art of good storytelling is to know what to leave out; and also knowing how to embroider enough as to heighten any inherent tension. (Think of this piece of writing as a semi-representational painting – the artist will have made decisions about what to exaggerate and what to leave out altogether, but the end result still bears a resemblance to the original subject.)

It's also about working out where an effective beginning place is, and where an effective ending might be – even if these differ from the original 'true' story (and the human memory being what it is, I assume that the past, once it *is* past, is not only history but already fiction).

Also, a story, when it's born, acquires its own life and energy. It can be shaped, but it may not always be manageable in the way that you hope or expect. That's a good sign!

So, having said that, it's important, in terms of making literature that you are able to let go of passages or even whole incidents that don't serve the story.

Some suggestions for reshaping or creating fiction from a piece of autobiographical writing:

Take one of your eight incidents from exercise 1 in 'Writing From Life 2'.

> 1 Work out what the 'thrust' of this story is – its theme (this will usually be simply a word or a short phrase, often abstract: 'loss', 'revenge', ' betrayal', 'a triangle', 'brush with death', 'adventure' etc), and its driving force – where does it or could it go and what propels it.
>
> 2 Summarise the heart of the story in just two or three sentences.
>
> 3 Forget the 'truth' of what happened.
>
> Identify a single strong motivation for the main character (whether this was really you, or someone else): what does s/he really want or need out of the situation and how is that being thwarted?
>
> Add (extra) drama and conflict – raise the stakes.

4 Consider using the third person, he or she, instead of 'I' if the story involves you personally (this will give you the objective distance necessary to see how to shape the story); or try using 'I' if in the original you wrote from someone else's viewpoint.

You could also:

5 Choose a new central character – come in at the story from a different angle.
6 Change the setting/central situation.
7 Try telling the story aloud – to yourself, to a tape recorder, to a friend. It will help you see what's significant, and address some of the questions above. If you do the latter, ask them to tell it back to you as they heard it – it can be illuminating.

It's as well to:

8 Think about where, from the point of view of making a good story, the story should open.
9 Avoid too many viewpoints – stick to just one if possible (or if it's imperative that there are more, be clear about whose thread is which, and when. Use line breaks to introduce a new scene or a different character's viewpoint.)
10 Avoid distractions such as digressions/subplots (at least if you are shaping a short story. If you're convinced that you have enough material for a novel, and the confidence to execute it, it's a different matter.).

Interestingly, you'll probably still find that the 'heart' of the story remains the same – but that the telling of it is stronger...

BEGINNINGS, MIDDLES & ENDS
A CHECKLIST

Decisions made or to be made
What's the theme? What's the story? What's the plot? Who are the main characters? What is the main character's major goal? What dilemmas and conflicts in this character's life will thwart that goal or purpose (without conflict there is no story)? How will they show up? What will precipitate the major crisis/climax? And, given this, what is the inevitable – albeit surprising – conclusion to the story?

Once you've answered these questions you have a summary of the book.

In general, aim for some kind of balance between narrative (telling) and action (showing). Scenes are more dynamic and engaging, but will be interspersed with narrative passages to fill in background/detail, and give the reader a psychological or emotional break from some of the intensity.

The beginning
>   Introduces the most important character(s)
>   Shows us something of their situation
>   Establishes the setting
>   Engages a reader/publisher.

Try
>   For a good strong opening sentence/paragraph – it needs to intrigue and invite
>   To begin in the middle of the action.

Consider
>   Opening with a dramatic scene
>   With dialogue
>   With a question.

Avoid

Unnecessary detail

Overmuch narrative/explanation; *especially* avoid spelling out things like the surname, age and general life history of the main character – a common failing (leave these things till later, where they can be introduced 'in passing', or as relevant).

Tip

Be prepared to use the opening as a psychological point of entry for you as writer. You may arrive at the end of the book and realise that the beginning is elsewhere; or that you simply need to let go of the first chapter or so, or reorder the narrative.

By the end of the first couple of pages a reader needs to know who the main character is and something of his/her immediate situation, and to be engaged with him or her and with the story.

By the end of the first chapter a reader needs to care enough about the main character as to be interested in continuing. Remember that weaknesses, as much as strengths, in the protagonist often hook our sympathy: viz. Quoyle in *The Shipping News*.

By the end of the first chapter a reader needs to be involved in the story.

Remember that you will need to deliver on all the promises you make/situations you hint at in the first chapter.

It's worth taking the time to work on the opening sentence, and then the opening page.

Opening sentences
Here are some classic openings:

'It was a bright cold day in April, and the clocks were striking thirteen.' (Orwell)

'All happy families resemble one another, but each unhappy family is unhappy in its own way.' (Tolstoy)

'The past is a different country; they do things differently there.' (Hartley)

'"Take my camel, dear," said Aunt Dot, as she climbed down from this animal on her return from High Mass.' (Macaulay)

'Mother died today. Or perhaps it was yesterday, I don't know.' (Camus)

'When Gregor Samsa awoke one morning from uneasy dreams he found himself transformed in his bed into a gigantic insect.' (Kafka)

And some less well-known ones:

'Every journey conceals another journey within its lines: the path not taken and the forgotten angle.' (Jeanette Winterson)

'"What am I doing here?" he kept asking himself.'
(Yvonne Eve Walus)

'There were no lions any more.' (Russell Hoban)

'Nothing is more deadly than a deserted, waiting street.'
(Harper Lee)

'Ours is a tragic age, so we refuse to take it tragically.'
(D H Lawrence)

'He looked at the policemen, and his eyes seemed full of sky.'
(Dick Francis)

'It had been happening to him every morning, recently.'
(Françoise Sagan)

'Much more than the card he slipped her at the last minute, it was the call of all those fortuities (the book, Beethoven, the number six, the yellow park bench) which gave her the courage to leave home and change her fate.'
(Milan Kundera)

'He sat drinking his tea, gulping and gasping, the fire drawing damp out of his clothes as if ghosts were rising from him.'
(Laurie Lee)

Starting points
The opening

1

Which – if any – of the opening sentences (above) caught your imagination? Why? Would it or they induce you to want to continue? If not, why not? (There is a difference, clearly, between something that can be seen objectively to be strong, and an opening that appeals to us personally.)

2

Writing: take one of the above sentences – preferably from a novel you haven't read – and run with it for a page. (You might want to compare this with the original book's first page later.)

3

Take a couple of contemporary novels and evaluate their opening chapters:

> How well does the opening sentence/paragraph/page work for you?
> Do you have a sense by the end of the first chapter of:
> Who the main character is?
> What kind of people, what kind of a story, and what kind of tensions the author is creating? (How are these things conveyed?)

Are we taken quickly into a scene, rather than given over-much explanation/ narrative?
Is there enough detail to intrigue us, but no more than necessary?
What about the diction and writing style? Is it fluent and fluid, or does it obtrude in some way?
If you had to award points out of ten for:

> Originality?
> Interest value?
> Suspense/hooks?

4

If you haven't already begun your novel, start *now* with a strong opening sentence; and simply carry on.

If you have, apply the above questions as objectively as you can; or exchange your work with a writing friend's and look at each other's.

The middle
> Develops the action
> Deepens the characterisation
> Adds complexity
> Increases suspense/intrigue
> Builds tension towards the climax
> Builds on earlier foundations
> Might introduce new situations/surprise developments.

> *Beware*
> The plot going 'flat'. *Try questioning*: what's happening to my main character? What might be the consequences of earlier actions? What's the worst thing that could happen? What if...? What could go wrong?

> *The climax*
> Represents the point of maximum tension/no return
> Is a culmination of what has gone before
> Shows and invites the reader to join in with the full impact of the results of past actions (or karma, fate, destiny etc)
> Usually involves such things as ordeal, exposure/revelation, choices/decisions, sacrifice, transformation.

The end
> Should come soon after the climax
> Needs not to be too drawn out
> Needs to be seen to be inevitable, albeit surprising
> Needs to be satisfying/appropriate, even if unhappy
> Needs not to be too contrived
> Doesn't need to resolve everything, or tie up all loose ends; though the major ones need to be addressed in some way.

Beware

Diluting the impact of the climax

'Going out with a whimper'

'Cheating' the reader by a 'pat' or too-neat ending, or by having previously withheld information that the reader should have had early on.

PART 4

WRITING FOR LIFE

THE NIGHT SEA JOURNEY
WRITING NEKYIA - ROSE FLINT

In archetypal psychology, the phrase 'night sea journey' is sometimes used to denote an entrance into the underworld, as experienced through depression or grief.

Jung gives us a powerful image of life when he describes it as a circle; we enter at the lowest point and spend half our existence climbing up – always towards life – until we reach the midway point at the top. And then we descend, always moving towards death. In the descent, he used the word 'nekyia,' from the Greek word that describes a 'night sea journey' as undertaken by Odysseus.

There are many deaths at the midpoint. Often we lose our parents, our children move away from home, our health or our marriage may deteriorate, our dreams diminish or our work decay. For a woman, this time is also menopause, the 'Change' when everything physical and emotional about ourselves may alter with frightening rapidity so we no longer know who we are. At this time many women experience a deep sense of loss, which seems to act like a fissure in the consciousness, allowing old, unhealed emotions to surface.

At this time of my life I had moved away from a much-loved house in the country where my husband and I had brought up three children. Family needs change and we had moved into the city, but it seemed that everything else was changing too. I could no longer rely on anything, I could keep no certainties and found myself deeply depressed, unmoored, feeling bereaved. I cried for a year and a day when I left and from then onwards, was stuck in regret – I just wanted to go back.

Sylvia Plath said that writing was her 'deepest health' and it always has been so for me. I continued to write, mostly poetry, searching for something I couldn't name. I was working hard, teaching creative writing and learning new things. I studied shamanism and alternative spiritual beliefs; later I trained as an art therapist.

One day, I read a poem by Jamie McKendrick about a road trip. And suddenly knew that I too needed to write a journey poem… I did not know then that it would be a book. I think I began it more as a way of saying something about the changing face of the land than about myself. I was working a lot in Wales and travelling up and down the country, I could bear witness to the huge amount of alteration – desecration – that was happening everywhere. I had been a very active member of the Green Party when I lived on the Borders but it seemed that what was valuable and beautiful in the land was daily being eroded by commerce.

Slowly I began to write more and more linked poems. I had a sense that I was taking a journey on an inner level and knew the direction was West. The poems revisited some events and landscape, but also established for me an inner world. I was not trying to write 'realistically' about my life; although based in truth this was a fiction, a story that allowed me freedom to discover more about myself. The collection now is not in the order that it was written. The first poem I consciously wrote – as a one off 'journey poem' – was 'Directions' but writing that quickly pushed me on to 'Freeway', then over that year – 1994 – another six poems were written. (I was still writing other work at this time.) Slowly I realised that I wanted to do something bigger than a sequence, that the work had a life of its own. Another sixteen poems were written, most of them in the following two years.

What happened next changed a lot of things for me. I was very depressed and not coping well with life. I remember going into my room one snowy day and sitting down by my window. I should have been on my way to a meeting in Wales but it had been postponed because of the weather. I began to write – not knowing where I was going with it, but with some of the themes that had already become part of the fabric of the book running through my head. I used the technique Peter Redgrove called 'Secret Writing', also known as 'free' or 'stream of consciousness' writing: that is, when you simply put pen to paper and don't stop until you have either covered the required amount of paper or completed a stated time. (This is a way of working that I had been using throughout the writing process, and one I value greatly.)

This time I could not stop. The poem became something beyond words – a vision. I saw within me and felt outside me the experience of the poem: of walking lost across snow and meeting a being I called Swan Woman.

This poem, 'The Blue Gate', deeply affected me. Writing it took my thinking away from the rigid fears and narrowness that had trapped me and gave me intense comfort. The poem was not finished, it was about half of the final text and I had no idea how to complete it or what it might mean. What I did not realise at the time was that it marked a halfway point in my own 'night sea journey'. It took me many months to complete, and itself represented a major journey within the journey for me. Now, finishing the poem, I realised that it was loss of soul that concerned me; here I found my way back.

I became more conscious of what I was doing on an inner, unconscious level. Working consistently with Secret Writing had given me a way of placing my life journey into a metaphoric landscape that reflected the many levels of my concerns at the time. I believe that this metaphoric land, this *innerscape,* resides in all of us, and is a place with huge potential to affect the outer world. I had not set out to write down how I was experiencing my life in the detailed, graphic terms of everyday language but I had needed to write, and the innerscape gave me great freedom to express those needs as poetry.

Trusting the process, I continued to allow the poems to form on the page but began to engage with them slightly differently, in a way that relates to the Jungian concept of working with active imagination. Sometimes I found a new poem did not seem to fit, and I would assume that it did not belong in the work. Often I found later that it was very much a part of it after all. The secret writing was placing things in front of me that I felt but had not articulated previously, taking me to places I did not always want to go, but needed to. Not just to briefly visit but to be inside, discovering texture, colour, beings, landscape, fears, joys.

Eventually I began to realise how much choice I had, how much I could alter my position; that I was not, after all, stuck in the depression and I could move on. Every sign and symbol in the poems, every living being and every landscape had been guides on a spiritual journey of renewal.

Although there were other finished pieces of work that I did not include I knew when the collection was finished: I did not need to write it any more. The last three poems felt very final. 'The Third Deer', using material from earlier sources, was a more conscious poem than the rest, and perhaps reflected that the journey I had made in the poetry through that inner landscape now had a value in my own conscious everyday reality.

When I came to put the work together it held many surprises. Other poems, which I had thought outside the book, fitted suddenly into different areas and every time that happened, I learned something new. An American Art Therapist has called paintings 'Angels' that come to visit us that we can dialogue with. I like this idea. I found my poem 'Blue City Angels', which had been written just before I began *Nekyia,* seemed to fit with the collection; in this poem the visiting angels are speaking but can't quite be heard. I now think that this was indeed an inner voice wanting to be heard – and also a voice of spiritual guidance, perhaps another guise for the Swan Woman.

Writing *Nekyia* has been important for me. It has changed the way I think about poetry – or the potential poetry has for healing. I know that making changes in that inner metaphoric landscape altered my being, healed the hurt that I had begun to write from, opened the narrowed world out again. I am still my age, still have my losses and griefs and mistakes. I am still a Green – angry at the abuse of the natural world, and I would still like to live in the country. But my journey is forward now. And when I walk near home, I usually see deer.

As a writer in healthcare, it has made me really *trust poetry*. What needs to be said, brought from the unconscious to the conscious, will be articulated by the voice of poetry if it is allowed freedom. It may not be obvious, it may even appear irrelevant or wilfully off-the-point; but it won't be. If you wait, quietly enough, meaning will come and in that realisation, that knowledge, lies the opportunity for change. In a sense, poetry can be the voice of experience that enlivens our innocence. When we hold certain things unconsciously, we are 'innocent' of them; I mean, that if we do not recognise what our feelings really are but just hold them, experience them, we are innocent in the way a child is. But when we are conscious of these feelings then the knowledge of the experience enables us to grow.

I also trust poetry as a spiritual ally that can provide the guides needed for any deep soul-journey. I don't mean necessarily that we all become spiritual counsellors when we engage with poetry in healthcare, rather that *poetry does this on its own*. Poetry has been allied to healing and to spiritual practice in many diverse cultures throughout history and sometimes little difference has been made between the shamanic journey to the Otherworld and the poet's ability to journey inwards. In modern medicine, the use of relaxation techniques such as guided visualisation are well known to have a beneficial effect Every time we engage others in either writing a poem – to an exercise perhaps – or listening to a poem, we establish that inner landscape within each individual. The very sharing of it, in a group has, I believe, therapeutic value. And what may be encountered there, and altered, can have a major effect in ordinary reality. Trusting poetry allows its healing qualities to surface and enrich life.

To go forward in life is to grow. We all need to take risks, open the gates, step onto new roads. We all need to search for that which makes our heart blossom, not wither. The poetry deep within us will guide us home and beyond.

Risk and the Heart

The year's inner hinge is opening towards the dark
and the cracks in the town are widening, allowing
a herd of dreams to come racing up from the marshes
under the city's heart. Some dreams are gentle teachers,
active in the last frail rays of the old sun, these
have a thoughtful dust-mote quality, a bee-dance memory;
we all become poignant in September.

Others grow spikes on their heels and come trampling in
with lies and a curt hardening. Last week
I saw a white deerskin stretched like a sheet
in a shop window: *Antiques and Curios* in fake Victorian,
the white deer's head and its nine tined antlers
gazing over the cigarettes cards,
the shelf full of chipped plaster Marys.

Now I never look that way; pass on the other side,
stepping over the crouching beggars and singers
my eyes low, my token coins like useless scraps of croissant
in this huge freezing wind. Winter wind that follows me home,
climbs numbingly into my body, enters the fires
so we sit on two sides of an ashy hearth, wondering
how we got caught in this place of flayed exhibits.
At night, I could weave a dozen nests for white owls
from the silver hairs I collect in brushfulls.

The dream of the deer goes on running into my sleep
drumming into my head, fusing into my heartbeats.
I can't find the deer's bones though I search
and search the windswept malls and terraces, listen
for its breath on the windows. Someone told me
it was severed to the Four Winds but once
in the river's quick reflection I saw its pearly ghost.
So real, I nearly stroked my hand down its back, or did so,
watching the leafy green of its eyes warm to me.

This morning, bee-dreams came. Faded now, they fell
like flakes of gold towards the shadow, dancing
a map within a shaft of early light. They know we are lost
here, and they tell me the way to get back home
is to risk the serpentine curves of the old road,
follow its flow of energy under the hill and leave
on the last of its breath. Go to the West: the deer's gift
of its white skin wrapped tightly around us for warmth.

Rose Flint[1]

WRITING FOR WELLBEING

Creativity and self-expression seem to be intimately connected with wellbeing. A healthy person is not simply someone who is mindful of diet and exercise, clearly. We know of the connections between psyche and soma; we know that psychological and emotional stress take their toll on physical health. 'Health' affects the whole person: body, mind, heart and soul. For full health, we need to be actualising our potential as human and also as transcendent beings. We need to live in the world of the senses, but we are not only creatures of the senses. We have other needs, too, 'meta' needs: for belonging, for a sense of purpose, for a life of meaning; we have an interior life that needs relationship and connection; solitude and silence; a moral and developed life of values.

A healthy person will also be a creative person in the way they live their life, communicate, and solve problems, even if they don't feel themselves to be creative in the more traditional sense. A person who is expressing themselves creatively will also be fulfilling some of their meta needs, which are connected with spiritual, emotional, intellectual and psychological health (these are usually lumped together as 'mental health', but I feel this is too narrow).

We know from research over the past twenty years that therapeutic writing is a powerful tool for coping with current life difficulties as well as for dealing with residual pain and unresolved grief and anger from the past. This kind of writing has a long list of benefits.

Therapeutic writing can improve your emotional and psychological wellbeing by giving you a safe place to express difficult thoughts and feelings, rather than either repressing them, or expressing them inappropriately at others through anger, violence or revenge, for instance. (This in turn minimises the chances of the repressed material emerging as physical illness, and alleviates the stress involved in 'holding down' those emotions which in itself makes us less resistant to illness.) These are some of the specific benefits that writing for health can offer:

It can allow you to gain insight into confused and confusing issues
It can act as a mood-enhancer by alleviating stress and depression, giving people a sense of being uplifted. Many people describe an upsurge in

their energy levels after having written about difficult issues, as the energy involved in holding them down is suddenly released

It can enable you, over time, to process trauma

It gives you a greater self-understanding, and therefore a deeper understanding of others, along with the associated compassion

It can raise self-esteem

It can enable you to live more authentically, and to truly know who you are – what you think, feel and believe

It can help you understand, integrate, learn and move on from difficult life experiences

In short, it can raise your consciousness; through greater self-awareness, transformation, self-acceptance and an increased sense of meaning can occur

Intellectually it can bring greater clarity, 'decluttering' and helping with perspective, so that what is important can be picked out

It's empowering: it can bring you a sense of greater control and choice in your life

By putting thoughts and feelings on paper sometimes issues that are bothering us at an unconscious level will become apparent, and as this process goes on, we can move out of feeling overwhelmed and confused into a place where we are able to feel more confident and act more decisively

It can also help one's powers of concentration and the ability to focus, with benefits from improved academic work to better prospects at job interviews.

All of these things can also affect the way we communicate, so that our interactions with others can be clearer and more assertive as we become more aware of who we are and what our desires, needs, true feelings and limits are. This in turn can make us better partners and friends, as we become freer of some of the more common 'games' people play in relationship, employed to get what we want through such means as manipulation, martyrdom, guilt or threats.

Perhaps the biggest surprise is the physical benefit. The initial manifestation is often relaxation: immediately after writing, the decrease in heart rate and blood pressure is measurable, and writers report feeling calmer. In the long-term, though, the benefits of writing in this way become significant: not only do practitioners report a reduction in the frequency of minor ailments such as colds, but immune function as shown by the white blood cell count is enhanced.

One of the early researchers into the benefits of writing from and about life experience was Professor James Pennebaker.[1] Working with a group of university students in the 1980s, he split them into two groups. Both were asked to write continuously for 20 minutes a day for four consecutive days. One of the groups was given a list of superficial topics on which to write. The other was asked to write about their deepest feelings and thoughts in relation to a personal trauma.

The first group had little to report. The second group, however, reported that although they felt much worse immediately after the four-day experiment (as can happen when writing about trauma, as it surfaces into consciousness and we relive it), over the next few weeks they experienced positive changes in mood and outlook, and a decrease, in comparison with both their previous experience and the other group, of minor ailments.

Pennebaker did not see therapeutic writing as a universal panacea, but rather a means of preventive health care that had the added advantages of being non-chemical, simple and free, even if not always entirely painless.

Starting points

1

Personal journalling
This is one of the most important tools that a writer has, both creatively and therapeutically. However, this is more than a 'daily diary', recording events. The aim is to record your deepest, most private thoughts, feelings and reactions to the day, or to an event, in as open and honest a way as you are able.

In a way, this acts as a kind of emotional and psychological barometer and pressure valve, simultaneously showing you areas of dis-ease and allowing you to process them.

It may be that, rather than writing about the day just passed, you have a specific issue or issues which is/are unresolved. If the issue is a deep-seated trauma, you may need to revisit it on paper more than once.

It is important that you are able to allow yourself to write in as close to a spontaneous stream-of-consciousness way as possible. If you have been using the exercises in this book, you should by now be familiar with the technique: just write, without pausing to think or judge what you have written, and without being concerned with grammar and punctuation. To allow yourself to 'go deep' with this, and for its benefits to become apparent, you need really to write for between 20 and 30 minutes at a time, and you need to make this regular practice. In effect, this is 'morning pages'.

This work is not for showing to anyone else. It is also not intended to produce beautiful results: it's about being as authentic as possible with yourself, for yourself.

We will look at journalling ideas and techniques in some depth in the next chapter.

1a

It can be very helpful to apply these or similar reflective questions to your 20-minute pieces:

What do I notice? What interests me? What am I really writing about? (These will hopefully be familiar questions to you by now; they are a fundamental part of reflective writing practice.) What might I learn from what happened and my reactions to it? Do I have the whole picture? Does this incident remind me of any other time or situation in my life? How might I handle it differently another time? What outcome would I like from the situation in which I find myself? Are there external changes I can or need to make, or does the change have to be an internal one? Can I 're-frame' the situation so that I am not so hurt by it? (I don't mean denying the truth, here; rather looking at it from a different angle.)

2 *Letters*

If what you are writing about relates to another person, or people (and it so often does, of course) you might wish to write a letter to that person or group of people – even if the person concerned has gone from your life. *This is not intended to be sent; you might wish, instead, to burn it.* It can be very cathartic to put these words down and then ritually destroy them. (I talk more about letters in the next chapter.)

What about writing a letter to yourself, from the (loving) you of now to the you of then (or the you of 80 to the you of now)?

3 *Someone else's viewpoint*

Another useful technique is to write 'in the voice of' the other party in a difficult situation. Allow yourself to simply write from their perspective in the first person, in whatever way suggests itself.

4 *Mind-mapping*

This one is adapted from Michael Gelb's book *How to Think like Leonardo da Vinci*[2] and uses mind-mapping as its basis.

Take a current or recurring challenging emotional theme from your life, and find a symbol or image to represent this. Put that symbol at the centre of a sheet of paper. Now, without thinking, scatter around that central symbol other images and symbols or pictures that come to mind relating in some way to the issue, connecting each one to the central symbol by radiating lines. When you reach a point of no more images arising, allow a keyword for each symbol to emerge in your mind, and print that word in capitals above or below the symbol.

Now look to see which keywords/symbols might connect with which others, and draw lines between them – curved or angled lines may be better than straight ones.

Do the same thing again, but this time choose your central image to symbolise what a solution to this issue would look like; and choose your other symbols and keywords accordingly.

When you've finished, simply put both maps away; and look at them in a few months' time... At which point you might want to write something.

6 *As if*

An extraordinarily powerful yet very simple technique, I find in my workshops, is the following.

Take a difficult and apparently irresoluble situation in your life.

Write out a typical playing-out of this situation.

Then write, in the present tense, a new scenario: now the situation has been resolved, and this is what it looks like.

Tips

Consider meeting with a friend either to journal together, or to explore some of these issues; someone who is not judgmental and whose support is reliable and honest.

Many people, often especially men in our Western world, feel uncomfortable writing in this way, seeing it as being self-indulgent. Break this habit! It's another way of judging yourself. And anyway, who's to know?

Be aware of any tendency to fall into habitual moaning and complaining on paper, or of a tendency to berate yourself as a failure. There is a balance to be struck here between being honest about negative feelings and simply reinforcing those feelings as a *modus vivendi*.

Also be strict without yourself about going deep into your inner life, rather than being pulled off track by fantasies, whether pleasant (i.e. erotic) or negative (i.e. vengeful).

A note of warning: there are some issues that are not easily resolved by writing, but may need the help of a professional.

A CANDLE AGAINST THE DARK
WRITING FOR SELF-DISCOVERY

"Make of yourself a light,"
said the Buddha,
before he died.
Mary Oliver

In the last chapter we talked about using writing as a tool for wellbeing. Here, I want to expand a little on the process of writing for self-discovery, again using journalling work for further reflection on your life's path.

Reflective writing is a spiritual discipline, a path of practice, and an effective way of increasing one's awareness. It's not an exaggeration to say that the world today needs as many aware people as possible if we are to have any hope of breaking the pattern of enmity and violence rife in our time (all times?). To 'Know Thyself', as the ancient oracular inscription at Delphi states, may still be the only injunction in which we can place any hope for real change. Knowing ourselves well may enable us to be less hasty in dumping on others material that belongs with ourselves. It also goes some way towards washing away the shadows and grime, wiping clean our 'doors of perception', so that we may, perhaps, start to see, or see again, things and people, ourselves included, as they really are, in their full and astonishing beauty.

Both creative and reflective writing initially involve, of course, a turning inwards. However, as I've said already, writing is about connection, our many relationships; first among these being our relationship with ourself. If we do not know and care about ourself, how can we extend that to others? Our relationship with ourself is an ongoing process of becoming conscious, and of moving from ignorance to wisdom – ideally, anyway.

Once again, the journalling work I'm going to mention here involves, as with all expressive work, a balance of, or creative tension between, if you prefer, subjective immersion and objective reflection. It also involves a balance of attention – or rather, a moving between – inner and outer, past and present, our own life and the places where our life touches, or has touched, those of significant others. Be prepared to write a lot; and don't stop just because you get to the end of this book – the process is a continuing one!

Lifeline – the overview

I suggest that you take your time over this – allow several days in all, or set aside some time each week. What about going away with a friend and taking a weekend over it?[1]

Part 1

I suggest that for all the following exercises you start by bringing your full attention to the present moment, and yourself in that moment. Find a comfortable sitting position, allow your body and mind to relax, and bring your awareness first to your immediate surroundings and their sights and sounds, and then gradually and gently bring your attention inwards, and drop it to your breathing.

> a) You'll need your journal or a notebook. Settle yourself somewhere where you will not be interrupted for around an hour. Allow yourself to sink into a relaxed frame of mind – you might help this by burning incense or essential oils (rosemary for concentration, lavender or melissa or neroli to relax, citrus, bergamot or lemongrass for uplifting), or playing soothing music (though you might want to switch it off if it distracts you when you're writing).
> Sit back, breathe deeply and slowly, and close your eyes. Picture your life's journey – the path to here – as a physical path. When you have a fairly clear picture, open your eyes again. In your notebook, write about the terrain – is it rough and rocky, smooth and lush, wooded or open, or none of the above? – on your journey to here. Were there patches of bog and wilderness, desert, water? Was the path winding and narrow in some places, wide and straight in others? And the actual track beneath your feet: how was it to travel upon? How is it now? Is your footwear up to the terrain? What is the landscape behind you like? And the view ahead? Dwell (I love that word) on these things for a while; allow images to arise that map out your journey to here.
> Write as much as you can about this.
>
> b) Then look back over it. Have you missed anything out?
>
> c) Look again. Here are those questions again: what do I notice? What surprises me? And finally, is there a unifying theme?
>
> d) How do you feel, looking back at those notes?

e) Is there a keyword or phrase for your journey, for the way you travel?

f) See if you can isolate a central image from the piece of writing, and write a little about your relationship to that image; OR underline strong or key phrases or images within it and draw together a short poem.

Part 2

a) Take a large sheet of paper, or stick several sheets of A4 together, and find some coloured pens. Again, find a quiet place and allow plenty of uninterrupted time.

b) On the paper, mark your moment and place of birth at one end, and at the other today's date, your age, and where you now live (I envisage these sheets placed horizontally, and the birth date being marked on the left, but of course you could work right to left, or bottom to top).

c) Mark between the two the track of your life, bearing in mind its nature – twisting and turning, hilly, or straight and smooth? Does it loop back on itself or press determinedly forwards? Are there detours and cul-de-sacs, tracks into forests or cities?

d) Then take your notebook. Sit quietly, eyes closed, allowing yourself to sink into passive receptivity. Allow your life to unfold in your memory's imagination, and allow key events in your life to arise into your mind – events that have shaped you and your life. There will of course be events that are common to everyone: birth, maybe birth of siblings, start of schooling, losing a pet, then a grandparent, moving house, adolescence, first love, further training, college or university, first job, marriage, children, etc. Note them all down. And there will be events that are unique to you, key events that have shaped you and the path you've taken. As you move on, you'll probably find that you become less concerned with the outer factual event and more aware of the underlying subtle processes: the connections between things, what drew you to a particular job/person/location, and so on. In your notebook make *brief* notes as an event suggests itself, then close your eyes and wait for another. (Note that you are only jotting a word or two, just to 'fix' the event in your memory. At this stage don't worry about chronology.)

e) Now choose about 10 or 12 of these events, the major ones, and, still in your notebook or journal, re-order chronologically, leaving space between each (about a paragraph). Make slightly longer notes about each, including the date, your age, the location, general circumstances and others involved.

f) Find a key image for each event, including where you are now – a concrete picture (for instance, an open door; a forest; a garden; a heart; a golden ball; a motorbike; a caged bird; a well; a snowstorm). Then find a keyword or phrase describing the event and the quality of it – this will probably include a verb. (Examples: 'I left home.' 'I fell in love.' 'I lost a key.' 'A door closed.' 'I forgot to laugh.' 'I learnt to fly.' 'I'm coming home.')[2]

g) A key tool in reflective writing is being aware of the balance of attention between being immersed in the writing process, and the feelings that are aroused by it. So now, read what you've written *aloud*. (It's helpful to read this to someone else, someone you trust; but preferably not at this stage your partner.) See how you feel about the writing and about hearing it. Make some notes about this.

h) Finally, mark these major events onto your Lifeline map. Add their key image/words.

Part 3

Over the next few days or weeks, choose one of these events at a time to write about in depth in your journal. Write about them as fully as possible, in the present tense, and with as much sensory detail as possible. (**A word of warning**: if you are feeling fragile or vulnerable, choose your subject and time carefully, or don't tackle events that may prove too painful to write about.)

Part 4

Once there was one continent from which the others split...
You are part of a long tradition: your immediate family, your ancestors, the tribespeople and clanspeople behind them; your nation, race, culture, continent and then of course your place in the human, and then the non-human, tradition. This is more a web than a line. Consider ways that might adapt the

Lifeline principles to extend your lifeline backwards into your origins, known or imagined – and also forwards, too… and to embrace your place on the planet and out into the cosmos, as well. Look for all your connections with others, whether or not you have 'known' them.

Working with relationships

For most of us, our relationships with other people are often the most rewarding and fulfilling, and the most challenging, aspects of our lives. Often, our relationships feel messy, unclear and confusing – that is, assuming we bring more than superficiality to them – and often it happens that stresses, anxieties and depressions are associated with unresolved feelings such as anger or grief in relation to others.

If we are honest with ourselves, we may find that the issues we have with others are actually, or at least additionally, issues we really have with ourselves. Remember the mirror principle, which I've mentioned elsewhere.

Once again, the work I shall offer below may need several days to complete – indeed it may be an ongoing process – and some quiet uninterrupted time each time.

a) Take some time to draw up a list of past and present significant others in your life, as far back as you know. This will include people of whom you have only the haziest memory – early friends, teachers – or maybe no memory at all, but whom you know existed in relation to you. Don't worry about the chronology yet.

b) As and when you're ready, choose significant individuals from your list, and write about them one at a time.

What we're looking for is not whether the relationship between the two of you was 'good' or 'bad', but rather whether it is/was significant in your life; a relationship with someone which involved the depths of yourself; an intense connection. Start with the person who first comes to mind after you have been sitting quietly, relaxed, just breathing.

Without thinking too hard, write a piece *about this person*, moving between their inner reality and your response to/feelings about them. (You might want to write imaginatively about them: if they were a colour? A weather condition? A garment? A vehicle? An animal? – Don't search for this; let your answers be spontaneous.)

c) Apply the questions 'What do I notice? What surprises me? What is the main theme?' to the way you've chosen to remember and record this.

d) Now write *about your relationship* with this person, starting with an image for it. Write a brief and direct statement, describing the essence of the whole relationship. What was or is this relationship about, at its core, for you? What are its particular qualities? What soul quality does it invoke in you? What did you learn or are you learning from it? This piece of writing may be several paragraphs long; it will contain the best and most nurturing aspects of that relationship as well as the harder more frustrating facets. What was fulfilling in it? What was negative? What was freely expressed, and what was hidden?

e) What outcome would you like/would you have liked? An image for that?

f) How did you feel, writing about all this? Monitor your response over the next few days, and jot it down.

Lifeline in relationship

It can be profoundly illuminating, liberating and moving to make a lifeline map of a path you've taken with a partner – loved one, friend or work colleague. Clearly, the longer that relationship has existed and the more intense the connection, the more the possibilities within the mapping process, and the more potential too for extremes of feeling.

Approach it as you would your own, mapping the terrain first. When you come to marking the line itself, be aware of the points where the separate lines of the two individual lives converge and diverge. It's useful to map three lines: yours, your partner's, and the line of the relationship. You might want to use different coloured inks; and it will be useful if you plot on paper first key events and significant situations and periods in your lives alone and together. Stay alert to transitional points of choice and direction; and of the paths not taken.

Be imaginative; experiment. Give yourself plenty of time; and be aware that you will be stirring up feelings and memories.

Continuing the conversation

An important tool in reflective writing, and for healing unresolved issues – as well as becoming aware of them in the first place – is letter writing. *I should emphasise here that you do not need to send these letters – it's the writing that is important.*

a) Choose someone from your list of significant others about whom you wrote in *Working with relationships* above; someone with whom you have unresolved issues. (It doesn't matter if that person is dead – you can still 'talk' to them through the letter, and redress imbalances from your side, in your heart.)

b) Spend some time quietly reflecting on the nature of your relationship with this person. Then summon up in your imagination the presence of that person, and when you are ready read back what you wrote about them and about your relationship with them. If it occurs to you that you've missed stuff out, add it now to the piece. (Don't think too hard about this; jot it spontaneously. Especially don't censor: if something occurs to you that doesn't seem to make sense or even be true, note it anyway.)

c) How do you feel, reading it back? Make some notes.

d) Now write a letter from the *you* of now to that person, as honestly as you can. Put in everything you think of.

e) And now write *their reply to you*, in the first person…

f) And finally, write a letter to the *you* of then from the you of now. Address yourself by name…

Mapping the world

a) This exercise, again a long one, depends on your making a pictorial map of your world. (Think about the mediaeval *Books of Hours*, and woodcuts of the cosmos from that era – look some up if you've never seen them. I'm not suggesting you use these as models, but they are both beautiful and inspiring.)

Use large sheets of paper, and colours, and map in pictures and images your life as it is right now. Put into and onto your map the people and things of which your day, and week, and year consist. Put in the habitual things, places and events as well as the special ones. Make it beautiful; you might want to stick photos, leaves, feathers, scraps of words, letters and so on onto it. Put in significant names of people and places, and dates. Put in words. What do you value? What gives your life meaning? How do you share out your life? What place do you give your relationship with yourself, the people you love – friends and family, your work, your interests, your immediate community, the wider world, your health, your creativity, your cultural life, your political life, play, your spiritual life?

b) Then take your notebook and look at the map you have made for yourself. What do you feel about this map? What does your personal cartography include, and what significant lacks or absences are there?

c) If you could redesign your life – and there is no reason why you shouldn't – what changes would you wish to make? Write about this. Give your imagination free rein.

d) And if you had only one year to live, what would you do with it?

e) Consider making a map of a special place from your childhood; and also one for your future self, based on c) above.

More on journalling

As I complete this book, I'm reading a wonderful article in the latest journal of the *National Association of Writers in Education*, by Christian McEwen.[3]

Just to remind you that journalling can take many forms:

'...I asked [my students] to consider some of the ways we can get stuck as journal-keepers, repeatedly using the same few tactics: self-analysis, summary description, emotional catharsis, till our diaries grow airless and egotistical. I asked everyone to note what they felt were their dominant modes, and then to come up with four or five alternatives. If they had always used lined (or worse) dated and divided pages, I asked them to imagine how different their practice might be if they were to try blank journals, and watercolour or coloured pens...'

Here are some of the suggestions from McEwen's group (some of which we've already covered):

Glue in photos, postcards, news clippings, flowers, leaves, scraps
Add maps, drawings, collage, marginalia (notes and drawings)
Include lists, questions, quotes, dreams, conversations, portraits, letters, guided meditations, detailed descriptions.

A TREE FULL OF BIRDS

If I were asked what I want to accomplish as a writer, I would say it's to contribute to a literature of hope... I want to help create a body of stories in which men and women can discover trustworthy patterns... Every story is an act of trust between a writer and a reader; each story, in the end, is social. Whatever a writer sets down can help or harm the community of which he or she is a part...
Barry Lopez

In the chapter on creation stories I laid out, briefly, a number of different approaches to explaining how we came to be here. Each of these viewpoints is unique; and yet many have features in common. Some have a gender bias; some seem loaded towards violence; some have humour and generosity; some establish the pre-eminence and dominion of humans; others less so. An individual culture's religious foundations – and, by implication, its creation narrative – has notoriously been fiercely defended as the only possible worldview, and arguably has been, and is still, at the heart of many situations of world conflict. What happens when one culture's adherence to its view of our origins, and the faith built on those, comes up against a different one?

When the idea of a spherical, rather than flat, earth was once again raised as a serious proposition in Europe in the Middle Ages (the ancient Greeks had already propounded this thesis), this view was condemned by the Vatican as utter heresy, and some of its proponents were excommunicated or put to death.

Later, Cromwell's troops destroyed the 'idols' and icons of the Roman Church in Britain. In the C19th, Christian missionaries destroyed the 'idols' of tribal peoples in the Commonwealth. At the turn of the new millennium, fundamentalist Muslims destroyed the sacred Buddhist images in Afghanistan.

Plus ça change... Some current fundamentalist Christian sects cannot accept any truth in other religions, nor in any Darwinian and post-Darwinian views on evolution. Some atheists cannot accept any notion of the existence of the sacred, in any form. Some people insist that creation narratives are literal representations of how things were and are; some say they are allegories; some maintain that, as metaphors, they constitute a vast and important body of 'wisdom teachings'; some dismiss them as childishly superstitious rubbish which should be stamped out.

Many so-called 'primitive' tribal cultures, ridiculed by our Western 'civilisation', have a profound awareness of the interconnectedness of everything, and live by laws of respect and reverence for all life, as embedded in their creation narratives. We, who consider ourselves sophisticated, have coerced, bullied, seduced or 'preached' many of these peoples away from these beliefs and into our worldview which, 'developed' though it may be, is hardly a sustainable, let alone a respectful, one.

What we do know is that we need to find a wiser, more sustainable way to live; not just for ourselves, but for the planet as a whole.

In 'Tongues of the Earth' Jeremy Thres raised these questions; and they are important enough as to raise again. What are the tales we tell ourselves? What underlying beliefs and truths do they portray? What stories support our values? How could we build on this? Do the stories in which we immerse ourselves enhance our view of ourselves, each other and life?

Here's another question: what responsibility does the writer have for what he or she puts into the world? No one wants chocolate-box stories and perpetual epiphany; you can't make stories about only contented characters in a perfect world. But when did you last see a film that portrayed people relating in a healthy, loving and mature way to each other? What is the attraction of watching TV shows and screenplays that centre on human dysfunction and people behaving badly?

What stories do we need? At the end of my first book I asked this question. Here I am again: nearly twelve years on, I am still asking this same question. In one way and another this question has been posed throughout this book, too: tacitly, or overtly.

How would it be to read books that support us in being more fully and compassionately human? Ones that give us tools to grow and change; offer us models of functional, healthy patterns of relating – whether to ourselves, to each other, to the wider human sphere or to the planet as a whole, rather than narratives that merely underline how grim 'reality' is, and how untrustworthy and self-seeking people are, thus confirming our view of the world and the human condition as basically beyond hope?

Perhaps our diet has become too thin, and we are looking for a different kind of nourishment. We need now stories that offer us healing, offer us the potential of wholeness, of coming through in the end. Empowering stories. Stories that show us human being at its best: its most courageous, generous, kind, loving, compassionate, wise, funny. Stories that celebrate the earth, wilderness, the diversity of nations, the diversity of species. Stories that allow us to imagine a new world order based on empathy, co-operation, kindness, discussion, negotiation, fairness, equality. Stories that celebrate what is green, what is vulnerable, what is innocent, what is childlike, what is wise, what is feminine, what is masculine; stories about co-operation and harmony rather than competition and conflict; about people making wise choices. Stories that celebrate magic, mystery, miracle. Stories that help restore some sort of faith, whatever that may mean for each of us.

I am aware that these things on their own do not make story, or even poetry. *But the way we deal with them, and the choices we make, do.* I am not suggesting that we pretend all is not how it is. I am not naïve enough as to assume that war will end in my lifetime; that violence will cease to exist; that poverty will be an extinct word; that pollution will be outlawed; that conservation will suddenly become more important to the corporate world than profit.

I am not at all suggesting that we pretend pain does not exist. On the contrary. Go to where the pain is. Write about it. Make a story of it. The pain will show you where the work is needed, and it will, in its unfolding onto paper, show you the path for healing. Human life will always be hard, in parts – that is the nature of the egoic life, which sees itself as separate and all-important, that judges and picks and chooses: 'I like this, but not that. This is acceptable but that isn't.' But the stories that matter, the big stories, are always a triumph over these limitations.

It is important not to give up. Human actions matter; they make a difference. Even one person's weight will make a difference. And who knows which of us will effect the final 'critical mass' moment at which a threatened downslide will wobble, pause, and start to right itself? And it is at that critical moment, when we are deepest in the darkness – maybe right now – that we need these stories of hope; when we need a lamp out of the cave. And we need to know we are not alone.

Find something you can really believe in; something that enhances your life; and a group of people who think like you, whether it's a writing group, or a politically active group, or an evening class, or an online discussion group, or people who like walking out on the land, or are involved in life-enhancing projects in the city. Find a community that supports you in your vision. Maybe they'll be flesh and blood people. Maybe it'll be the books of poets or authors writing passionately about things you care about. It's crucial. Make it the next thing you do. 'Never doubt that a group of committed individuals can change the world; in fact it's the only thing which can,' said anthropologist Margaret Mead. And 'Better to light a candle than curse the darkness,' goes another saying.

Where do you start? Find a moment of glory. I'm thinking of Seamus Heaney's 'Postscript' poem, of R S Thomas' 'Bright Field', of Brendan Kennelly's *Glimpses*. Early in her book *Pilgrim at Tinker Creek* Annie Dillard mentions a tree, an Osage orange, which, ostensibly empty, suddenly flames with an eruption of blackbirds, previously unseen; then another, then another – hundreds of blackbirds from what looked like an empty tree. This was a moment of glory for her, to which she returns in the course of the book. Reading her passage, many years ago now, that tree became a moment of glory for me, too; one which I have not forgotten, to which I return, a metaphor against which I measure, or by which I name, other moments – including, of course, my own personal remembered gloriousnesses. The tree, in the book and in my imagination, is both itself and a metaphor for something else. It has become mythic in size, and that way contains magic.

It happens that many bright moments occur outside, when alone in nature; and many occur in the little 'lost' moments between people. These events, I realise as I get older, are not the huge dramatic moments of intense revelation or passion, as they seemed to be when I was younger. Instead, they're often tiny and easily missed; clichéd in their everydayness: a smile, a hug from a loved one, a touch on the arm, shared words or silence, extraordinary light on the water, the glimpse of a kingfisher, an unexpected gift through the post, a card with kind words, pony's breath or dog's wet nose barely touching your hand, catching the dawn, an instant of total and spontaneous openheartedness. Sometimes you are prepared, maybe in a heightened state of some sort. Usually, though, these moments occur in mundane circumstances – and, let's face it, much of our life is mundane; yet this, this *quotidiennité*, is the terrain of miracles. It's the present moment that we inhabit – the *now* that is the only time we have. The writer's job is to pay attention, pay attention, pay attention. Cultivate that kind of looking.

Slow down. Stay open, stay alive. Stay awake.

Writing is a process that never stops. There is no destination; there is only the journeying. Sometimes it works; sometimes you're off track. You're always searching for the next step. '…It can take a lifetime to convey what you mean, to find the opening,' says Lopez. 'You watch, you set it down. Then you try again.'

So you find something that inspires you and you let the pen catch fire. Find that moment of glory. Stay alert for it. Catch it out of the corner of your eye as it streams past, and slide it onto the page. Write what you're passionate about. Really passionate about, deep inside. Let it have soul. Let your words matter. Make them count. Don't waste them, and don't underestimate them. Don't worry whether anyone else cares about your writing. That way, you can't fail. 'People are hungry,' says poet David Whyte; 'and one good word is bread for a thousand.'[1]

FOOTNOTES & REFERENCES

Introduction
1 Peter Abbs: 'The Responsibilities of the Poet', *Writing In Education* 34 (NAWE)

Eau de Vie
1 With acknowledgement to Kate Thompson for the first two of these questions
2 This poem appears in Julie-Ann Rowell's book *Convergence* (Brodie Press)

Telling Tales
1 E M Forster, *Aspects of the Novel* (Penguin)
2 Rainer Maria Rilke, *Letters to a Young Poet* (Everyman)

Writing From Life 1
1 W S Graham, 'What Is The Language Using Us For?' in *Implements in their Places* (Faber)

Tales of Wonder
1 From an article by Selina Mills in *Resurgence* 211
2 Phil Cousineau, *The Art of Pilgrimage* (Conari Press)
3 From *The Creative Writing Coursebook*, Julia Bell & Paul Magrs (Macmillan)
4 Michael Symmons Roberts, 'On Dyeing' from *Raising Sparks* (Cape)
5 From an article in *The University of Sydney Gazette*
6 From William Fiennes' *The Snow Geese* (Picador)

Catching the Wave
1 From an article in *The University of Sydney Gazette*
2 Adam Nicolson, *Sea Room* (HarperCollins)
3 ibid.

Car Mechanics
This essay appears in David Keefe's book *Writing Your Way* (Windhorse Publications)

Begin Anywhere, Begin Somewhere
1 Marge Piercy, *The Moon Is Always Female* (The Women's Press)

'Spoon' – How Do You Spell It?
1 Paul Matthews, *Sing Me The Creation* (Hawthorn Press)

One Foot in Front of the Other
1 Clarissa Pinkola Estes, *Women Who Run with the Wolves* (Rider)
2 From an article by Selina Mills in *Resurgence* 211

The Writer & Threshold Consciousness
1 Jane Hirshfield: 'Writing and the Threshold Life', in *Nine Gates: Entering the Mind of Poetry* (HarperCollins)
2 Czeslaw Milosz: 'Ars Poetica?', from *The Collected Poems 1931–1987* (Ecco Press, translation © 1978 by Czeslaw Milosz and Lillian Vallee)
3 Arthur Rimbaud, 'Le Bateau Ivre', tr. Samuel Beckett, in *Collected Poems in English and French* (John Calder)
4 James K Baxter, 'Recent Trends in New Zealand Poetry' (Caxton Press)
5 Tomas Tranströmer, *Collected Poems*, tr. Robin Fulton (Bloodaxe Books)

Sauntering
1 Phil Cousineau, *The Art of Pilgrimage* (Conari Press)
2 *see also* Roselle Angwin, *Riding the Dragon – Myth & the Inner Journey*, (Element 1994/Chrysalis 2002)

Silence
1 This is also the title of an anthology of Beat Writings edited by Carole Tonkinson: *Big Sky Mind* (Riverhead Books)

Tongues of the Earth
1 From *The Sacred Mountain*, Steven Foster & Meredith Little (Lost Borders Press)

Dark Matter
1 Federico García Lorca, 'The Havana Lectures', from *Obras Completas* (Aguillar)
2 Jason Webster, *Duende*, (Doubleday)
3 Ben Okri: *A Way of Being Free* (Phoenix)
4 Stephen Nachmanovitch, *Free Play* (Tarcher/Putnam)

5 Roselle Angwin, *Riding the Dragon – Myth & the Inner Journey* (Element 1994/ Chrysalis 2002)

6 cf. James Pennebaker, *Opening Up: The Healing Power of Expressing Emotions* (Guilford Press)

7 Robert Bly, *A Little Book on the Human Shadow* (Element Books)

8 Ben Okri: *A Way of Being Free* (Phoenix)

9 Peter Abbs, *Personae and Other Selected Poems* (Skoob Books) *Poem used by kind permission of the author*

Perspective, Perception and Preconceptions
1 Ben Okri, *A Way of Being Free* (Phoenix)

2 John O'Donohue, *Eternal Echoes – exploring our hunger to belong* (Bantam)

'Only Connect'
1 The explanatory sentence comes from *Leonardo da Vinci's seven principles of learning – their relevance to mental health* by Judith Lee; Northern Ireland Association for Mental Health – an inspiring little publication, itself based on a book by Michael Gelb, *How to Think like Leonardo da Vinci* (Thorsons)

2 From an article in 'Foundations of Physics', Vol. 5 (1975), D Bohm and B. Hiley; quoted in *The Marriage of Heaven and Earth*, Gregory Szanto (Arkana)

3 Manus J Donahue, http://www.duke.edu/~mjd/chaos/chaosh.html

4 *The Marriage of Heaven and Earth*, ibid.

Thinking Wild
1 Henry Beston, *The Outermost House* (Henry Holt)

2 Wallace Stegner, 'The Wilderness Letter'

3 Barry Lopez, *About This Life* (Harvill Press)

4 Gary Snyder, *The Practice of the Wild* (North Point Press)

5 Andy Fisher, *Radical Ecopsychology* (State University of New York Press)

Eternally Opposite, Eternally Connected
1 Betty Edwards, *Drawing on the Artist Within* (HarperCollins)

The Power of Dream
1 For more on all this, see Dr Jung's works; for example, *The Archetypes and the Collective Unconscious*, and *Man and His Symbols*. Joseph Campbell has furthered

this work with books such as *Hero with a Thousand Faces, Myths to Live By, &*
Creative Mythology

The Creative Process
1 See Betty Edwards, *Drawing on the Artist Within* (HarperCollins)
2 Clarissa Pinkola Estes, *Women Who Run With The Wolves* (Rider)

Altered States
1 Stephan Nachmanovitch, *Free Play* (Tarcher/Putnam)
2 In Brewster Ghiselin, *The Creative Process* (Mentor)
3 Ibid

Fractured Light
1 Kenneth Steven, *The Missing Days* (Scottish Cultural Press)

Wrestling with a God: Making Poems
Note: *This piece started life as 'What I Want From A Poem', a brief presentation I
gave at the Arvon Foundation's Totleigh Barton centre in 2000. Versions of it have
appeared in* Rialto, The Reader, Stride *online magazine, and I have come across it
on other Internet sites.*

1 Ruth Padel, *52 Ways Of Looking at a Poem* (Vintage)

Whole Fragments
1 Ruth Padel, *52 Ways of Looking at a Poem* (Vintage)
2 John O'Donohue, *Eternal Echoes – exploring our hunger to belong* (Bantam)
3 Neil Astley, (Editor), *Staying Alive* (Bloodaxe Books)
4 'Memory & Imagination', The Allott Lecture, reprinted in *The Reader*, no 14
5 Stephen Burt, 'Close Calls with Nonsense' in *The Believer*, May 2004
6 Ann Lauterbach: in *What Is Poetry: Conversations With The American Avant
Garde*, Daniel Kane (Teachers & Writers Books)
7 If you don't know where to start, look out for books (in the UK) from these poetry
presses to start with, where there is a wide range and the standard is high: Anvil,
Bloodaxe, Cape, Carcanet, Enitharmon. There are a number of other presses you
should also look for: Arc, Peterloo, Rockingham, Stride, and some new smaller
ones, such as bluechrome and Brodie Press, that are gaining strength. Get a feel

for the individual lists. The Poetry Society and The Poetry Book Society exist, of course, to promote poetry. Anthologies make good starting points, where you can start to work out which poets you enjoy; two recent wide-ranging ones are *Staying Alive*, and *Being Alive*, both edited by Neil Astley from Bloodaxe. Other personal favourites are *The Rag and Bone Shop of the Heart*, (HarperPerennial) edited by Robert Bly, James Hillman and Michael Meade (this says 'Poems for Men' but I love it); *wild reckoning*, edited by John Burnside and Maurice Riordan, 'an anthology provoked by Rachel Carson's *Silent Spring*', and published by the Calouste Gulbenkian Foundation, is another; also *The Spaces of Hope*, edited by Peter Jay (Anvil). There are various others, some more innovative, but this handful offers a flavour of the contemporary poetry scene.

Magazines: look at www.poetrykit.org for a list of magazines; also Dee Rimbaud's online list: *The AA Independent Press Guide*: www.thunderburst.co.uk; 'information on nearly 2,000 lit mags and presses'.

The Unsettling of Language
1 Andrew Duncan, *The Failure of Conservatism in Modern British Poetry* (Salt)
2 Charles Bernstein, *My Way* (University of Chicago)
3 Rupert M Loydell, *A Conference of Voices* (Shearsman)

Lakes and Rivers
1 Roselle Angwin, *Looking For Icarus* (bluechrome)

The Pearl from the Gravel
1 Kenneth Steven, *Iona* (St Andrews Press)

Late September
1 Mario Petrucci, *Heavy Water* (Enitharmon)

The Poet's Career: a short gallop at full speed, or the flight of a bird
1 A longer version of this essay first appeared in *The North* magazine in 2003

Haiku, Tanka and Haibun
1 Noragh Jones, *Stone Circles – Haiku and Haiku Prose* (Pilgrim Press)

Joy and Grief – One Brush
1 *Every attempt has been made to contact copyright holders. Sincere apology is offered where this has proved unsuccessful*

Exploring further

A good start – spanning over three centuries – is to immerse oneself in 'the Four Greats' – Basho, Buson, Issa and Shiki and their contemporaries. Although haiku occupy only a third of *The Penguin Book of Zen Poetry* it is still a good buy, thanks to Lucien Stryk's sympathetic translations. Another of his Penguin translations is *On Love and Barley: Haiku of Basho* (1985). Shorter, but lavishly illustrated and including more contemporary *haijin* is *British Museum Haiku* edited by David Cobb (British Museum Press, 2002).

The Haiku Handbook by William Higginson (Kodansha, Japan) is an indispensable old favourite. A valuable learning resource is Lee Gurga's *Haiku: a Poet's Guide* (Modern Haiku Press). *The New Haiku* is a Western selection edited by John Barlow and Martin Lucas (Snapshot Press). And a classic collection that concentrates on North American poets is *The Haiku Anthology*, edited by Cor van der Heuvel (3rd ed W W Norton).

It is well worth joining the British Haiku Society. Your subscription brings you four copies of the *Journal* plus benefits. Visit the Society's website: www. BritishHaikuSociety.co.uk

The other indispensable UK journal is *Haiku Presence* (12 Grovehall Ave., Leeds, LS11 7EX). Prominent in the USA are *Frogpond – Journal of the Haiku Society of America*, and *Modern Haiku*.

There are a great many websites.

Haibun

1 Pamelyn Casto in *The Art of Haiku*, Editor Gerald England (NHI)
2 ibid.
3 Ken Jones, James Norton, Sean O'Connor *Pilgrim Foxes* (Pilgrim Press)
4 ibid.
5 Rupert Loydell & Roselle Angwin, *A Hawk Into Everywhere* (Stride)

For more on haiku, tanka and haibun, see:
Gail Sher, *One Continuous Mistake – Four Noble Truths for Writers* (Arkana)
Editor Gerald England: *The Art of Haiku* (NHI)
Editors George Swede, Randy Brooks: *Global Haiku* (Iron Press)
Harold G Henderson: *Haiku In English* (Charles E Tuttle)

Also:

Ken Jones, James Norton, Sean O'Connor, *Pilgrim Foxes* (Pilgrim Press)
Ken Jones, *Stallion's Crag* (Iron Press)

Where Boundaries Blur: The Prose Poem

1 Peter Johnson, Editor, *The Prose Poem: An International Journal*, English Dept., Providence College, Providence, R1 02918, USA.
2 'Michael Benedikt Talks About Prose Poetry' interview by Dennis Stone in *Poetry Society of America Newsletter* 19 (Sept. 1985)
3 ibid.
4 Michael Benedikt: 'The Future of the Prose Poem' in *The Prose Poem: An International Journal* (1993)
5 ibid.
6 Andy Brown, *Hunting The Kinnayas* (Stride)
7 Rupert Loydell & Roselle Angwin, *A Hawk Into Everywhere* (Stride); Rupert Loydell & Roselle Angwin, *The Present Where* (Spirit_Level); Rupert Loydell & Robert Garlitz, *Snowshoes Across the Clouds* (Stride)
8 Roselle Angwin, *Looking for Icarus* (bluechrome) *first published in an earlier version in* Fire 15

Heart of Story

1 Barry Lopez, *About This Life* (Harvill Press)
2 Roselle Angwin, *Creative Novel Writing* (Robert Hale)

Out of the Labyrinth

1 Barry Lopez, *Crossing Open Ground* (Picador)
2 Clarissa Pinkola Estes, *Women Who Run With The Wolves* (Rider)

Once Upon a Time

1 *Penguin Dictionary of Psychology*

See works by C G Jung, Marie-Louise von Franz, Joseph Campbell and James Hillman

Creating the Universe

1 Bill Bryson, *A Short History of Nearly Everything* (Black Swan)

Themes

Further info: check out on the web: Polti; Murray's Manifest Needs; the Karpmann Drama Triangle

Plots

1 Ronald Tobias, *20 Master Plots & How To Build Them* (Piatkus)
2 'Building the Otherworld', *The Guardian*, 11.10.03

Characters

1 E M Forster, *Aspects of the Novel* (Edward Arnold/Penguin)
2 V Propp, *The Morphology of the Folk Tale* (University of Texas Press)
3 Celia Brayfield, *Bestseller* (Fourth Estate)
4 Marina Oliver, *Writing & Selling A Novel* (How To Books)

See also
Roselle Angwin, *Creative Novel Writing* (Robert Hale) & *Riding The Dragon* (Element/Chrysalis)

The Night Sea Journey

1 Rose Flint, *Nekyia* (Stride)

Writing for Wellbeing

1 J W Pennebaker, *Opening Up: the Healing Power of Expressing Emotions* (Guilford Press)
2 Michael Gelb, *How to Think like Leonardo da Vinci* (Thorsons)

See also:
Abraham Maslow, *The Farther Reaches of Human Nature* (Pelican)
Piero Ferrucci, *What We May Be* (Mandala)

LAPIDUS
(Association for the Literary Arts in Personal Development)
BM Lapidus
London WC1N 3XX

A Candle Against the Dark

1 Under my *Fire in the Head – creative & reflective writing* programme I run a number of weekend and longer courses that often include such work. For more details please send an SAE to Fire in the Head, P O Box 17, Yelverton, Devon, PL20 6YF; or check out my website: www.fire-in-the-head.co.uk

2 Ira Progoff, *At a Journal Workshop* (Tarcher Putnam)

3 Christian McEwen in the *Journal of the National Association of Writers in Education* 34, Winter 2004

See also:

Tristine Rainer, *The New Diary* (Jeremy P Tarcher)

Louise DeSalvo, *Writing As A Way of Healing* (The Women's Press)

Kathleen Adams, *Journal to the Self* (Warner)

May Sarton, *Journal of a Solitude* (The Women's Press)

A Tree Full of Birds

1 David Whyte, *The House of Belonging* (Many Rivers Press)

NOTES ON CONTRIBUTORS

ANDY BROWN is co-ordinator of Creative Writing & Arts at Exeter University, Chair of tEXt Festivals and was a Centre Director for the Arvon Foundation at Totleigh Barton. His five collections are *Hunting the Kinnayas* (Stride, 2004), *From a Cliff* (Arc, 2002), *Of Science* (Worple, 2001, with David Morley), *The Wanderer's Prayer* (Arc, 1999), and *West of Yesterday* (Stride, 1998). He edited *Binary Myths* Vols. 1 and 2 (reissued Stride, 2004) and also writes and publishes short stories and criticism.

ROSE FLINT is a poet and artist. She works as both an art therapist and a creative writing tutor. She is the Lead Writer for the Kingfisher Project, working in the hospital and community of Salisbury, and a regular tutor for Imaginative Writing at Liverpool John Moores University. She has been co-tutor for several 'Writing and Spirituality' courses with Alison Leonard at Ty Newydd. She has three collections: *Blue Horse of Morning* (Seren), *Firesigns* (Poetry Salzburg) and *Nekyia* (Stride). Her poetry can be found in many anthologies and magazines.

KEITH JAFRATE is a poet and musician living in Huddersfield, where he's one of the directors of 'The Word Hoard'. Stride published his *Songs for Eurydice* in autumn 2004. He's currently working mostly with the text-music quintet orfeo 5.

KEN JONES is a co-editor of the annual volume *Contemporary Haibun*, and contributes regularly to UK haiku magazines, as well as being represented in British and American anthologies. For his contribution to *Pilgrim Foxes: Haiku and Haiku Prose*, co-authored with Jim Norton and Sean O'Connor, he was awarded the Sasakawa Prize for Original Contributions in the Field of Haikai. Recent collections are *Arrow of Stones* (British Haiku Society, 2002); *Stallion's Crag* (Iron Press, 2003). Jones is a Zen practitioner of thirty years' standing, and author of books on socially engaged Buddhism. He lives in Ceredigion, Wales, with his Irish wife, Noragh.

DAVID KEEFE (Manjusvara), originally a composer, now edits Weatherlight Press, publishing the American poets Robert Bly and William Stafford. His poems and essays have been published in leading journals throughout the English-speaking world. 'Car Mechanics' is extracted from his new book drawing together writing and Buddhist practice, *Writing Your Way*, published by Windhorse in 2005. David co-leads 'Wolf at the Door' writing workshops and is a long-standing member of the Western Buddhist Order.

ANDIE LEWENSTEIN, poet and storywriter, has taught creative writing in Adult Education centres, on Emerson College's Word Work course and on a health centre programme for people recovering from long-term illnesses. She is a co-ordinator of the Poetry *OtherWise* week at Emerson.

RUPERT LOYDELL is the Managing Editor of Stride Publications, Editor of *Stride* magazine, Reviews Editor of *Orbis*, Associate Editor of *Avocado* magazine and a regular contributor of articles and reviews to *Tangents* magazine. He is a Royal Literary Fund Project Fellow, following a RLF Fellowship at Bath University, and also a Visiting Fellow at Warwick University. He lives in Exeter, Devon with his wife and two daughters. Recent publications include *The Museum of Light*, *Endlessly Divisible and A Conference of Voices*, and four collaborative works: *A Hawk Into Everywhere*, with Roselle Angwin; *The Temperature of Recall*, with Sheila E Murphy; *Eight Excursions*, with David Kennedy, and *Snowshoes Across the Clouds*, with Robert Garlitz.

PAUL MATTHEWS runs *Word Work*, courses in Creative Writing, at Emerson College in Sussex, where he has also established *Poetry OtherWise*, a summer week of writing workshops. *The Ground that Love Seeks* (Five Seasons Press) is a gathering of his poems, and is available from him via Emerson College. He's also the author of *Sing Me The Creation* (Hawthorn Press).

CHRISTOPHER NORTH was a well-known figure in the English poetry scene until he left to live in Spain. Founder of 'Metroland Poets', he has read his own work on the BBC, at the Poetry Society and at *Ways With Words*, and been placed in major poetry competitions. With his wife, Marisa, he now runs a creative writing and arts centre in a converted olive mill at Relleu in the Marina Baja mountains near Alicante.

STEPHEN PARR (Ananda) was born in 1944 in Darwen, Lancashire, the only son of a printer on the local newspaper. He moved to London in 1966 to join the BBC as a sound engineer. He has been writing poetry and fiction since the '70s and has been published in many small-press magazines. He has self-published ten pamphlets of his poetry, and has had poems in Bloodaxe's landmark anthology *The Long Pale Corridor*. In 1999 his first full-length poetry collection *North of the Future* was published by Windhorse Publications. He is the co-director of the 'Wolf at the Door' writing programme.

MARIO PETRUCCI is an Arvon tutor, freelance writer, songwriter and the first ever resident poet at the Imperial War Museum, and is also poet in residence for BBC Radio 3. His poetry has won numerous awards and has been described as 'Heartfelt, ambitious and alive' (Jackie Kay). 'Late September, 2001' was published as text and audio on BBC News OnLine (BBC.co.uk/ news, Oct 4 2001), in *The Spectator* (under the title 'Weave', 7 Sept 2002) and is due in *Flowers of Sulphur* (Enitharmon, 2005) which has already secured major awards both from London Arts and the Arts Council of England. 'Last Wish' appears in Mario's Arvon prizewinning collection *Heavy Water* (Enitharmon,) available from www.enitharmon.co.uk or through the author's official website, where further information on Mario and his work can be found: http://mariopetrucci.port5.com.

JANE SPIRO has combined a full-time career in higher education with creative writing for 20 years. She runs an MA for international teachers of English at Oxford Brookes University, and develops language skills with teachers and international students through creative writing, poetry and story. Pioneering this strategy, she has run workshops worldwide, including Belgium, Switzerland, Hungary, Poland, India, Mexico and China. She was consultant and co-editor for the first poetry anthology of learners' voices, *Poetry as a Foreign Language* (White Adder Press 1999). Jane has written collections of stories for language learners: *The Place of the Lotus* and *The Twin Chariot* (Thomas Nelson 1991), *Travelling Light* in *London Tales* (ELI Naples 2003), a novel *Nothing I Touch Stands Still* (Crucible Press 2002), had poetry published in the US and UK and shortlisted for several poetry prizes, and has written and presented 6 programmes on cross-cultural issues for Carlton television. *Creative Poetry Writing*, a retrospective of 70 creative writing workshops, was published in 2004 with Oxford University Press.

KENNETH STEVEN is a full-time writer living in Perthshire. He takes part in numerous residencies and literary events throughout the UK and abroad. He has many books in print, the newest being a poetry collection, *Columba* (St Andrews Press) and a children's book *Imagining Things* (Lion). *Atlantic* will be coming out from Peterloo in 2006. A fluent Norwegian speaker, Kenneth has translated the Nordic prizewinning novel *The Half Brother* by Lars Saabye Christensen. With Roselle, he has established the annual *Into Blue Silence* writing retreat on the Hebridean Isle of Iona.

JEREMY THRES is a student and practitioner of wilderness passage rites, these seeming to hold so many of the keys for him to the regeneration and reintegration of Land, People and Spirit. He has contributed articles to several magazines around this work: *Sacred Hoop, Common Living* and *Circles on a Mountain*. He is a founder member of the not for profit organisation Regenco, and, more recently, the Earth Mystery Initiation School (EMIS). He is based in Devon, England.

I would like to thank Julie-Ann Rowell for the time and care she brought to this book as copy editor. Julie-Ann, like other members of my Two Rivers poetry group, has also been generous in permitting me to use her poetry in these pages. Look out for her book, *Convergence*, published by Brodie Press. Elisabeth Rowe, another member of the same group whose work has been reproduced here, also has a collection: *Surface Tension* (Peterloo).

Thanks, too, to Susanne Worsfold for layout and typesetting, Fred Hageneder for the cover design, and Eloïse Sentito for the cover image. Amy Shelton contributed some beautiful brushwork; sadly there has not been space to use more of her work.

Thanks also to Peter Abbs, Ken Jones and Neil Curry for permission to use their poems or excerpts.